ANDY COLE
THE AUTOBIOGRAPHY

Andy Cole with Peter Fitton

CONTENTS

ACKNOWLEDGEMENTS

When I was asked by my publishers André Deutsch to put my autobiography together, it was, I have to say, the first time I had really sat down and reflected on my life and career to date. Having now finished the book I realize, at times, how many twists and turns, ups and downs, I have faced on the road to a wonderful balmy night in Barcelona. I am obviously proud of my achievements and the resilience and strength of mind it has taken to fulfil my dreams. But along the way, I have been fortunate to receive love, advice, strength and support from some people who will always remain important to me, who I feel are worthy of an extra special mention.

First and foremost, I would like to thank my mother and father for helping me through those difficult formative years. Their guidance laid the foundations that helped me succeed in life and appreciate what this wonderful game of football has given me – love and thanks.

To Shirley, my partner of nine years and my beautiful son, Devante. I know you are always there for me, even through all the moods and difficult moments. It is in reflection that I realize how important your support is – thanks and lots of love.

To my Grandad, such an important figure in my life, who knew the value of listening. You will always be in my heart and thoughts. I will always love you and never stop missing you.

I have six sisters and a brother who have always shown their love for me – love and thanks.

To Paul and Margaret Stretford, when things seemed to be at their worst, you were always there for me – thanks for everything.

To all the mates both in London and Nottingham – respect. But, a special mention for Marcel and Clive – thanks for the support chaps.

I would also like to thank everybody at Proactive Sports Management for taking care of all the day to day requirements of Andy Cole – the Footballer.

Finally, there are some, without whom this project would not have come to fruition. Peter Fitton, the wordsmith, Nicky Paris, my Commissioning Editor and Tim Forrestor, Managing Director at André Deutsch – thanks for the opportunity to put all this down on paper and last but not least, my team-mates from Arsenal to Manchester United, without whom there would be no story to tell – thanks.

Enjoy! I hope I have not missed anybody out.

FOREWORD
by Sir Alex Ferguson

In writing the foreword for Andy's autobiography, I do so with great zeal, as this is right up my street and I am delighted that Andy has asked me. Now I am going to go all nostalgic.

As a school lad, I had this fascination to be a striker, or centre forward as they used to call us, and my early years were spent modelling myself on the great Scottish heroes; Willie Thornton of Rangers, Willie Bauld of Hearts and Laurie Reilly of Hibs were my idols. As a player, I became a striker of reasonable repute but I had an absolutely blinkered view of who my idol and hero was, and it was Denis Law. There was no one who could measure up to Denis as far as I was concerned, although other famous strikers of the time held my admiration.

I have had the great pleasure to work with and coach some wonderful strikers in my twenty-five years as a Manager, and if you read the following list you will understand what a privilege it has been for me. At Aberdeen, I had excellent strikers: Mark McGhee, Steve Archibald, Eric Black and John Hewitt. The latter pair scored Aberdeen's two goals when they defeated Real Madrid in the Cup Winner's Cup Final at Gothenberg. Archibald and McGhee were first class but with different talents, abilities and temperaments.

Now, since I have been at Manchester United, I have had the pleasure of working with a wonderful collection of great strikers such as Mark Hughes, Brian McClair, Eric Cantona, Teddy Sheringham, Ole Gunnar Solskjaer, Dwight Yorke and, of course, Andy Cole. This is, once again, a spread of different talents, abilities and temperaments, but all great Manchester United players.

When I signed Andy Cole there was a wonderful feeling of springing a surprise on the rest of England, as it was done so secretly. Not one of the press had an inkling of our raid on Newcastle, and that is very rare when Manchester United go into the transfer market. There has been nothing but gratitude since the day Andy joined us in January 1995 and that gratitude is not about what we have achieved or the goals he has scored, but is more to do with the character of the person, and that is why I can set down and appreciate his qualities.

One of the additions to my list of essentials as a Manager has been observation. As I have gathered experience, I have also learned the art of watching players' behaviour in training, in the dressing room, hotels and whilst travelling, and it is amazing what you learn about them. With Andy, I see a person of good ethics and manners. We don't always see that with our younger generation and it is refreshing when you do come across it. He has also proved he is a man of great moral fibre, as has been shown in his determination to overcome a succession of injuries and illness. Now that told me a lot about Andy and tells you that you are dealing with a person of substance. He has had to dig deep to overcome early difficulties at the club and now we are benefiting from that resilience, and that benefit has been the development of him as a total footballer whose lightning reflexes give defenders a headache. His movement can create so much space for his team-mates and his goals mark him down as one of Manchester United's all-time greats. There are many of his goals we will always remember, but it is the variety of these strikes which I can instantly recall. His overhead kick to score a decisive goal at Middlesbrough to win the League, his dribble to beat two men and score at Anfield, his combination with Dwight Yorke to score at Barcelona in that epic 3–3 draw last season, his first time strike against Newcastle United from an Eric Cantona pass in the 2–0 victory in 1995. Can we forget those five goals against Ipswich or his four against Newcastle United? We could go on and on to analyse all his goals: and what it tells you most of all is the variety of them. Supporters are never fooled and that is why they have always got behind Andy Cole. They know that, apart from his play, he is a trier, and all the world loves a trier.

It has been nothing but a pleasure to have signed him, worked with him and shared in great moments at the club, and I wish his book an enormous success.

Alex. Ferguson

Chapter One

Was it going to be the splendour of an open-topped bus to parade my career achievements? Or, apparently more likely in those earlier, sullen and defiant years, the possibility of an open prison where I might reflect on my downfall? And I am not being over dramatic, either. I am, in fact, being utterly and deadly serious. Because these two options were very much a part of life's big risks for an immature, bucking-society, right-on rebel of a character. I'm not particularly proud of the admission, but that was me until at least the age of twenty. Tearaway, first class, and didn't I know it. Hey, mate, the world wasn't big enough, not if somebody had a notion of getting in my way. Now here I was, seven incredible years later, able to declare the answer. Instead of the personal nightmare that beckoned so dangerously, I had seized the fantasy. I was aboard the bus, even if it seemed more like a golden chariot, as Manchester United celebrated a unique treble, the most historic achievement of all time in club football. They were even talking about us being the game's immortals. Steady on, I thought, but whatever that meant it sure felt good. It was the spectacular evening of 27 May 1999, and less than 24 hours earlier I had been in Alex Ferguson's front line in Barcelona when the Germans of Bayern Munich had seen the nigh impossible hurled in their faces. United had raised the European Cup to the heavens, coming from behind and scoring twice in injury time through substitutes Teddy Sheringham and Ole Gunnar Solskjaer to win it. Bayern were traumatized, very much in a state of stunned disbelief; so, might I add, were we. They raised their eyes to the heavens and questioned whether greater forces were at work. Even the benevolent hand of the late Sir Matt Busby, United's last winner of the trophy in 1968, and now, they speculated, looking down from above on what would have been his ninetieth birthday. Whether it was fate, or the freakish destiny of a simple football encounter, all I know is that life had never felt better. The sporting folk of Manchester shared the moment; sensing the emotion and filling the streets; a million strong, they said, as we nosed slowly towards that civic reception. And I was just grateful to be a part of it.

Eternally grateful, in truth, because here was the final, indisputable justification that my decision to leave home at just fourteen had been absolutely correct. In a sense, it had saved my life. I wanted to be a wage-earning, big-time footballer, desperately so, too, and yet if I had stayed in Nottingham, running wild in the streets and mostly out of control, I might well have reached no more than the sad destination of some of my closest friends. A prison cell. That's not a gesture of bravado, it's a fact. And for a few of my contemporaries in the city-fringe community of Lenton it was their reality. I was born there on 15 October 1971, into an expatriate Caribbean family of eight kids, older brother Desmond and six sisters, Marva, Sybil, Joy, Jackie, Patsy and Lorraine. My parents, Lincoln and Alynite, hailed from Jamaica. Like so many others from the West Indies, they arrived in the 1950s and 1960s as part of the post-war demand to fill jobs for a nation that had lost so much of its workforce. London was the landing place, but not for long. Even now, my dad can't fully explain how he arrived in Nottingham. He just drifted north, following a chain of beckoning fingers, and ended up down a mine shaft. From the sunshine island, in fact, to the darkest place on earth. Still, as he has reminded me so often, the money was good. It had to be, in order to keep safe and secure such a large family, and he worked in the pits until they started closing them down. Dad did the graft, I got the glory, and for a long time the family swap didn't look too fair an exchange. Mainly that was down to me; I was something of a pain in my developing years. There wasn't too much excuse for my reckless, selfish behaviour either.

Maybe I was spoilt. Maybe I was indulged a little too much. Certainly I was a central figure for so much all-embracing love. From my parents, naturally, and from my sisters, predictably. Being the second-youngest Cole was like winning a prize every day of your life. OK, the finances were a bit tight. Eight children don't come cheap, even on a sweat-browed miner's wage packet. But, as compensation, there were always strong, daily-imposed family values and much of it came from the religious background and beliefs of my grandparents and my mum. But, you know what it's like as a growing, learning, street-smart, working-class kid: you get to a certain age and you forget all of that, because you just want to run with the gang. I was no different. The Sunday school, man, well that was just history. Only now, fifteen or more years later, have I gone full circle. I have returned to my own very private, but very sincere, beliefs in God. I'm not born again, or any of that stuff. And I don't go to church every weekend either, but now religion has returned with real significance to my life. At ten or eleven I wanted out; now I very definitely want back in. It's no big deal, but it does help me with guiding principles. And once, oh boy, there

3

was a desperate time when I needed them more than I do even now. Douglas Infants and Primary School should really have been a fine starting point on the great learning curve. It was five minutes up the road from home, every one of the family was taught there, and it was a good place, a real good place. Well, it was while I spent my time in the free-and-easy environment of the infants' department.

Then, very rapidly, it was brat-pack time. Up the ladder to the primary school and very much down the scale in how not to win friends and influence people. I was a very disruptive, argumentative, and uncooperative little chap in my younger days. Authority was there to be challenged, and I challenged it every minute I possibly could. I was always rowing with teachers, even at eight and nine. I wasn't the type to listen to too many people. Well, nobody to be exact, except myself. I was downright belligerent and plain rude. When I look back, recalling the boy I was back then, I just cringe. I got everything wrong, big style. I was slung out of class a few times, banished from school a few times more. You are, supposedly, expected to grow out of that kind of wild-boy act very quickly. I didn't. I was the exception, I just got worse. When my comprehensive education began at Sandfield Secondary School, I was, more or less, a law unto myself. How much worse than before? Well, in the next couple of years, I was suspended four or five times, but the rebel wouldn't be tamed, or even curbed. School was not, you see, on my agenda. I didn't appreciate discipline. Football and anarchy were my favourite games. I was a plain and simple tearaway in those days. It was the only description that fitted. I caused so much grief and heartache for my mum and dad they should have started a campaign for the prevention of cruelty to parents! Lessons, whatever the subject, just got in the way of the football. And, on reflection now and being absolutely honest, the school allowed me to get away with murder. They indulged me when, with greater responsibility, they might have cracked down. And hard. What they did, in fact, was turn a blind eye simply because I had a talent for playing football. They would never expel me, even though I might well have deserved such a punishment, because they feared losing me to another school's football team. Crazy, but true.

Consequently, I got away with liberties as an almost daily event. I believed I had a licence to do exactly what I wanted to do. I exploited the weakness of any so-called authority to the full. I was out of control. I am not proud of it now, but that's just the way it was. I fought with the teachers. I even started fires in the biology and chemistry lessons. Thinking about the whole episode all these years later actually makes me wonder why they didn't call for the men in white coats and lock me up. What I did was maniacal, honestly. Do you remember the bunsen burners that were fixed in the labs for doing the odd experiment? Well, I thought of a very different experiment – a lesson in scaring the living daylights out of the duty teacher and one that might have burnt the whole school down if I hadn't been spotted quickly. I pretended to be cutting a piece of paper, very deliberately so everyone could see, but that was all a bit of kidology. Behind the paper, I had hold of the rubber piping connected to the gas supply. Snip, and the job was half done. Next a match, strike it before the teacher could work out what was happening, and, whoosh, the whole lot went up in an incandescent roar of burning gas. The classroom scattered, but I stayed, rocking with laughter as they tried to douse the flames. I thought it was an absolute hoot but, on refection, they should have drummed me out of the school and never let me back. Yet I got away with such madness. A lot of my friends, involved in the same kind of misbehaviour, weren't allowed to escape. No way. They were expelled.

I was always forgiven for no other reason than I was a gifted footballer. It was a cycle of doom, really, because I just went from bad to worse. When I look back, the whole situation strikes me as very wrong. That, obviously, includes me as the basic problem, but also it involves the people in charge of me. The whole issue drove my parents to the point of despair. My mum was never too bad. She attempted to understand my frustrations. But my dad fought from the opposite corner. He was aggressive, as I saw it then, authoritarian and hellbent on getting me back in line. He used to bark at me: 'I sent you to school to get an education – not just to play football.' He was very much a disciplinarian and typical of his Caribbean upbringing. I didn't conform to the pattern. Rebels never do. Families from Dad's part of the world have always been blessed with a dominant father figure ruling the roost. But he was suddenly dealing with a changing society, with vastly different temptations and dangers, and very definitely a different son. Now I can only shudder and grimace, and repeatedly apologize, for what I did to them, what I put them through. So, for the record, sorry, Dad.

By this stage, I am sure, you will have gathered I didn't concentrate too much on any studies. The only other subject, apart from football, that met with my total approval was the PE session. Maths, English, geography and all the other stuff, forget it. It wasn't for me. Even when the the teachers gave me wise encouragement I refused to change. They used to tell me, 'Andrew, if you put your mind to this subject, you could do really well.' I just wasn't fussed. The brains, they told me, were there, but only I could decide to use them. I chose not to. Self-respecting tearways don't behave that way, do they? I revelled in the role of being the classroom joker, the guy who clowned around and didn't give a damn. At that age, around twelve and thirteen, my sporting successes meant everyone else appeared to look up to me. In a way, I was on a pedestal. So, as I figured, with that kind of popularity, I could do exactly as I wanted to do. I played for the school team at least two years in advance of my age. We didn't, admittedly, have too many other good players and the standard of the side, compared with neighbouring schools, was never very good. The teachers again bowed the knee. They let me play exactly where I fancied playing. As a striker, in midfield, at the back, anywhere as long as it kept Andy happy. I was the best footballer they had and I could do exactly as I pleased. Another mistake. Once again, there was no control. But such is life.

The result, academically at least, was that I have ended up without a single qualification. Not one exam pass, not even a little certificate for woodwork or something. That is a reality I have always regretted. Even now I have arguments with my girlfriend, Shirley, about it. Her view is that it still isn't too late for me. She wants me to enrol at college. She still believes in getting those all-important bits of paper, even though my career has largely made them unnecessary. Maybe, when the football is over, she can persuade me to walk back into the classrooms I once hated so much. For the moment, I simply emphasize the real need for learning skills on my young son, Devante. He is very definitely not going to be allowed to take my hellfire route, with the consequent risks; no way, no how. His school work must always come first. He has been made to understand that I don't care if he has the ability to be the best footballer on the planet, or the finest sportsman we have ever produced, there can be but one priority. He has got to get his basic education right. Then we can go from there. Devante is not going to do it my way, because my way was wrong. I've just been lucky. Dead lucky, in truth. I happened to be blessed with a talent and, no arguments, that's the fundamental reason why I am where I am today. Without football, I could well have been in dire straits by now. I appreciate I have been fortunate. I had a gift, and in the end thankfully I used it, otherwise I could have faced the very same dead-end situations looming over so many of my generation. It stares me in the face every single day. There, the very gamble of life is exposed by the fate of some of my closest mates. So many of them are in terrible situations. I feel for them, I really do.

When I pop back to Nottingham to see the folks, I look up the old wild bunch. They just have nothing to do, no targets to achieve, no ambitions to fulfil. Sad, man, sad. Some of them might well have just been released from prison. That's not an issue, it doesn't matter to me. They are still my friends. I grew up with them. That could have been me. Yes, there but for the grace of God and an ability to play football, I might easily have ended up in jail. As I readily admit, I was a tearway, one of the best at that. But, years later, a certain newspaper delivered an article to my doorstep which I considered shocking, completely and totally wrong. It was all about my early lifestyle. It was also libellous and they paid for their lack of discretion in a court action. Their outrageous claim was that if I hadn't made it as a footballer, I would have ended up being a pimp. Think about it. I have a loving mother and six sisters and yet they still placed that astonishing slur, that gutter-level insult, against my name. I had to challenge them and I had to win. I immediately called Paul Stretford, officially my agent but also very much a personal adviser whose close support I have always been grateful to have, and we decided on a straightforward course of action: to pursue the newspaper concerned – it was, no surprise, the *News of the World* – aggressively and quickly. It meant an expedient phone call to my solicitors, where Paul instructed them to appoint George Carman, QC, one of the most prominent barristers in England. Within two days we met him at his chambers and I was very surprised, initally anyway, at the appearance of this nationally famous lawyer with such a respected and fearsome reputation in the highest courts in the land. He reminded me of a favourite uncle, small of stature, white hair, those half-moon glasses and a very benign smile on his face. He didn't quite live up to my mind's eye image of someone who was capable of taking on the sharp-practice merchants at one of Britain's most powerful Sunday newspapers. But we talked to Mr Carman for a couple of hours, his only reaction being an occasional nod of the head as our complaint unfolded, followed by an even rarer question. Suddenly, he rose from his deep considerations and said to us: 'This is an outrage and they will pay.' Now, that was more like it. A plan of action was quickly agreed and a writ duly served on the newspaper.

I thought it was only right I defend the honour of myself and my family and, if need be, I was ready to march into court to do it. Deep down, and being absolutely honest now, it was the last public appearance I wanted in all the world. I dreaded such a prospect. Paul made a call to Mr Carman and alerted him to our fears. The case, we worried, might develop into a media circus with the allegations and counter claims of such a case. Particularly with the certain evidence I have put before you already in admitting I was not exactly an angel during those formative years in Nottingham. My lawyer was full of reassurance. As Mr Carman put it to Paul, 'Don't be concerned, old boy. Tell Andrew not to worry his head with such matters, but just keep scoring for those wonderful Geordie folk. This will never go to court. This newspaper has scored an own goal.' He thought the pay-off was very humorous and laughed at his little joke, chuckling as he put down the phone. Within seven days Mr Carman had been proved right. He achieved an utterly comprehensive victory: no court appearance, a prominent apology in the newspaper, and no legal costs, plus a significant sum of money in damages to help heal the wounds. Some of the cash I paid to certain charities and the rest was diverted for my family to go on holiday. The allegations, I have got to say, hurt the people closest to me as much as they wounded me and they deserved some comfort from winning this court action. Unscrupulous newspaper editors, in attacking a young and successful footballer to produce a cheap headline or two, don't really consider that it is not just the principal who suffers. All those close to him, even more unfairly, have to bear the pain as well. The whole experience is something I wouldn't like to endure again, but on occasion you have no option; you can't walk away and let the scandalmongers get away with their injustice. That's why the vindication, far more than any financial reward, was by far the most important result of this piece of litigation.

In the offending article, there was one element of truth. They said that, for a time, I was completely off the rails. No quarrel with that at all, but the rest of it was a heap of garbage. I have never tried to deny, or cover up, my crazy years. Back then, everyone said I had a chip on my shoulder and I don't deny that either. It might not be too wise to concede it now, but at that developing age I held a view: I'm good at football, I know to the soles of my boots I am bloody good, so why not be arrogant, why not play on the edge? You need self-belief as a youngster, a bit of swagger, or you don't get acknowledged, particularly when you come from the community where I was born. But, surely, there is also some merit to be recognized that I managed to come through all that stuff and not only survive it, but, more importantly, I succeeded. The reason was basic. At fourteen, I made the single, most momentous decision of my whole life. I decided to leave home, quit the thieving and the have-a-laugh anarchy of the streets, and go to soccer's school of excellence at Lilleshall. Without that decision, the most constructive move I'll ever make if I play until I'm fifty, I would have been doomed. You see, at that time, I was still running with the mob. I wasn't getting anywhere, except into more and more trouble. I was out with my mates all the time, motivated only by making mischief. It was a restless, never-satisfied society that I was involved in back then. There were no silver spoons, cushy opportunities or easy answers. So, filled with frustration, I was just your average hooligan, mostly involved in local aggro and vandalism, but never any serious or vicious crime. It was the pastime, more or less, of so many teenage boys growing up, being cocksure and defiant, and having too much energy to burn. I got in bother with the police, of course I did. But when you are so young, you tend to get away with it. I never actually landed up in court. That, I'm afraid to say, was to come later. When it did, it scared the hell out of me, too. Much earlier than that experience, back in 1985, I knew I had to make a radical change. If I had failed to do that, I might well have been another no-hoper, a statistic of failure. I said to myself: 'You can stay in Nottingham and keep getting in bother, more serious by the week, or make a break – and try to do something with this life.' Given that choice, there was no choice. I left a lot of people behind, people who were close to me, and yet I just knew it was something I had to do. Be determined, be focused, that was my new code for survival. It was, like, making a statement of intent on my life. I had to turn the key and, then, quite dramatically almost close the door forever. When I return to Nottingham now, which is admittedly a rare event, I don't shun my long-time friends or feel uncomfortable, even wary, in the old environment. Folk down there, thankfully, don't see me as some kind of superstar. First of all, I am one of them. I'm the mate from way back, a little bit more distant, but fully aware of where they are coming from.

Some of them may now feel trapped by circumstances. Maybe if I had stayed, that would be my reaction as well. But I still like to be involved in the area and not lose the sentimental connection completely. Even if I am in town for just a few hours, I still feel the special atmosphere. I think it's something within me; I suspect it won't ever go away. My parents are still very much part of Lenton. It's as if they are anchored to the spot and that, occasionally, is a focus of good-humoured arguments between us. I want to move them out. My idea is to buy them a house in what I might regard as a better area, but they won't budge. They don't see why they should. In a way, I suppose, it's spin-off from football, part of the trappings of the job I do. They see it as making a whole lot of fuss, a song and dance about nothing. I see it as helping them financially because I have the power to do it. Ultimately, though, they must have the final decision, just as I had mine back in the 1980s in reaching for a better, richer, less hazardous life.

To make a mark, to do something with your natural ability, you have to graft. And I had to take that decision by myself. My anti-social behaviour had caused so much conflict in the family. It escalated to the point where there wasn't really a shoulder to cry on, nowhere I could seek advice. It was all down to me. That was when I opted, very wisely I have got to say, for Lilleshall, where in the space of two vital years I was given a whole new career perspective, even if that infamous rebellious streak remained half-buried inside.

The person I most have to thank for getting me there was Andy Marriott. Or, more precisely, his dad, Ian. Andy, a year older than me, became a goalkeeper with Arsenal (he's now at Sunderland). He was also twelve months in advance of me in enrolling at Lilleshall. We first bumped into each other playing in junior football teams around the Nottingham area, particularly with Forest when Brian Clough was their manager. Once Andy started getting involved in the trials, locally at first and then nationally, I was, very gratefully I must say, invited along. Fortunate, too, because without Andy's dad driving me around, I just wouldn't have been able to take part in the sifting process at all. It was a very big break for me. First of all, I was committed to the eliminators in the East Midlands, gradually building towards the ultimate test when just sixteen very envied places at the school of excellence were up for grabs. At first, the competition was in thousands drawn from grass-roots football all over the place. Then it was hundreds. Finally, it was me and a handful of others. We made it, the chosen few. I was there with Ian Walker, the Spurs and England 'keeper. Brian Small, of both Villa and Stoke, was also in the same class of 1985. So, too, were Scott Houghton and Jason Kavanagh. Not forgetting that Vietnamese boy, Hung Dang, who was at Tottenham for a while. They used to rave about him and, yes, he was brilliant. I don't know what happened to him. He just fell away and then, apparently, dropped out of football altogether. That's not unusual. The casualty rate among young, aspiring footballers is colossal. In our year, you could count the survivors on one hand.

But the whole experience was invaluable. It drilled into you the core beliefs of what it takes to be a professional footballer. You couldn't be wild, you couldn't be lairy, and you certainly had to forget any notion that you were owed an easy living in this life. It was a case of buckling down and taking the discipline, a bit like an army camp existence I suppose. Basic, but very important, values were instilled into you from the moment you checked in to the day of departure twenty-four months later. In that process, a certain Dave Sexton was invaluable to me. He might have been a touch over-technical for young kids but, without any shadow of doubt, he had an encyclopaedic knowledge of football and was one of the best coaches I have ever worked under. As an AP – football jargon for an apprentice – you rapidly learned the score. You were told to do this, clean that, shift this, and don't argue. You couldn't turn round and give a mouthful of abuse, or two fingers, otherwise you would be outside the main door looking in, with no second invitation coming. Not nice. So that, back then in the 1980s, was what Lilleshall was all about. Teaching you the fundamentals of being a footballer while, naturally, measuring and honing skills that might be good enough to secure a place in the big time. I, predictably, had to change – and fast. If I had retained my earlier independent, even insolent, attitude I couldn't possibly have survived. I would have been turfed out. Sure I had my problems, a few skirmishes and run-ins with the instructors from time to time, but nothing too heavy. A rebel, it seemed, can't be distanced from his cause, no matter how misguided, in just a couple of years. Not in my case, anyway. But, let me say very quickly, I did mostly abide by the rules and regulations. It was a school regime, too, apart from the practice pitch and regular football training. Not many of us bothered with the lessons a great deal. We had an hour's homework each day and, dutifully, we all completed it. Trouble was, we never let it sink in! It was an exercise, a ritual, and that was all. As footballers, we all just felt we had a foot on the ladder. For some of my mates, sadly enough, the rung proved a bit slippy and they fell off, never to be seen in the game again.

If it had been left to my dear old dad, that might well have been my own fate. With all his heart and soul, he wanted me to be a cricketer, not a footballer. Perfectly natural, I suppose, with his Caribbean background. He understood, too, that I had the potential. From a very young age, under his caring tutelage, I showed I was fairly handy with both bat and ball. Part of the family heritage, really, because both my old man and my brother played the game to a decent standard. As a schoolkid, I got myself into the Nottinghamshire county side. I impressed influential people there. They put me in the team. I turned round, and staggered them all, with the reply: 'I don't want to play for you any more.' And that was that. I was around thirteen at the time. My father has never let me live it down. He was mortified with my totally unexpected reaction, but I had gone as far as I wanted to go in cricket. I just wanted to prove to myself, more than demonstrate to anyone else, that I could make it to such a high level. Once that had been achieved, I was satisfied. I haven't played the game competitively at any time since. I could run, too. Not that long-distance stuff. Much too time-consuming and boring for me. But the quick, go-for-glory bit down the track was a real buzz. I broke the schoolboy record in Nottingam for 200 metres and it was a breeze. I can't remember the time I set, because it never seemed too important. I just loved sporting activity. I used to play basketball as well back in those days. Anything to get me out of the classroom.

But football always remained the priority and, of course, the true passion. For as long as I can remember I was obsessed by the individual satisfaction it granted the better players and how, if you honed natural skills, you were able to impose your presence on a game. Because I was prepared to put so much into the game on a personal level, I had to be a winner. Always. Losing was not my bag. I remember being beaten in a cup final as a schoolkid and not being able to take it. First I ripped my shirt off. Next I burst into tears of frustration and fury. Then I refused point blank to collect my loser's medal. I was just *ten* at the time. That medal, as far as I'm aware, is still tucked safely away in a drawer at the Douglas Road Primary school. It can stay there. I don't want it. I never did, no matter how much embarrassment my little protest caused at the time. I can remember the sportsmaster, Mr Peter Wilson, collecting the medal on my behalf. They locked it away until I apologized for my behaviour. Some chance! They're still waiting for the S-word to this day. But I also recall that same Mr Wilson saying some time later, 'I was annoyed with Andrew. But even at that age, he didn't want to be a runner-up, only a winner.' Dead on. They still tell tales down there about my supposed petulance on the pitch. I was just a stubborn so and so. Like how I stood by a corner flag in an Under 12s' game and refused to move because I wasn't happy with the way the team happened to be playing. They accused me of behaving like a five-year-old, of sulking, and being too much of an individual. And of terrifying my team-mates and calling them 'crap' if they didn't perform properly. Being completely out of order, merciless in truth, with those who lacked my natural ability. Now, for that behaviour and lack of understanding, I am prepared to say sorry. But in making such a concession, there is the flip side. I know the people around me back then are never slow to mention my match-winning technique and, what they termed, my 'precocious skills'. If that's flattery, then it certainly can get you anywhere. I'm very proud that a troublesome, confrontational, awkward, cussed character like myself can, eventually, learn from their immature mistakes, detect the route to the top, and take it.

Chapter Two

Highbury, those historic marble halls, Double winners, great football tradition, so many trophies and all that major business. Couldn't fail, could I? Arsenal just had to be the place for a confident boy like me. They had the players, real, special players, too, and they had another secret that was an even greater trap for somebody with my ambitions for reaching the top very quickly. You only had to take a look at the teamsheet. Arsenal, no question, was the place where young footballers were made, not born. They were always granted early, first-team opportunities. That was priority number one. Number two was the very obvious fact that so many of them were black players. I couldn't resist the invitation. I had to be a Gunner. From the moment I embarked on the Lilleshall course I knew my destination in the pro game. Then came George Graham. Gorgeous George, no less. And what a nightmare for me he turned out to be. But when I signed associate schoolboy forms with Arsenal at fourteen the manager was Terry Neill, not that he had much to do with shaping my decision. The really important influence was seeing so many young players in their side. Players like Michael Thomas, David Rocastle, Tony Adams, Paul Merson and Kevin Campbell. And, of course, Paul Davis, who was something of a mentor for me. He used to tell me Arsenal was the only club I could possibly join. It was the place where, if you had the talent, you just couldn't fail. It was the place where superkids always got their chance. Everyday, Paul, Michael and the rest would invite me to their dinner table in the canteen and fill me with the magic of Arsenal Football Club. They were the quiet persuaders and, soon, I was hooked. I fancied the London scene, too. I could stay with my sister, Jackie, and be in the big city. It all stacked up. Everything else was out of the window.

There were, of course, other clubs in the chase. The usual, tempting approaches were made by Sheffield Wednesday, Aston Villa, Celtic and late on the rails came Nottingham Forest. Of every single one of them, Forest had absolutely no chance. Sad that, isn't it, just wiping off your home-town club without a backward glance, or a split-second of regret? But Forest had been eliminated years before, never to be forgiven in my opinion for an incident targeted at a twelve-year-old boy trying to make his way in something of a forbidding football world. That boy was me. At the time Brian Clough was the manager, although he was completely innocent in what happened to me. In truth, I doubt he ever knew anything about it. The guilty men were a high profile player who was an important member of the squad, and a member of the coaching staff. I loved it at Forest. Always thought I might be a real player there one day. Then came the incident. I strolled into the dressing-room area after one training session to be met by the player in question. 'Hey, Chalky,' he said. 'Can you go and do this job for me?' Just a yard or two away, the coach stood and said nothing. He was, I have got to say, laughing his head off. It was clearly an unacceptable jibe. The coach should have dealt with it immediately. He did nothing. I glowered back at at them. Maybe as one of Forest's stars, the big man or so he thought, he figured he could say what he wanted and get away with it. Not with me, he couldn't. I turned to him and said, 'Nah, that's not for me. Not the way you talk.' Immediately, I was out of there and I never, ever went back. I just quit on the spot. They lost a potential, home-produced talent because of that one small-minded comment. If I had been just a little older, I might well have been tempted to report everything to Mr Clough. I never had a problem with him. Years later, when Forest were playing Arsenal at Highbury, I was clearing the dressing-room when Alan Hill, his assistant, pulled me over. 'Brian, this is the local boy we missed out on. Good player, too.' Cloughie just seized me in a bear hug and planted a great big kiss on my cheek. The episode was all so regrettable. When I look back, I know I would have enjoyed nothing better than playing for Forest, where initially I learned so much. I also fully understand now that, no matter how high you aspire or what you achieve in football, you have still got to treat people properly.

Mind, at around sixteen and two years after signing for Arsenal on my birthday, my own values were not exactly flawless. They put me in charge of the rest of the apprentices in my year at Highbury. It was something of a foreman's role, if you like, and it carried very necessary responsibilites. Generally, I'm afraid to say, I ignored most of them. I was supposed to organize the other APs in their jobs around the club. Instead I allowed them to do exactly as they pleased. I should have controlled the other lads; all I did was allow them a free rein and, consequently, much of the time little got done. Pat Rice, the left fullback from Arsenal's trophy winning teams of the 1970s and 1980s, was the youth coach. He had to crack down and he did. I got the sack and Ray Parlour, a year younger than me, was put in charge. It was the first hint of more conflict to follow with Rice. But, far more seriously, I tangled with a far tougher opponent and one that invariably proves to have the upper hand. You've got it, the long arm of the law. And, after many years of trying, they finally had me in their grip. I was lured, for all my street-smart background, into a situation involving a family issue that rapidly ran out of control. It ended with me in the dock of the local magistrates' court trying to explain my side of events. On a weekend break as an Arsenal apprentice, I decided to head back home to Nottingham to spend some time with the folks. All cosy, all innocent. What I hadn't appreciated was that one of my sister's best friends was trapped in an unwanted relationship with a certain young man. He decided it was time to turn up at our house as I hit town. There was a disturbance. No, in fact, there was more than that. A fight broke out between the two of us outside my family home. Subsequently, I was arrested, accused and placed on a charge of inflicting grievous bodily harm. I was still sixteen and just embarking on my apprenticeship with Arsenal. Suddenly, everything, my career and every ambition I ever had, was at stake. For the first time in my life, for all the madness of my youth, I was hauled into court. Several appearances later, they threw out all the accusations against me. I was, rightly, declared innocent. It was all very scary. I understood that something very precious might be instantly taken away from me. Like, to be exact, the life I had planned for myself and the dreams I had treasured for years. The risks were obvious. If I had been convicted on such a serious charge, Arsenal would understandably have taken a dim view. They probably would have been left with little option but tossing me out on my ear and that would have been another football career over. So when the verdict was delivered, I had tears in my eyes. They were tears of total relief. Praise the Lord, it all got sorted out in the end. But very soon, back at the club, I was pitched into more uncertainty.

There was upheaval, concern and a feeling of deep frustration. In my eyes I had a big problem. I was banging in goals on a regular basis, but I didn't see any tangible rewards. I seemed to be getting absolutely nowhere. Remember, it was the very idea of Arsenal being a fast-track outfit that tempted me to join them in the first place. I was an explosion waiting to happen, full of anger and resentment. All that was needed was for someone to ease down on the detonator. That person turned out to be Rice. He kept chivvying, needling and having a go at me in training. I couldn't control my emotions any longer and I snapped. There was a whole salvo of effing and blinding, then I snarled at him: 'I'm off. That's me finished here.' And I stormed off the park. The rest of the lads couldn't believe it, but I was in the shower, towelled and on my way before they could take another corner kick. I made the dash to Jackie's place to pack my bag, raced for the train and made the grand escape for Nottingham. It might well have been another more ominous destination, like oblivion.

Back home, my mum and dad could barely believe what I had done. They thought I was out of my head. Maybe I was. Within a day or two, Stewart Houston, then the assistant manager at Arsenal, was on the phone. Bluntly, I told him, 'Forget it, I'm talking to no one. I'm packing everything in. That's the end. I am just getting nowhere with you down there.' He advised me, rightly, that I was being impetuous and overreacting and, again correctly, that it would be an act of rank stupidity to waste my football talent. I refused to listen, warned him again that this was farewell time and that I did not see any worthwhile future for myself with Arsenal. Next news,

Terry Murphy, the club's youth development officer, was back on the phone. This time, correctly, he spoke to my parents as he tried to resolve the stand-off. He pleaded with them to get me back to Highbury, insisted that any outstanding problems would quickly be sorted out, and, would you believe, even offered an apology. The rebel, miraculously, had been pardoned again. Stubbornly, I still stood my ground but slowly my parents broke down those youthful barriers of defiance. They said a football career was all I had ever wanted, which was true, and why, then, should I just chuck it all away in a fit of pique. They were right, the persuasion sank in and slowly made sense, and ultimately I was coaxed into a return to Arsenal. It was apologies all around and words of reconciliation by the dozen. But, deep down, I knew the long-term consequences. That was my first real spat with the club and from that moment I suspected I would get nowhere at Arsenal. I was right. I had committed the unforgivable crime in taking on the establishment of George Graham and there could be only one eventual and lasting survivor.

I played in the youth team and got goals. I played in the reserve team and got goals aplenty. What happened? Zilch. Once again, maybe a little rashly and impatiently, I felt I was being held back. Certainly I was getting nowhere. The first team appeared as remote as ever. At sixteen I felt I had no chance of progression, at seventeen I figured I should be moving on, and in the next couple of seasons those views were hardened by events. There was another aggravation, too. Young players that I considered not to be in my class were handed pro contracts at seventeen. Why, then, did I have to hang around until I was eighteen for the same career guarantee? That narked me. I was disillusioned. I thought it showed a lack of respect. After all, I was doing the business and yet my fellow APs were gaining greater recognition. Think about it. There were boys like Ray Parlour, top player, and Neil Heaney, once of Southampton and Manchester City and now I believe with Darlington. Where are the rest? I couldn't handle the frustration of it all. It was a grievance that bit deep into me and filled my mind with resentment. There was only one answer – knock on the door and see George. So I did and he was waiting. Predictably. I wasn't even nineteen and this was showdown time with one of the most famous and successful managers in the game. Inside his office, I challenged him immediately: 'Look, I should be in your first team. And now. Understand that? I'm a confident lad, you see.' George Graham didn't budge. His reply: 'I don't see it that way, son. I just see it that you have got a chip on your shoulder. You walk around this place like you are the bee's knees.' Answer: 'I don't think I'm the bee's knees. But what I do think is that I am good enough for your first team. Right?' The next volley had already been loaded: 'No, I don't think so. You have got an attitude – the wrong attitude. You start knuckling down and then you might, just might, get into my team.' I shut the door behind me. I might as well, in a way, have closed the final page on our relationship. You only had one chapter of confrontation with George Graham.

From that very moment, a relationship didn't exist. I never saw eye to eye with George in all my time at the club. He just seemed to have his favourites whom he wanted to play to the exclusion of everyone else. I was the outcast. Sure, I was a confident chap, I had an assertive edge about me at the time, and I had certainly told him the uncomfortable truth as I saw it. I can well imagine how that may have goaded a man of George's dominant nature, and rubbed him the wrong way. But when you are of a certain, still-maturing age you don't look for explanations, or even a reasoned argument. All you want to do is play the game. You think you deserve it, that you have earned it. George Graham's so-superior attitude just rankled with me. I had a chip on my shoulder, and I now realize that, but I can't have been the only truculent teenager in football at the time. He would never grant you an inch. No, that's wrong, he would never grant you a fraction of an inch. Yet young footballers need to be aggressive and assertive in a very competitive environment. If I had remained head-bowed and subservient, touching the forelock and all that, I would still have been getting nowhere at twenty-five. So, it was inevitable that conflict, George and I would always go together because I felt it right to speak my mind. It was fatal to question his authority in any way.

As a young man, very much on the outside of such a formidable organization, he appeared a very autocratic, aloof figure. George could walk blindly past you in a corridor without any acknowledgement. He would just blank you. That's hard for a kid to take. One day you were in, the next, well, you were nothing. Or that's the way it appeared. At a young, vulnerable age, even when you put on an act of bravado like me, you want the golden arm around the shoulder and some comforting, encouraging words. That just never happened in George's regime. He was a hard man, maybe too hard, and his methods were enforced with a fearsome authority. It was Tony Adams who christened him Colonel Gaddafi. No nickname has ever fitted better. George was all powerful, the ruler, the dictator, and he wanted everyone to know it. You just had to toe the line with him, no ifs and buts. It was never a case of having a ruck with George. You couldn't argue with him because he just didn't tolerate debate. He was the manager of Arsenal Football Club and you, the humble peasantry, had better believe it. His control was forever laid down the only way he knew how – with an uncompromising iron fist.

He shifted the high profile men, the characters of the club you might say, double quick. When I first signed, Charlie Nicholas, that wonderful showman, a player of immense popularity on the terraces, was still there, fleetingly, and then he was gone. Graham Rix, another player with flair, didn't survive much longer. Soon he went through the door. Their types, for all the skill they possessed, just couldn't be accommodated. It was a way of George placing his own well-determined imprint on the club. George had a very low tolerance level. If you didn't do it his way, you were history. And that, in the long run, was my fate too. To be honest, I don't think George Graham ever felt I was good enough to get into his team. At the time, Campbell, Merson and Alan Smith were in front of me. So, believe it or not, was Perry Groves. Now that was just too much to stomach. I used to think to myself: 'I'm as good as him. Easily. Yet I can't get a game. Now that pisses me off.' I couldn't get the negative vibes out of my head . . . like, I'm waiting, I'm smouldering, I'm fed up to the back teeth, and I'm twenty. I made sub for a few minutes against Sheffield United and had a run-out in the Charity Shield. Wonderful! Apart from that, absolutely nothing, no bait dangled to keep me happy and hungry for more. So the inevitable happened. I was back knocking on George's door. He told me, fair and square, if he could get rid of me, and the offer was right for Arsenal, he would have me on my way. By then I was coming up to twenty-one, convinced I wasn't ever going to emerge from relative obscurity. If I had stayed, I might well still be there, very much condemned to the shadows. Because I don't think I would ever have made it under Graham. Never, ever. He wouldn't have granted me a chance; he had made up his mind, full stop.

A lot of people suggest now that I was too abrasive, too argumentative, and too arrogant for Graham in my early years. It wasn't that at all – it was simply a case of being seriously committed to my ambition and having great self-belief to make certain that the dream eventually came true. When I was at Arsenal, men in powerful positions there used to ask me regularly why I wasn't in the first team. I could only raise my eyes as an answer. One of them was David Dein, now the club vice chairman. He was my great boardroom supporter. He would sidle up and say: 'You are going to be a star, Andy. You are going to make a big name for yourself in the game one day. Keep going.' I still reflect on his prophetic words to this day. If he could see it, as a director of Arsenal, why couldn't the manager he employed see it, too? Only George can truthfully reveal his reason, but I have long suspected there is a fairly simple answer. All he could see was this chippy, confrontational, very challenging young man in front of him; he could never, more's the pity, look beyond that and recognize a footballer desperate to make his mark. I always knew I had the ability, had the belief I could succeed. All I wanted was for someone in authority to reaffirm those convictions. That man had to be George Graham, but he was too involved in himself to make that critical step. You can't even say it was a consistent rule he applied to everyone. He was certainly forgiving of other Arsenal players, as a number of controversies which made the tabloid headlines in the 1990s was to underline. And yet, for all Graham's outstanding achievements with Arsenal, there doesn't appear to be overwhelming or wholehearted respect from the major players who claimed those championships and cups. Certainly, that's the impression left with me after reading Tony Adams' book. Not many, I suspect, would be rushing to play for him again.

When he refused to grant me an opportunity, the explanation was always that Kevin Campbell was a better player, or that Merse was playing out of his skin. So, consequently, there was no room left for me. They were the usual, very obvious alibis, all delivered pat, the trademark excuses of the management business. And then he went out and signed Ian Wright. Now Wrighty is a top player and 200 Arsenal goals underline the calibre of the man. But I like to consider myself very similar in attacking style, just a younger version. Why, then, didn't George allow me, a home-produced striker without a fee, to lay down my first-team credentials before investing so much in Ian? Hey, look, I might have failed, and I might well not have lived up to Wrighty's considerable achievements, but at least I should have been given the chance. Maybe I was just a name on the hate list. Surely, though, that's taking personal dislike and intolerance to ridiculous levels. Long after my departure, when the goals were flowing at my later clubs, George insisted he never regretted the decision to release me. But then, when I was on the way towards winning the treble, I read an unlikely newspaper admission from the great man. It stated: 'If I had known he would turn out this way, I would never have sold Andy Cole.' Vindication at last! It was time for a quiet chuckle and yet, too late was the cry, far too late. There can never be any dispute that George Graham was an excellent manager for Arsenal. In the end, I can't complain about what he did for me either. Because he did me a genuine favour – he let me go.

Initially, it was only a temporary move across the city to Fulham. The loan was merely for three months, but it meant a great deal to me. It meant, of course, regular competitive football in the first team and a platform from which I could finally build a professional career. I relished the opportunity and then, suddenly, I was confronted by two characters who seemed to loom out of football's dark ages. Jimmy Hill, whom I couldn't stand, was one. He was the chairman. The other was Alan Dicks, the boss, and frankly I had never heard of him. The players at Craven Cottage seemed to trample all over him; it was a sad sight to witness. Just arriving from Arsenal, where Graham was a boss to be obeyed and never questioned by the majority, it was incredible hearing the Fulham players speak so dimissively to Dicks. I just couldn't believe it. They ran the training themselves and did precisely as they pleased. It was like a holiday camp. My immediate reaction was: 'I can't take too much of this – but, then again, I need to be playing steady football. You have to stay awhile.' At Arsenal, it was demanded that players didn't step out of line by as much as an inch. Down at the Cottage, they were taking liberties by the country mile. That provoked a few bust-ups and, inevitably, I figured in most of them. I just didn't approve of their lack of focus. Then there was the hapless Mr Dicks. He kept trying to tell me how to play the game. Was he kidding, or what? It seemed to me that here was a guy being pushed around by everybody else, yet he still felt equipped to advise me what football was all about. He wasn't exactly speaking from a position of absolute authority, was he?

Now let's move on to old Jimmy. I could never take to him. No, correction, I have to admit I disliked him with a passion. I think he quickly sensed it, too. I had been at his club – he was the man in charge, back then – for a matter of weeks, and I had scored a few goals along the way, when I received the summons to his office. We had, previously, kept our distance and, despite my feelings about him, there hadn't been any grief or a wrong word said. Then, without warning, it was gloves off, rather than any meeting of minds. He suddenly said to me, 'I don't think you will ever make a player.' I was taken aback. 'That's your opinion, but I've also got my own opinion and I'm confident in my ability,' I replied. 'No,' he said, 'you have got a bit of an attitude. You're not going to make it.' When this nasty little dialogue was all over I thought to myself: 'And who do you think you are to give me such a hard time?' It seemed to me that he wanted to bludgeon any ambition out of me. To this day, I haven't the remotest idea why Hill attacked me in such a way without, to my knowledge, any history between us. No hassle, no arguments, no insults – all I can assume is he was having a bad day. Still, it reinforced all my instincts about this opinionated man who clearly considers he has a right to put the rest of the world in order. I don't forget his contribution, of course. He helped the players during that period of, ahem, stone-age football when he campaigned successfully for the abolition of the minimum wage. It was a cause well fought. But these days, be serious, he is a bit out of touch. He is a man of another time. He did his bit, and thanks a lot, but we have to move on, surely. Watching him on the box, lambasting another player, any player, I think: 'Yes, mate, and that's exactly what you said about me when I was younger.' Now here I am, an England player, a Manchester United player, with the treble in my hands, the happiest footballer on the planet. What, Mr Jimmy Hill, is your verdict? Am I ever going to be a player, or not?

The brief escape to Fulham was followed by an even shorter return to Arsenal. It was as if I was being recycled and very swiftly I was on my way to Bristol City. Once again, it was a loan job; three months from March to May in 1991 and the mission was to help them avoid relegation. Their manager had just been dismissed and Denis Smith, a huge and helpful influence on my development, had been appointed. I did OK for him and Bristol, scored a few goals, and we just about stayed up. They considered me their lifeline. Even more important, for the first time in a while, I had revelled in my football; the West

Country experience was really enjoyable and it proved, on reflection, to be the place where my career slowly changed course. At one time, if only briefly, it seemed to be heading in the direction of Derby County. While I was still based in Bristol, Pat Rice called me. He said Derby were in for me, he didn't know the fee, but he would ring back to confirm the finer details. I asked him if the Arsenal manager was prepared to let me go. A momentary silence and then the indication that it would be a yes. So I just sat back and waited. And waited. Nothing happened. The first major transfer of my life had disappeared down a great black hole before I had even got round the bargaining table. It seemed I was booked in for another summer of uncertainty with Arsenal. Not exactly part of my plans because I had reached the point of desperation and my decision to leave had long been forged in my own mind. Salvation came while I was away on holiday. Arsenal had finally agreed a £500,000 fee for my transfer to Smithy's mob and I was now free to travel to Bristol for talks. They lasted no more than a couple of hours. OK, it wasn't exactly a club with a name up in lights, or a particularly glamorous destination on the football map, but it did offer hope and significant opportunity. It wasn't Arsenal, true, but that's where I had been largely ignored. It wasn't Fulham, either, where I felt I had been abused for no good reason and now regarded it as no more than a joke outfit. This was Bristol City, where I knew from recent personal experience I would be valued for my ability. I would be helped and encouraged as well, and I would be able to express myself as a player. It was an offer I couldn't refuse.

Denis Smith had bold plans, too. His determined campaign in dodging relegation had delivered the right kind of allies at Ashton Gate. The budget was hastily provided for him to erect sterner foundations. When I arrived on a permanent transfer, I genuinely considered them to be, OK, a team in transition but also a team on the upward curve. I felt that promotion to the old First Division was a realistic target. I was calming down as well, I was far more focused, and the desire to play meaningful football for a living was being fulfilled. For that Denis deserved congratulations, essentially from me. So, too, did his chief scout, Tony Thorthorp. Smithy was quite a character and had a marvellous, highly personal method for developing my career and turning me into a better pro. He felt I needed toughening up, so he used to kick the living daylights out of me at every training session and took great delight in this very original, one-on-one coaching method. It did harden me to the basic realities of living in a man's world; you just don't survive unless you are prepared for both the mental and physical demands. And these two guys were of immense help in building my confidence, no easy matter after the way it had been put through the shredder at Arsenal. An element of flattery, for any of us, can take you a long way. There was the psychological impact, another great benefit for me, in the knowledge that the manager was prepared to stake his reputation, and a sizeable amount of money on me when so many other people were asking, 'Who is this guy, anyway?' And, yes, there was some risk on my part in that this was football in the backwoods and I might disappear there forever. At Arsenal, a number of my closest mates questioned whether I was doing the right thing. I never had any doubts. It wasn't a tough decision, it was a decision in which I had no choice. I got a signing fee, a few quid extra in wages, and always felt I was about to realize my potential. Denis and Tony are two helpers along the way whom I will never forget. Sure, as always, I got in bother with Smithy a couple of times. It happened first when he granted me some Christmas leave to see Shirley my long-term girl-friend, even if it was only for a matter of hours. We trained

Christmas Day morning, then I was released to get back to London. I stayed a bit too long and smuggled my way back in with the rest of the squad a few hours behind schedule. I thought Smithy hadn't noticed, but then a letter arrived. I had been hit with a hefty fine. I dawdled over the payment and, in the end, didn't have to cough up. Smithy, sadly, got the sack before I ever got round to paying his fine.

Mostly, though, I coasted through life with City. Every Saturday morning was a real buzz, in the knowledge I would be out there doing the business in front of 15,000 fans instead of being in the reserves with a few old pros going through the motions. It was a decent team, too. I played alongside Leroy Rosenior, who was a very experienced forward recruited from West Ham. Gary Shelton, a hard-working boy in midfield, and Mark Aizlewood, also gave us some resolve and quality. The pity was that that side, which had cost around £800,000 and was big, big money for Bristol, just never knitted together. At the back of my mind, though, I had plan B as a backup. Down in Bristol I lived by a single motto and that was self-preservation. My motivation was: 'If I am as good as I think I am then, within a year or two, I'll be destined to finish at a much bigger club'. Bristol City, and this is not being patronizing, was my stepping stone. So it proved to be. First of all, Forest, who might have signed me for nothing, entered the fray. Smithy told me immediately of their interest, but warned: 'So far, they haven't offered enough. But if they come back with the right figures, you can go.' It was Cloughy who had stepped in with the bid. Six-hundred grand, they said it was, and a clear profit for Bristol in less than a year. But they wanted more. Cloughy, the old fox, had other ideas. He was being threatened with relegation, and eventually Forest took the drop that season, so he was desperate for a goal-scoring striker. But everybody in the game knew his way of doing business. He liked to recruit a player cheaply, work on him and then emerge the other end, a year or two later, like some kind of miracle man when the signing turned into a major star. He, clearly, had a price in mind for me. Smithy kept me in touch with developments and I felt I would soon be on my way.

That weekend we played Birmingham, strolled it 3–0 and I was very happy with my performance. When it was all over I was out on the pitch doing a virtual lap of honour. It was a salute to the fans because I figured it would be my last appearance in front of them. Straight after the match, Smithy grabbed me and informed me that Forest had tabled a bid of £650,000. I thought, that's it, I'm on my way, but he told me to sit down and sit tight as the offer wasn't good enough and added nonchalantly that he was confident that by Monday they would increase the bid to a level more to his liking. But Forest apparently didn't pick the phone up and I was once again back in limbo. Next we played Luton in the FA Cup, on a Wednesday night, and Smithy told me that it looked like Forest had certainly cooled but not to worry, because Newcastle had been on the blower about me. After the game, once again, he declared that he was confident that Newcastle would match his valuation of £1.5 million. I couldn't believe the size of the fee. As a player, there was nothing to do but wait. But then catastrophe. Smithy was sacked. I owed him so much. He, arguably more than anybody, provided the guidance that was to prove of such benefit later on.

The Smith philosophy was blunt and basic: if you want to throw away a career, that's fine with me, but if you intend playing at the top, this is the way to go. He shaped my destiny in a very crucial way. He was the first to under-pin the shaky, uncertain confidence of a young player; the first to make me believe I could be special.

With Denis gone, another month went by and no bid

was on the horizon. I hadn't a clue what was going to happen to me and by then Russell Osman had been appointed in Smith's place. For a while, the transfer business was kept deliberately low key. Even so, whether in the long or short term, I figured they would want to trade me to Newcastle, as long as the price was right. Lesley Kew was Bristol's chairman at the time, very much a juggler of finances and a dedicated hard bargainer. He wanted every penny because he knew Arsenal's sell-on clause would also bite into his club's profits. It was about this time that I heard a very strong rumour that Aston Villa were keen to do business. Nothing happened, though. Years later it was suggested to me that the reason was that Doug Ellis, the Villa chairman, couldn't locate Ron Atkinson, his manager at the time. Not surprising, really, when he has a reputation for having roughly a boss a week in charge of his club. Anyway, even without Villa's presence at the bargaining table, the opportunity for something of an auction developed when Newcastle started talking big numbers. They originally proposed a deal at £1.5 million. It was politely turned down. Eventually the figure reached £1.75 million and it was handshakes all round. My value had more than trebled in little more than ten months. The problem was City couldn't conclude the transaction for a while. The reason was that they just couldn't track me down. Actually, I was in the local launderette doing my washing – humble boy, you might notice! – when they finally put the package to me. I didn't need to think twice, not with Kevin Keegan as the man in charge at St James's Park.

Chapter Three

The mobile rang. 'Can I speak to Aidan, please?' Strange call, I figured. This is somebody, surely, trying to set me up. 'Wrong number, mate, there's no Aidan here. This is Andrew Cole.' The guy at the other end spluttered in obvious embarrassment: 'Hey, sorry, I'm very sorry, it's Andy Cole I want to speak to.' And that bizarre little exchange added up to my first ever formal introduction to Kevin Keegan, an extremely influential figure who helped transform my life. Crazy, I thought. Here's somebody who has just invested some mind-boggling money in my football future, and he doesn't even know my name. I've pulled his leg about it many times since, and he's not stopped apologizing for his mistake. But from that wrong-footed beginning developed a manager–player relationship I suspect has to be envied by many a pro in the game. It remains on a sound basis of mutual respect to this very day, despite the inevitable points of friction and fall-outs along the way. You're bound to have a barney with him sometime, because he is an emotional, heart-on-sleeve type of character. I cannot see anything wrong in that, either. Yet so many uninformed outsiders portray Kevin as a walking, talking, giant-sized ego and only that. They're so way off the mark. He has an ego, no doubt about it, and a sizeable one at that. But the secret about Kevin is that he understands that most other people, certainly within football, also have egos which don't exactly demand a microscope to detect their existence. And he allows for those frailties and chinks in the armour. He is prepared to accommodate their egos, too, unlike some I could mention who can only be described as ego-maniacs. The breed of manager, and you know who I mean, which forever demands only absolute power, to the cowering disadvantage of everyone else. You've got it – the control freak.

That is one indictment that can never, at least fairly and objectively, be levelled at Kevin. He might easily have got heavy with me, for instance, in that first conversation. Because, initially, I knocked him back in what was an almost typical response from me at that time. As we chatted, Kevin told me I must head north for Newcastle immediately. He wanted to get the details sorted and have me in the squad without any further delay. 'Nah,' I said. 'I can't do that – I've got something on today.' It was, I have to say, being economical with the truth and most probably he held that view while we were talking. But he didn't push the issue aggressively, even though he has ribbed me mercilessly about it ever since, suggesting I threatened to turn him down and gave him a hard time over the transfer. Not many people have dared stall on Kevin, so maybe I was chancing my arm once again. But the opposite, in fact, was true. I was desperate to play in a Keegan side. He didn't need to convince me about anything and the following day I grabbed the shuttle and signed everything in a matter of hours. Really, I had no decision to make. When you think of Keegan, his fantastic achievements as a player and the kind of inspirational personality he is, then you simply say, 'Oh yeah, that's the money, fine, and how long do you want me here?' And then you shake hands on a done deal. The money I earned was undeniably well in excess of my wages at Bristol, but that, honestly, wasn't the point of the exercise. I knew with Keegan I could go places. I've never made any secret of the fact that I joined Newcastle, long before I understood the fanatical desire of the place as a football heartland, because of Keegan, and nothing or nobody else. Lee Clarke, an old-time mate from playing together at junior and intermediate levels with England, had never stopped preaching the Geordie gospel to me, but KK loomed above all other considerations. I couldn't turn him down, ever. He was a player I revered when I was growing up. He was my idol, you wore his named boots, had his posters on the wall, hell, he was THE man. When the offer came, inwardly I knew ... I've got to play for him. The true measure of the manager was, frankly, one of the significant reasons why the Newcastle board had recruited him for the job. They understood only too well that he was the magnet, the personality able to lure major players to St James's Park due to the power of who he was, his reputation, and what he stood for.

He had, apparently, been tracking me from my very early days at Bristol and first tried to buy me within weeks of being appointed at Newcastle. Strange as it may appear, his conviction about me hardened when he saw me playing little more than half fit. I played in a fixture against West Ham. To be honest, I shouldn't have played as I was nursing myself back from a knee ligament injury I received against Watford a few weeks before. It meant I had been laid up for weeks and on my comeback I could barely run. Kevin was in the stands scrutinizing that below-par performance. Now, most managers, certainly those ready to invest millions, would have decided to take another look when, probably, I would be in better shape and not operating at a level above no more than 70 per cent. Not Kevin. Maybe he's a lateral thinker, but he reckoned that if I was prepared to play while still crocked, sacrificing myself for the team as he saw it, then that made me a footballer he wanted to buy all the more. No wonder he was never anything other than a terrific influence on my career and, unlike a few others I might name, never tried to change the way I played. He was always content with what he got for his money. The bottom line is that he asks players to express themselves. Some suggest he is not a tactical or technical man. That's wrong. Kevin likes to say his piece, but he is more convinced by the idea of creating a team in his own ideal of how the game should be played, and then letting them get on with it. Another strength is that he surrounds himself with close confidants like Arthur Cox and Terry McDermot, who share a huge knowledge about the game between them. That allows Kevin to deal with the man-management side and, let me assure you, there is nobody better. He polishes the ego, instils confidence as a daily ritual, building players up and never destroying them, even when they might well be enduring a nightmare. Most managers have the habit of building you up, only to knock you down. A bit like the good guy-bad guy syndrome and the art of psychology I suppose. Kevin's secret was to be positive all the time and that made players perform as if they were prepared to die for him.

When I first moved to Newcastle, I don't mind admitting I was a little star struck. Most of the players at the club I had only previously seen on the box. Kevin Sheedy, who had a left leg that was unreal, and Kevin Brock were great for the side until they fell out with KK. There was also Steve Howey and Killer Kilcline (Barry Kilcline) and Rob Lee who had just signed from Charlton and Scott Sellers who had signed the day before me from Leeds United. My future strike partner was Dave 'Ned' Kelly and there was also Gavin Peacock who, it turned out, I basically replaced. The first game was against Swindon, away, and KK just told me to watch the players and the pattern of play. I came on but, to be fair, it wasn't a great performance. Next up was Notts County. I scored on my full debut. And after that was my home debut against Barnsley – my introduction to the Toon Army. We won 6–0 and I scored a hat-trick. Newcastle United was about flair and playing to the sound of the bugles. We would win 6–0 here, 4–0 there, and 5–3 at our place, it was gripping, exciting stuff. We were so superior to anyone else in that division, it was like being involved in a blood sport. The manager wanted goals from me and, from day one, I was able to provide them. They were, not being too modest, something of a factor in hauling Newcastle into the élite competition of the Premiership, which we achieved with a fantastic home win against Leicester, and I finished the season the way I started, with a hat-trick. It was hallelujah time, a carnival of celebrations and backslaps all round. It was a fantastic day – not just on a personal level but also as a professional, as it was my first ever professional medal and the hat-trick meant I'd scored twelve goals in twelve games since joining in March. But very quickly, Kevin stopped me dead in my tracks. Matter of factly, he ushered me to one side and said, confidentially, 'I'm looking to buy Peter Beardsley to play with you next season. He will help you get goals and make you a great player. All right?' Now that was a head-scratcher. What did he mean . . . trying to buy a player for me, just for me? I had hit the net often enough and so did Ned, certainly enough times to secure promotion, and I felt that Ned and I had played very well together. We had blended well together, I told the manager, and he readily agreed. But he ordered me not to worry, that was his side of the business, and he went out and signed Beardsley anyway. And was he a signing! Boy, did he know how to play! He was a gift from the gods, a player of true creative genius and, unhesitatingly,

I nominate Peter as the best striker I have ever operated alongside. It's not even an argument. I appreciate I have subsequently forged a great attacking bond with Dwight Yorke at Manchester United, but Beardo, well, he was just a phenomenon, a footballer who deserved to have the cliché 'out of this world' patented as his personal logo.

He could do the lot. He could almost read your mind, and certainly plot your next move. He could deliver the pass at precisely the most dangerous and effective moment, create space for himself on or off the ball, and all this was based on the platform of an outstanding work ethic. This fella flogged himself to death for the rest, even though he was the best footballer in the team. There is not a single superlative that Pete has not earned in his career. For me to be placed alongside him was a pleasure. I'm tempted to suggest I should have paid for the privilege, but that's likely to give some directors the wrong idea. What I will say is that I got fifty-six goals in that Newcastle team in no time at all and they wouldn't have been possible without his remarkable contribution. He understood Keegan's underlying system which, hopefully not being big-headed, was to base the whole team around me. The briefing always amounted to 'Get the ball to Andy, and he'll put it in the net'. So the majority of goal-scoring chances meant I had to be played in and, fortunately, nine times out of ten I lived up to that individual pressure and put them away. I was the fulcrum while Beardsley was the catalyst. Wide of him we had Scott Sellars and Robert Lee, bombing in the crosses or angling the ball back to me from the line. We all understood the simplicity of a very dangerous strategy, yet it was a very easy framework in which to get the results and feel comfortable. We used to terrify the opposition because of the rapid movement of the ball and the explosive pace we possessed on the counter-attack. Peter would drop off very stealthily, slip me in with a perfectly paced ball, and BANG. That's how simple it was. It was Kevin who clearly envisaged the smoothness and efficiency of the partnership and it was a great compliment to me that he actually signed such a fine player for my benefit.

It was a relationship of great trust that I enjoyed with KK. So close, in truth, that he took me into his confidence over the purchase of players and even sought my advice on who he might buy next. He consulted me very closely on at least two of the big names who helped take Newcastle so agonizingly close to the Premier League title. One night I was rushing into the ground, on an errand of private business, when I bumped into the boss. He asked me where I was heading and I told him I was off to collect my mail from the office. 'No, you're not, sunshine,' he said. 'You're coming with me.' He dragged me into his car and slammed the foot down hard. Next, we are hurtling past Carlisle on the motorway. 'OK, joke over,' I said to him. 'Let me into the secret. And, by the way, where are we going?' KK laughed and shrugged, 'Sorry, I forgot I hadn't mentioned that part, but we are off to watch Liverpool play QPR.' Then, with more seriousness, he added, 'I want you to have a look at this certain player for me.' I was perplexed. 'What are you on about? How I can be watching players for Newcastle United? I've not been at the club five minutes.' Anyway, we rolled into Anfield and at that stage I still hadn't a clue about the supposed Mr X under scrutiny. I sat down to watch the game and it was purgatory. It was a windy, horrible, winter night and there was only one thought entering my mind. Like, what the hell am I doing in this place right now? I was freezing my nuts off and, increasingly, I felt more and more brassed off. Still, almost with a smirk on his face, the manager wouldn't let me into his secret. Suddenly, he blurted out: 'I am looking to buy a centre half. Who have you found it most difficult to play against, would you say?' I ran through a few names, reeling them off one by one. KK shook his head, no, it wasn't him, or him, and definitely not him. Then he revealed the target. I hadn't mentioned him on my list, I have got to say, and yet I had just watched him in action. 'It's Darren Peacock,' says the gaffer. 'I think he can do a good job for us.' I agreed and that was that. Daz signed for us shortly after that unwanted night on Merseyside. The question remains whether Keegan kidnapped me for a second opinion or just because he wanted a bit of company in the car.

But that was KK. He would phone up out of the blue and ask for my verdict on certain players in the league. Did I think the individual would be helpful to the team, would he be able to fit in, things like that. Remember, I was only twenty-three at the time and yet the manager was ready to take me into his confidence on such important matters. I was very flattered and it naturally helped our relationship. He dropped another famous name in my lap on another morning after training. This time it was Ruel Fox. Did I feel he might help increase the scoring ratio even further with his contribution from the flank? 'He's a tricky player,' I confirmed. 'He will get the crosses in and he will certainly create chances for us. Yeah, I would go for him.' A couple of days later Foxy arrived from Norwich. Many times, KK consulted me on such matters and I don't think I am being too naive in saying I might have had some influence on team affairs during that period. I was flavour of the month on Tyneside, and I happened to be scoring plenty of goals, but I believe the manager bothered to speak to me principally because he thought of me as an honest and straight boy. We were very close. In fact, as a player you really could not ask for anything better. KK has been really good for me in many ways, not just in my development as a footballer but also planting my feet more firmly on the ground and helping me become a far more rounded, stable and mature person.

Sometimes, mind you, I seriously wondered if ever that state of mind would be possible among the Geordies. Up there, man, it was totally manic. I had never experienced anything like it before. It was like being beamed up to another planet after my life in London. In the south there are other interests, other distractions. Up there, in bonny-lad land, it's football, football, and then more football. Nothing else, I swear, matters. They could drop the bomb and the only question to be raised would be whether it meant they now had to walk to the match on Saturday or would the buses still be running. It was such a culture shock. I was brought up to enjoy life, and football is always going to be very much a sport for me. Not to the Geordie boys. For them it's the whole point of their existence. There is just no escape. A pastime has become an obsession, and it can be both wonderful and brain-damaging at the same time. When I first arrived in town, my soulmate Clarkey naturally volunteered to show me the sights, if you understand the drift. The whole place was heaving. I had just never seen so many clubs so busy. Every place you hit was absolutely mobbed. And everywhere you looked, there was the Toon Army in force. You entered a disco club and the only topic was football; you booked for a meal and it was football again; you headed for the shops and it was more football. Hey fellas, I thought to myself, I can't take much more of this. But the goals kept coming, and promotion became a certainty, and I was trapped like a captive hero. Soon, too soon, they hailed me their king, just like Jackie Milburn and Malcolm Macdonald in earlier eras of Newcastle success. I didn't want such acclaim, I really didn't. I shunned the very notion of being an idol, but that's what I was forced to accept and acknowledge. Centre-forwards are the very core of Newcastle football culture. If you score goals for Newcastle, and give 100 per cent effort as part of the bargain, your destiny is shaped for you. You are placed on a pedestal, and there you remain until they want to talk football. And then they squeeze you into a convenient corner and there's no way of dodging the ambush for at least a couple of hours swapping opinions on *the* game. If anybody asks what is the price of fame in Newcastle, there's one notable answer: you are transformed into a twenty-four-hour football chat line if you're lucky, and a jibbering idiot if you are not.

Which brings me to the point where I almost assumed the latter role. It was a place called Crook, a quiet, little mining village. And, arguably, trying to settle in there was the most short-sighted mistake of my life so far. The place itself was OK, even if in my eyes it was like something out of the dark ages. But, in truth, I was the one at fault, not the village or the very nice people who occupied it. I was young, I was living alone, and I decided to rent a five-bedroom house in the back of beyond. As daft as you can get, really. If I had been with my family, it might well have been a sound arrangement. Cast as bachelor boy, it was madness. They rolled the pavements up in that place at nine o'clock and that was it. It reminded me of things I watched on telly as a kid when they tried to portray a clichéd version of living in the north. You know what I mean, all cobbled streets, smoking chimneys, and stone terraces; a bit like the famous Hovis advert really. For me, it was all a bit too weird. I landed in Crook merely because the manager suggested I would be much better with my home on the south side of the city, making it far more convenient for the training ground near Durham. It was in the countryside, as well, which had a certain appeal. There were four shops in the village and mistakenly I thought I was getting away from it all. Peace and quiet, switching off from the big, flash world of football, yeah, that's exactly what I decided I wanted. But soon reality moved in and joined me. I started to get pestered with passers-by banging on my front door every minute of the day. The rest of the time I was either in front of the television or in a state of hibernation. One night, Paul Stretford, then my newly acquired agent, popped round to discuss some career details. When he arrived all he could see were the kids in the driveway, almost swinging from the guttering, and screaming through the letter box for autographs. I was slumped in a darkened living room, with both sets of curtains drawn and the television notched up to full volume to drown out the palaver going on outside my front door. It felt as if I were a pop star, and if that's what they have to deal with they are welcome to it. This all happened very quickly, within a couple of weeks I would think, and Crook had taken on the proportions of the village of the damned. I had to get out. The city boy just couldn't take any more. Paul advised me to get my bags packed because we were leaving, and fast. He booked a suite at a hotel outside Durham, where my Newcastle team-mate, Scott Sellars, another of his clients, was also staying. Then we headed off to discuss the accommodation arrangements with the club. Paul never revealed exactly what went on behind those locked doors but within a week I was relocated to a club apartment in an upmarket area of the city. It was a sensible move back to the place where I really belonged, a very nice place, too, in a refurbished Victorian block with a great deal of privacy and security. I was now on the doorstep of the real action in the heart of Newcastle. It was a huge release for me. There, in an environment I related to far more easily, I was truly at home.

And then there was Clarkey. I'm not sure whether this zany, off-the-wall character threatened my sanity or helped me keep it. Whatever, he was always a great mate and my closest dressing-room confidant at the club. He also introduced me to the spectacularly active nightlife in the north east which is just something else, definitely of a different dimension to anywhere else I have lived. When, ahem, football responsibilities permitted, we certainly went out there and enjoyed it. Back at the club we had a ball, too. I was what you might describe as Clarkey's silent partner in crime. He was such a funny guy, larger than life, and very much the joker in the pack. We used to get up to some tricks between us, but because Lee was famously marked down as the dressing-room prankster he always took the rap. I – nice, innocent Andy – was never fingered for the blame. But it was Clarkey who, indirectly at least, led to my first major confrontation with KK. And it was an incident which got hugely out of control and might well have led to my very early departure from Newcastle. Everything erupted in probably the most explosive week of my time in football. We had played away at Southampton over the weekend and it had been a very poor all-round performance from the whole team. But Clarkey, as far as some of us saw it, was singled out as the scapegoat. KK had grabbed him on the touchline after the first forty-five minutes and given him the blowtorch treatment. Back in the dressing room, the poor boy got some more. Early in the second half, as we all expected, Lee's number went up and he was subbed. I didn't have a clear view of what happened next but, apparently, Clarkey walked over to the dugout and, without too much ceremony, booted the physio's water bucket into orbit. Then he turned on his heel and strode off in the direction of the dressing rooms, and that's where he ended up a touch unlucky. First of all, because the game was live on Sky and, secondly, because the tunnel for Southampton's changing rooms is sited in a corner of the ground. You can't just duck up the tunnel and escape. So, as Clarkey stormed off, KK followed him double quick. He caught him, too. Next came one of the most astonishing sights ever witnessed on the playing fields of England, or at least in pro football, as Kevin seized Clarkey by the ear and marched him right back down the touchline to our bench. He looked like a naughty little schoolboy off to detention, and Lee was ordered to watch the rest of the game from our dugout. With such a public humiliation, it was inevitable the relationship between manager and player could never be the same again. I, for one, wasn't happy at what was happening. When we eventually lost, and deservedly so, Kevin really took to the warpath. He stormed in, clearly blazing mad, and literally went berserk with the lot of us. Nobody was safe. He went absolutely nuts. But, yet again, Clarkey took the brunt of the manager's anger. It reached a crescendo when Kevin banished him from the team bus for the trip to play Wimbledon in the Coca-Cola Cup on the following Tuesday night.

That decision shifted me to centre stage. We were holed up preparing for the game with the Crazy Gang. It was Tuesday morning and, as for training, well, I just didn't fancy it one bit. Whether I still had the treatment of Clarkey buzzing around in my brain, and couldn't stop brooding over what had happened to a very close mate, I don't exactly know. Maybe I had just switched off completely after the blown-fuse events of the previous weekend. But one thing was a fact, I wasn't interested in anything KK had planned for us on the training ground that particular morning. He knew it, too. Kevin obviously believed I was just fannying around, the way footballers do from time to time to get a point across, and he challenged me directly. At first he was quite calm. He asked me what was wrong. I told him: 'I'm just not up for it.' Kevin's face changed and he snapped back. 'Right, then, if you don't want to be here any longer, then eff off.' From that moment the dialogue was brief, Anglo-Saxon, and not too subtle. 'You saying that to me?' I asked. 'That's right – you.' I had always been taught it was rude to decline an invitation, particularly from the man in charge, so I turned and replied: 'OK, then, I will eff off.' And I was gone. I stalked off, watched by the rest of the bemused players, little knowing I was heading for the biggest hue and cry you would ever believe. I was only in my hotel room for seconds. Changed, yet still in a turmoil, full of a roaring anger and other emotions, I just ran for my car and, before I truly realized what was happening, I was hurtling down the drive. And also out of Newcastle's team. The most obvious hide-out was my girlfriend Shirley's home in London. I was sitting there, in front of the box, when the news broke. The TV announcer, much to my surprise, wrapped up his news bulletin by stating: 'Andy Cole has walked out on Newcastle.' It seemed very dramatic, and quite strange, as if I was looking in on the fate of someone else.

I still don't know whether Kevin deliberately released the story or, more likely, it had just leaked out to the media. When questioned, he said, 'We don't exactly know where Andy is now. He has gone missing from the squad. The chances are he is still in London somewhere.' I spoke to Paul Stretford. I seem to remember I was in a minicab when he tracked me down, and you don't get more anonymous than that. Bluntly, I warned Paul, 'I am just not having that treatment. And you have no chance of me going back up there. It's all over.' I sat it out for another day or so, despite Paul's persuasion and insistent advice that I must return to Newcastle sooner rather than later. By now, all hell had broken loose. The story of runaway Cole was plastered over every newspaper. The chairman, Freddie Shepherd, and other big-hitters at the club became embroiled. They all begged me to go back. I was adamant I was staying put. It was another stand-off. Immediately, there was talk that I was forcing an issue and just wanted out. That the disagreement with the manager had, maybe, been engineered in some way to get myself placed on the transfer list. It was all a nonsense. I wasn't unhappy generally, I had been enjoying my football, but I just needed time to myself. There never seemed any relief. My folks would come up to see me, we would pop unannounced to some nice restaurant and next the world and his wife would want a piece of the action. I was under continuous bombardment. I needed some form of refuge to be with Shirley and my family. But that was interpreted, even distorted to some degree, that I wanted to quit the club.

Anyway, at the height of all the drama, an immediate promise of a new contract was raised, which had incidentally been on the agenda for some weeks, and that stirred another grievance. I believed they had been stalling on that subject for their own purposes for a while. In the meantime, other first-team players were being signed up on expensive packages left, right and centre. It rankled with me. But, in the days that followed, during which talks to try and resolve the impasse never stopped, both Paul and Shirley urged me to think again and return to meet the Newcastle directors. Finally, I relented and took the plane back north. Paul was going to act as the buffer in an ongoing crisis. It was OK on the flight north because the home-going Geordies only wanted autographs and handshakes and the occasional back slap. That was the show of public support I needed. Because I did feel, I have to admit, a certain apprehension about how the supporters might react. When we landed, the Jockweiller was waiting. Let me introduce Freddie Fletcher, Newcastle's chief executive and a decent bloke, who earned his nickname because of his stocky build and the fact that he didn't flinch in the toughest of negotiations. He could tear your head off, too. In a phone call, he suggested to Paul that I stayed put in my plane seat and he would try to get his car through security and on to the runway. Paul then had to make a run for it, hopefully collecting our bags along the way, before we went Hollywood for a minute or two and made the great, dramatic, tyre-squealing escape.

Honestly, it was unreal at the airport that night. The whole place was under siege. You couldn't move for fans, photographers and other media people. TV crews swarmed everywhere and it looked as if the Beatles had decided on a comeback. I scrambled into a car which had been moved out on to the tarmac, the idea being to smuggle me out of a back exit at the airport. Suddenly, there was Paul, scampering like hell in front of the mob, bags under his arms and my inevitable load of London shopping between his teeth, and I figured he was going to lose the race. He was two stones overweight, panting like hell, and looked as if he was doing an audition for a remake of Abbot and Costello in one of those fabulous old movies. But he made it, and the Jockweiller, boot down like Schumacher, was ready for him. So were the snappers, strewn across the road and waiting to complete the ambush. They, and the onlookers gathered with them nearby, made one highly dangerous mistake. They seriously underestimated Mr Fletcher and had to learn the lesson that the Jockweiller was, quite literally, not for turning. Ever. With a manic stare, his hands gripping the wheel and well ready for the white-knuckle ride, he slammed down his boot and headed straight for them. Man, was that scary. I'm sure Freddie even let out a blood-curdling laugh as he aimed the bonnet straight at the photographers. Most jumped for their lives, one stayed brave to grab the all-important snap, and Mr Fletcher,

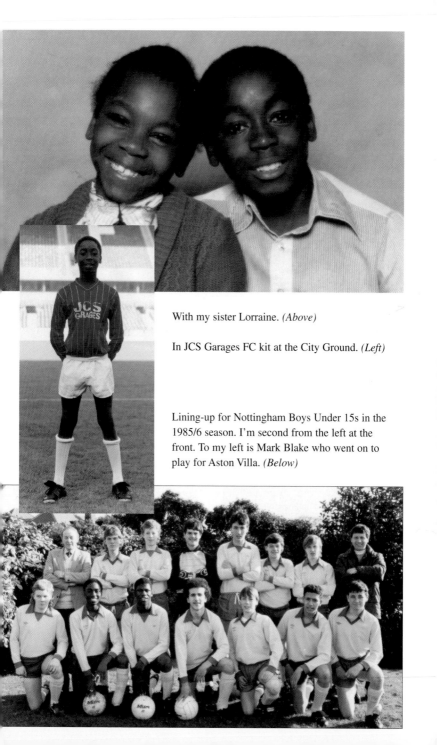

With my sister Lorraine. *(Above)*

In JCS Garages FC kit at the City Ground. *(Left)*

Lining-up for Nottingham Boys Under 15s in the 1985/6 season. I'm second from the left at the front. To my left is Mark Blake who went on to play for Aston Villa. *(Below)*

I'm third from the right along the back, and very happy to have made it to Lilleshall. Ian Walker is on my left. *(Above)*

The decision to go to Lilleshall was one I was determined to make on my own. *(Left)*

A proud moment as I collect my Lilleshall cap on graduation. *(Above)*

Off to a good start. Plying my trade as an apprentice with Arsenal. *(Left)*

Appearing for Arsenal in August 1991, in the Charity Shield against Spurs.

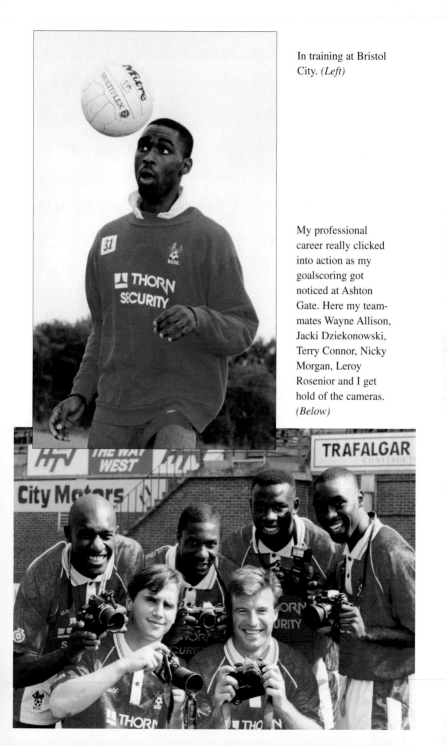

In training at Bristol City. *(Left)*

My professional career really clicked into action as my goalscoring got noticed at Ashton Gate. Here my teammates Wayne Allison, Jacki Dziekonowski, Terry Connor, Nicky Morgan, Leroy Rosenior and I get hold of the cameras. *(Below)*

It all started to happen. Here I am playing for England Under 21s against San Marino.

Tucking away the goals for Kevin Keegan's Newcastle United, against Leicester City *(above)* and Southampton, against an old school-mate from Lilleshall, Simon Charlton *(below)*.

Celebrating another Premiership goal with Scott Sellars *(inset)*, picking up the North East Sports Award *(left)* and posing on a bike for a soft drink campaign *(above)*.

mercifully, swerved at the very point of collision. Blinded by the flash, the fastest chauffeur in the north east just about managed to negotiate a roundabout, approaching at something close to the speed of light, and we were off. A few detours, the usual back doubles to shake off the pursuing pack, and we arrived at the meeting point.

They took me straight to Mr Shepherd's house. Waiting there with him was Douglas Hall. Also at home was Lorelle, Freddie's wife, and his youngest son, Warwick. A quick glance around revealed no KK. I was a little concerned at his absence. It looked to me as if the riot act was going to be read, I was the accused in the dock, and it had now become a board-level issue, not a footballing matter. Change of underclothes, please! The Shepherd family, apart from Freddie, was dispatched to another room. I wanted to leave with them. Mind you, it was a splendid place for a bollocking. Full of memorabilia, equipped with a fine solid-oak bar, and decorated almost completely in red. Better to hide the bloodstains of the victim, I figured. The atmosphere wasn't helped when the other Freddie, namely the Jockweiller, declined a drink as I accepted a Coke and vanished into the kitchen. There, apparently, he actually nicked the dog's dinner. He returned, spraying the room with chunks of chewed meat as he demolished a ham shank. He couldn't open any dialogue because his mouth was full at the time, so Mr Shepherd moved in. Paul, naturally, was by my side as the ice was broken by the Newcastle vice-chairman. He asked me what was at the root of my problem. The answer wasn't hard to deliver and I explained: 'Look, I can't live the way I am living. I am in a gold-fish bowl too much here. I know the fans are terrific and they mean well. But it's me, only me, every day of the week. I feel like a captive all the time.' It was true. I felt I was being stifled, almost submerged until I had no other life, by the adulation of the

Toon Army. It was too restrictive. They didn't seem to want any other player; it was me all the time. I was being taken over by the monster. In truth, I knew I was too young to deal with such celebrity – I just couldn't handle it at the time. My only wish was to play football, enjoy it, and do as well as I might for the benefit of the whole team. But, in a matter of a few meteoric months, I had been elevated to the status of local folk hero. There never seemed a moment, no matter how carefully I tried to engineer it, when I could escape that identity, that awesome responsibility. It drove me mad. I told the directors I needed my own space and, if they would grant it, I also needed precious time down in London to spend with my family and friends. That would be my retreat from madness. The opportunity, if you like, to be Andrew Cole and be an ordinary guy taking it easy. At that meeting, the whole confused affair was thrashed out.

At the start, it was the vice-chairman, in that wonderful Geordie accent, who opened up. I expected a blast, but it wasn't like that at all. 'Hey, Andy – man, what yer gan an don this for like?' he asked. Before I replied, he continued, 'We've been worried sick, man. You don't want to leave, do you? This team's built for you, man.' I tried to make a point and got as far as 'yes, but', before he was off again. 'I've chatted with Kevin and thought it best he wasn't here. Not because he doesn't want to be, mind, but perhaps we can sort the real issues out without too much emotional charge in the room. Is that all right? If you want Kevin here, not a problem, because he's sat at home waiting for me to ring.' Pause. 'Right then, bonny lad, what's it all about?' I backed off, just slightly. They were just too nice to do anything else. 'To be honest,' I explained, 'it's all got out of hand. One thing has led to another and before you know, I'm here in front of you. I've no problems that can't be sorted out. I love working with the gaffer.' It was what the chairman clearly wanted to hear. 'Well, that's not a problem then. We can sort this mess out, nay bovver. Do you want something to eat? Listen, why don't I have a chat with yer man here. If you want to stay, it's not a problem, but maybe you can go and have a cup of tea across the way with Lorelle and Warwick.' Now that was an offer too good to refuse. An hour later, Paul came into the room. I was playing a computer game, but knew by the look on his face there were more urgent matters to be sorted out. It transpired the directors had believed there were insurmountable problems and the disappearing act was all part of a contrived plan to leave the club. With their minds put at rest, they were very responsive when Paul suggested immediate discussions on a new contract. They were also able to inform the fans that, following a hard night of discussions, they had persuaded me my future was still at Newcastle. So we reached an agreement that suited all parties. I was to be allowed an escape route from time to time, at my convenience and with the blessing of the board and management. And the only remaining obstacle was a conciliatory chat with the gaffer. I knew he was a man you didn't cross lightly and there might be retribution. I told him on the phone: 'I'm sorry, things had just built up too much. Right, I'll see you in the morning, normal time. Cheers.' I put down the phone, and that was it, the runaway was back in the fold. The board and the manager now fully appreciated the pressure I felt under at that time. Even better, they had been prepared to listen and help. The unfortunate episode seemed to bring me closer to the fans and the people at the club.

The day after the meeting, I trained. It was bedlam. The ground was under siege. I spoke to Kevin as soon as I had squeezed my way through the mobs. He reassured me that he approved everything that had been agreed the night before. There were no grudges, no sullen agendas that somehow I had rebelled against his authority, just an acceptance that there had been a workaday problem and now it had been resolved. He confirmed: 'I will give you more time to get away from being the centre of attention up here. You can be your own man. And what happened a few days ago is now history. It's forgotten.' I've reflected on those words many times, so just pause and think again what he was really saying, mostly about himself in a way. Because that reaction was 99 per cent different to most other managers'. They would have fallen on me like a ton of bricks. I would have been fined a fortune and slapped on the transfer list. Yet, with Kevin you could always work with him on a more human level of understanding. He was a mate, as well as the boss. If there was trouble on the park, and you weren't playing too well, then he figured there was probably trouble off it. And he would meticulously take time out to solve it. It was a rare quality that I found so important to me during the crisis. That was, after all, my first season in the Premiership and the sudden fame had left me feeling a little claustrophobic and unsure. KK understood that and dealt with it in his own, unique manner. I'll forever be grateful. I have so much respect for him because, as the manager dealing with a player who had walked off his training pitch, he was entitled to crack down hard. Instead, it was all water under the bridge. You are very fortunate as a player to have Kevin in charge, because it is not in his nature to be a vengeful person who stores things up and then waits for his moment. He could, with no little reason, have held one hell of grudge against me for the rest of my spell at St James's. But that's not the makeup of the man. Consequently, I felt, as the other party in the little squabble, that I owed a great deal in return. There was an obligation, if you like. So you played the game and didn't abuse his generosity of spirit, or his fairly flexible authority. Just a little footnote to this whole saga that might interest you: both Clarkey and I were restored to the team the following Saturday for the return against Wimbledon. We won 3–0 and, dead on, the pair of us scored a goal.

Peace reigned for quite a while after that little skirmish. That Newcastle side, full of flair, excitement and always living on the edge, captivated the nation's attention. On Tyneside it was a team worshipped with almost blind adoration, but nationally, too, there was a growing respect and a recognition that we played the game the right way. We were the knockabout entertainers, the people's choice after their own favourites. And it gave you a good feeling. Always, though, there is a dark shadow that temporarily stops you in your tracks for a moment or two. Mine was unfortunate – the second brush with racism in my career. It was made worse on this occasion in that it affected my family and friends and was a direct spin-off from what was happening to me at Newcastle. Allow me to provide the background which, on reflection, might be an explanation – if not an excuse – for this disturbing incident. The season before, in the wake of the Wimbledon affair and the walkout, I had enthusiastically signed that four-year contract and felt reassured that I was destined to spend a few more years in KK's front line. But I hadn't legislated for a rather worrying physical problem that affected my calves. It was caused by restricted blood flow, diagnosed as compartment syndrome, not the shin splints that everybody talked about, and it gave me a great deal of pain during games. I tried, gingerly, to nurse myself through and, to be honest, I just couldn't be my old self. I wasn't able to train and that combative edge, vital if you are to look good against the best players, was inevitably eroded. I remember playing against Crystal Palace and hunting down a forward ball with their centre-back, Chris Coleman. The ignominy of it all, and I couldn't really take it in then, was that the big Welshman got there first. He had actually outsprinted me. Unbelievable! I was known to be quick and he wasn't meant to be, and Rob Lee gave me some terrible stick. 'You know I'm not fit – I don't do anything in the week, no workouts, no nothing now except wait for match day,' I reminded him. But it didn't stop the muttering from the usual cynics, the smart-alec brigade who always, supposedly, have the inside track and know more than anyone else. They had it that I was deliberately dodging games, that I was just swinging the lead. Once the rumour started it rapidly got out of hand and I was smeared with claims that my heart was no longer in Newcastle FC; that, to put it bluntly, I wanted out of the place. Nothing could have been further from the truth.

I shut my ears to it all. Or at least attempted to focus on what was really important. I knew the only solution in the long term was to seek medical advice and probably take a rest. Anyway, we had Manchester United to play in a mid-week Coca-Cola Cup tie at St James's Park. I tried to go for it, but it just didn't happen for me. It was impossible for me to play to the standard I demand of myself. There was no movement, no acceleration, no spark. Mercifully, for both the team and myself, they dragged me off. We still managed a 2–0 win. No shame in that. I had tried my best and the physical limitations left me well short. I spoke to the manager. There had to be a serious discussion because three days later we were playing Alex Ferguson's United at Old Trafford. I told KK that to play on would do me no favours; it seemed to me that rest was the only cure. And that's when the rumour factory really started to churn out fabricated stories by the dozen. Now, plain and simple, the media insisted I wasn't happy at Newcastle and, furthermore, I was looking for a move. None of it was true, but that didn't appear to matter. The knives went in, big style. I am sure that kind of hostile misinformation sparked the racism flare-up. I can't recall the specific game, but my brother and a few mates were strolling up to the ground before kick-off when they were viciously targeted. A few Geordie fans in a passing car thought it was some kind of twisted entertainment to start jeering at them and aiming racist abuse. It was black this, and black that. As much as I loved the city, and the vast majority of people living there, that was a despicable act and unforgivable. I warned the manager I wasn't going to tolerate such behaviour. I also stressed to the Press the same message. I didn't threaten to walk out, but I felt I had to make a stand so the general public understood how horrified and concerned I was about such an incident in their city.

The word on the street will always tell you that the Geordie fans have somewhat of a racist tendency about them. Whether it's a myth, or an established truth, I don't really know. But what I can say is that, personally, I never had a significant problem with them, until this incident. OK, since leaving the club, I have experienced a little bit of stick from the expected reception committee at any return match. And mixed in amongst it I could a hear a few monkey sounds coming from the terraces. But a very small, brain-dead minority is not going to change my overall view about the vast numbers of supporters on Tyneside. They were a wonderful asset for me, always very supportive and grateful for what I tried to do for them, and I respect them totally. I had a tremendous rapport with them and that remains undamaged by the mindless bunch who betrayed the great majority by attacking my friends and family. At least, it was a feeling that remained unaltered in my mind, even after I left in 1995. And what a strange affair that was, carefully juggled by KK without my knowledge until the very last moment. Even then I was reluctant to pack my bags and leave.

Things, as I discovered later, started to rumble when we played Blackburn in an FA Cup tie in January. I wasn't playing well and the form of the whole team was not too impressive either. Yet I was still very much in the dark about what was happening above my head. I went in for training the morning after the game. Kevin kept his silence. But by that stage he had clearly determined in his own mind that drastic steps needed to be taken in revitalizing his jaded and predictable Newcastle side. He figured, probably correctly, that we had been sussed out by the Premiership and countermeasures were being employed to stop the supply line to me. The side found it difficult to create the prolific opportunities of the past and, as a unit, we were very much in the doldrums. Too many rivals were able to pick us off quite easily. For instance, I don't think I had scored a goal for something like fifteen games. Proof enough, really. KK knew by pure gut instinct it was the moment for another revolution, a time for positive action. That was his trademark. I still hadn't got the vibes, though, and didn't have a clue my departure was already being arranged in secrecy. Previously, I had repeatedly stressed to Paul that I wouldn't ever leave Newcastle for just another club, but if ever the fantasy came true and it was Manchester United then he could count me in. Otherwise, I wouldn't even contemplate deserting Tyneside. Mention had been made of Tottenham at an earlier time when stories were being circulated that I was homesick for London. I had made it perfectly clear I wasn't interested in any move to White Hart Lane. But never, not in my wildest dreams, did I consider that Kevin would allow me to sign for his great rivals in Manchester. Then it happened. Like being hit by an Exocet. Just incredible.

I was sitting down at home, preparing to watch Ferguson's outstanding team play their own FA Cup tie against Sheffield United at Bramall Lane, when the phone went. It was Paul. 'You know you said you would only leave Newcastle for one club in England . . . well, sit down quietly, because they are in for you.' I thought it was a wind-up. Man. U., in for me, no, I just didn't believe it. He was insistent: 'Just get some gear together. I'm on my way up to collect you. We have to be back in Manchester by the morning to sort out the personal details. OK?' That call was around 7.55 pm. By midnight I was hurtling down the motorway, a little disturbed, even uncertain, that my whole life could be pitched into such unbelievable turmoil in just a matter of hours. It wasn't that I didn't wish to join Man. U. No, that wasn't exactly the feeling. I was just bewildered by the speed of it all. Earlier that same day I had had no concept of moving away from Newcastle; now I had been sold, sealed and almost delivered without having a say in the whole business. I had no control over events. It was weird and unnerving. Kevin must have sensed my mood when he finally called on the mobile. He was heading in the opposite direction to us with Keith Gillespie, Manchester United's young winger who was part of the deal, alongside him in the car. The dialogue between us was a little stilted, I suppose, but he was only too willing to give his reasons for the transfer. As I suspected, he thought that the Newcastle side was looking lightweight. Too predictable, also, with so much of the attacking play based around me. If they stopped me by defensively dropping a little deeper, or smothered Beardsley, then Newcastle could be contained and beaten. The strategy needed to be altered and that's why, first, he moved for Chris Armstrong and ultimately signed Les Ferdinand. That was the future; the present was dealing with my troubled mind and a serious reluctance to be on my way, bags packed and a suit for the interview, without any warning. It was a bit too swift in execution for my liking.

I challenged him: 'Yeah, I know what you are saying, gaffer, but I still can't understand why you have agreed to sell me.' That's when KK mentioned the size of the fee, close to £7 million, and that blew me away. I told him: 'My mind's in a bit of a whirl. I'm not saying I don't want to go to Manchester, but this has come out of the blue. I'm just disappointed to be leaving Newcastle like this.' To a great degree, I was in effect questioning myself. If I had been allowed a week, or even a day or two, to mull over what was happening, it wouldn't have been a problem. There was never any thought that I didn't want to go to Old Trafford. The issue was more . . . Why do Newcastle want to get rid of me? I'm a top player for them. What could I possibly have done wrong? He tried to reassure me and replied: 'Now, Coley, it's very big money and, just remember this, you have done a great job for this club. Now I need to change things, with the help of your fee. I'm sending you to Man. U. because it's an outstanding club with a smashing team. You will become a better player there – you will learn so much more. Don't worry about it.' And then he added more personally, 'You have always wanted to play for them. It's a great move for you. Anyway, my mind is made up. It's the best thing for both of us.' When Kevin says something like that, it's better to accept you're history and get on with life. I did. I never ever went back to that beautiful penthouse, which had been completely revamped by an interior designer, once I flicked the light switch for the last time. Someone even went back there to collect all my gear. The door had been firmly closed on that chapter of my career. Sometimes decisions are made beyond your control and, reluctantly, they have to be accepted for the good of your future.

It was only later, when I spoke to Alex Ferguson, that I was granted some insight into that weekend of transfer intrigue. He revealed that it was a comment from Joe

Royle, who had been talking with Kevin, which put him on the trail. During the conversation, the hint was dropped that, if the price was right, I could well be bought from Newcastle. Apparently, Joe explained that Kevin was looking to change things around in the belief he could quieten a bit of unrest around St James's Park. First of all, though, that same morning Mr Ferguson attempted to make a sounding-out call for Stan Collymore at Nottingham Forest. He was thwarted when he couldn't make contact with their manager, Frank Clark. So big Stan was out of the frame. Without delay, the next call on the scribble pad was KK. The offer was made and promptly accepted. Kevin just needed to clarify the position with the bigwigs in the boardroom. There was, from what I hear, some fairly rigorous resistance, along the lines of 'We can't let Cole go. If we do that, we will all get lynched'. But Kevin refused to budge on his decision. He told them he would take the consequences and protect them from the wrath of the fans, if there happened to be an uprising. And indeed there was. As I watched TV that night, there was KK, alone on the steps, facing the wrath of the fans and pariently explaining his reasons and motives. He wanted the cash for another spending budget to enable Newcastle to move on to another era and, furthermore, he wanted it done quickly. I suspect KK had chewed things over for the previous four or five days, while the rest of us remained in the dark, but once the decision had been reached, that was it. I have got to say it showed his great courage again. Not many managers would have been brave enough to sell one of their better players, a crowd hero at that, to such an obvious rival. That's a measure of the man. He was prepared to have a few arguments upstairs to get his way; one phase was at an end, another football day dawned.

I belonged to a different United, as far as he was concerned, and that is the bottom line in Kevin's world.

That's why he was fully prepared to stand on the stadium steps, surrounded by angry and protesting supporters, and persuade them to have lasting faith in him because he would never betray them for one minute. He never did. KK does exactly what he wants – or you find someone else to do his job. The directors discovered precisely that after I left, when Kevin, defiant and determined as ever, made that other famous stand. This time it was his future at stake, not mine. But the unblinking, never-flinching decision was still made. He didn't like being pushed around, with ultimatums being laid down over a new contract. It disturbed him the way the Newcastle emphasis seemed to be more directed to a period of powerful empire-building – big business in other words – rather than the football side. That signalled the time for him to go and, unsurprisingly to me, he went. It was shame, because if he had remained in charge Newcastle would have been champions by now and years of trophy frustration might have been at least satisfied. Instead, it all went a little pear-shaped when this combination of showman and strongman left town, didn't it?

Chapter Four

There was only one emotion filling my mind the day I joined Manchester United. It wasn't quite in the proportions of sheer terror, but I was scared, definitely scared. S-E-V-E-N MILLION POUNDS. Now that's scary. Third-world countries have debts less than that and they get hounded to the farthest corners of the planet unless they pay up. So a transfer fee of such monumental, telephone-number proportions was really beyond my comprehension and, yes, it did bother me. A lot. To the very soles of my boots, in fact. At Newcastle I had arrived as a young unknown, relatively expensive, OK, but still with everything to prove. Here, on Wednesday, 12 January 1995, I was being paraded as the hired gun for the wealthiest, most powerful, fiercely ambitious and exalted club in the land. And I had cost more than they had ever invested before. That record fee, since eclipsed by any number of players, was a very heavy burden. It might have crushed me, if I hadn't shown a certain strength of purpose and slowly put it in perspective. Like, I hadn't paid it, they had, so all I could do was perform. In the end that approach worked best, but it was a philosophy which was well and truly tested along the way. And occasionally pushed to extremes. But the more immediate threat was just as awkward and unnecessary in the week I left

Newcastle. Yet another controversy came rumbling over the horizon. Football fate had decreed, as so often happens in such circumstances, that Mr Ferguson and his team's next Premiership fixture happened to be, where else, but back in Geordieland. They told me, in no uncertain terms, that at St James's Park on that Saturday I would be banned. It was strictly out of bounds. Forbidden territory.

That decision not only disturbed me. It also nagged at me deep down and hurt. Let me explain. Without my knowledge, or approval for that matter, the two clubs had agreed during their transfer negotiations that I wouldn't be allowed to play. I was to be excused boots. Fine. What they didn't say was that I would not even be allowed in the ground. All I wished to do was to turn up, watch my new team, and show my deep-felt appreciation to the fans I had left behind and who had given me so much loyalty. Not possible, sir. Too risky. Officialdom had spoken. I couldn't believe it. But on police advice, or at least that's what they claimed, it was decided it would be too dodgy for me to show my face on the very same terraces where I had been such a favourite. To this day, nobody has been able to persuade me that the Newcastle supporters would have turned nasty with me and provoked crowd disturbances, or tried to run me out of town. I think the club officials were more concerned and too sensitive about the media's determination at whipping up an anti-Cole campaign. And that, they feared, might have inflamed the odd nutter into attempting something really out of order. I have to agree that the newspapers, particularly those mainly focused on the north east, didn't waste the opportunity. Within hours of my departure, they were hitting the streets with hyped-up accounts that I had lacked genuine commitment to Newcastle for months; that I had been playing for away; that I hadn't been trying a leg. They questioned my loyalty and I was portrayed, quite wrongly, as some sort of traitor to the Geordie cause. Now that kind of unforgivable, snide comment did dig deep, a blow aimed right under the ribs. Consider the facts. I had given far more than a record haul of goals for Newcastle. I had played when injured and sworn my allegiance to KK when it might have been easier to leave. During the Wimbledon skirmish, for instance, he asked me if I wanted to bail out permanently. I said, very adamantly, I didn't. Did I wish to sign for Ossie Ardiles, who had made an inquiry, at White Hart Lane? Once again I had delivered a firm no. Was my preference living in London? Again it was a no. Mine, in truth, was a very reluctant exit from St James's. Despite all of this I was being placed in the public stocks and pilloried with wild information that was totally out of order and completely false.

So, when the formalities were carried through in Manchester, I was still confused and almost in a state of shock. It seemed, too, that I had been placed uncomfortably in the middle of a no-win situation. On the one hand, I didn't want to leave Newcastle, yet entirely the opposite impression was created, and, at the same time, I didn't want to send out the vibes that I was unhappy to join the other United. My mind was in a whirl. The truth is I was disappointed at Newcastle's decision to sell me, particularly when I had never been consulted on the matter, and yet any footballer would be a born fool if he rejected the opportunity of signing on at Old Trafford. It was very definitely an uneasy time in my life. An extra hassle, as I have already mentioned, was the actual fee, which immediately placed six zeros behind my name. Nerve-jangling, scary stuff, you must admit. There it was, crazy figures and the great unknown of a transfer-market record. I was alarmed, almost intimidated, by what was happening. I knew it would have a lasting impact, maybe a dangerous, threatening influence as well, on my immediate future. I wasn't wrong. Just a few months earlier, Chris Sutton had moved to Blackburn Rovers for £5 million. Now that was a big package, and it attracted a fair amount of attention because of Jack Walker's involvement and the fee being the highest ever paid. Now here I was, something close to £2 million more expensive, and also joining a club with a far grander, more important profile. The media hype was immense and very daunting for me to deal with. This was a huge transfer, with so many obvious implications for the people involved, and it might well have destroyed me. The predictably fearful and dark scenario was constructed to make me feel even worse. You know what I am talking about. All that media imagery of Old Trafford being the graveyard of famous strikers. The names of past failures, big men with even bigger reputations in their time, filled every headline – and that was before I had even kicked a ball for my new team. I tried to ignore it but, inevitably, it does creep into your consciousness and you can't escape the most chilling thoughts. You dread being condemned as another wasted statistic, another cursed and insulted flop. And that's when you might easily clamber aboard what could be described as the cycle of doom.

You put yourself on permanent trial. You just try to prove your worth every single second and, consequently, you try too hard, perilously hard in fact. You attempt the impossible out on the park to such an extent that mistakes are inevitable and you are in danger of being considered a complete mug. I've just suggested it was like a public trial; on reflection it constituted more of an inquisition. Believe me, I know, because I was that man. And I was as guilty as any other player in the history of the game in betraying myself with such misguided behaviour. At United, I initially tried desperately hard to make it work, too hard in fact, and that is why it took me so long to adjust to a different team pattern and way of playing. When that happens you start getting criticized, even mocked. And when you get knocked, guess what, you try even harder. It's the entry ticket to a vicious, self-destructive circle. All the time, you are battling against yourself and that way you can't ever win. The next grim stage is shutting out the demons, and that is certainly never easy, as they crowd in and create more despair and desolation. Block out all those cynical comments, you tell yourself, or you won't survive. But all the time they are there, preying on your mind, wrecking confidence and undermining the natural fighting spirit. You end up simply as a disaster waiting to take place. The pressure, the fear, the demands, the self-examination, the expectation, it all finishes up churning through your daily thoughts and turning you into something close to a mental wreck, unless you are very careful. There's only you who can handle it, only you to go out on that pitch and perform, only you able to justify yourself. And, of course, that enormous pile of money placed on your shoulders. Sure, a lot of people wander by and vainly persuade you not to worry about the fee because it's not your business anyway. They were always well-meant platitudes, easy words to offer, I have got to say, and yet they never provided me with an ounce of protection. They couldn't do. It was all part of the deal, the punishment that comes with the fame. And, yes, the fortune.

I was still a young guy, only twenty-three and with plenty to learn, and it was a mean, depressing experience. I had to live up to top billing. You know something else, too? It doesn't matter whether it's showbiz, rock and roll, or football, you are duly exposed, an easy target, and there are plenty of folk out there prepared to pull the trigger and shoot you down. How did I cope with it? Well, in all honesty, not too well in the early phase. If you want to know exactly what happened, the only sensible explanation now is that I tried to become the invisible man; I turned myself into a recluse. I stayed with Paul Stretford, my agent, and his wife Margaret in their family home during my first year in Manchester. They were brilliantly supportive, but not even they could completely ease my months of abject misery. I had my own torture chamber. It was my bedroom. Every day I would return from training, quickly smuggle myself in through the front door, and get to that private sanctuary as fast as possible. Then I would stay there, locked in with my own very confused thoughts. I felt isolated, and just a little desperate, persecuted as well, and I had to overcome all those messed-up emotions. It wasn't easy and it took time. Probably eighteen months followed before I had truly come to terms with life at United and I wouldn't want to go through such an ordeal ever again. During that period, I resolved that the only escape route was through a policy of hard work and getting the head down. So I grafted, and grafted, and then grafted some more. The other players had packed in, showered and dressed, and I was still out on that training pitch, burning up both energy and all my frustrations. It was all I could do.

Away from the club, I literally opted for the hermit life. I shut myself away from the rest of the world. Since the age of fourteen I had always pursued the independent path, so I felt I had really no one to talk to despite Paul's very supportive role. He provided a great deal of helpful advice, how to cope with various dilemmas and those periods of anguish and uncertainty, but one unavoidable fact just stared me in the face: I always understood I was the only one who could make sure I walked through the tunnel of fear and failure and make myself a success. No matter what well-intentioned friends said to comfort me, to build a very battered sense of self-esteem and confidence, or polish the ego, in the end it was down to me. I needed to confront all the nastiness, and there was a fair amount of that flying about. There were plenty of insults, sneers, and people were generally mouthing all kinds of unpleasant things about me. I had to get my head around it, control it, and try to be objective and focused. Even when they muttered that I was a waste of money and worse. Like, for instance, when I had surgery on my suspect calves and that led to some lippy guys suggesting the operation meant cutting off my feet and stitching them back on the wrong way round. It was all cruel stuff. Always, though, there was a buttress. My resistance remained intact, based on the belief that I was a genuinely good player and such qualities were never lost overnight. The more the nastiness and vilification of my football ability was thrust in my face, the more bloody-minded I became in the determination to prove my detractors wrong. It was, in a way, more fuel to add to the fire of resentment burning within me. I knew in the end it would come right for me.

But along the way, naturally I suppose, I made one or two flawed decisions. The most serious was the moment I opted to be very much a social outcast. I just felt I didn't want to mix with people or join in the normal life. And it reached the extreme situation where I wouldn't even drive my favourite and highly expensive car to safeguard myself from any unwanted, extra attention. The car, a Porsche 911, was admittedly a bit of a fashion statement and some people might have considered it a little over the top. When I drove around, passers-by would stand and stare at me. Or even point their fingers. I felt I had to stop using it, so I stuck it in the garage to try and protect my anonymity. Instead, I borrowed a club Audi saloon, quite literally a middle of the road vehicle which nobody would notice, and so joined the ordinary folk again! The Porsche remained under wraps for months, sparing my embarrassment. It was another indication of my insecurity at the time and the difficulty I found in resolving my troubled situation. I felt a lot better in the Audi. Lower profile, not so many gawping eyes, and it helped remove me from so much public attention. Now, if not at the time, I can well understand outsiders being less than understanding and prepared to show little sympathy. All they saw was a highly-paid footballer, not someone enduring something of a personal trauma. How could they view it any other way? They might even have been a little contemptuous. Their attitude could be summed up in one sentence: 'He's not doing it on the park, so what right has he got to roll around town in a sixty-grand Porsche? He must be a right flash so and so.' Anyway, whatever their opinions, that's the way I read the script and so the motor had to go.

Cutting myself off in other ways, though, was not a wise move. Since my early teenage years I have grown up virtually on my own. The major decisions had all been mine alone, and mostly my life had taken the upward curve, barring a few rucks with authority along the way. But when you are confronted with something quite different in the rougher, rawer, less pleasant aspects of a football career, it's all suddenly very different. You don't know in which direction to turn, who to confide in, who to trust. So I became Fortress Cole for a while, barricaded and shuttered against the world. Nobody really got close to me in that period. In doing that, I made the whole experience a lot tougher than it should have been. My team-mates, when I allowed them to be, were extremely supportive. Senior pros like Steve Bruce, Gary Pallister, and the two Pauls, Parker and Ince, were brilliant. All of them offered a comforting arm to help me through the crisis and, let's not kid ourselves, that's what it was. A crisis that came near to claiming the victim, too. You see, when I first arrived in Manchester, I never suspected the dream I had been involved in at Newcastle was in danger, that I would be exposed and not score the buckets of goals I had promised myself. It never occurred to me that I wouldn't be rampaging past defenders and hitting the net as I had done for most of my career. When you hit the wall with a wallop, it hurts. These were horrible, tormenting, menacing months for me. Every single day I was being tested to the limit. If I had buckled, not shown the mental strenth and resilience to cope, that would surely have been it. I would have crumpled and faded away like one or two United strikers before me. Only a powerful work ethic – and this is not meant to sound arrogant – saved me. I grafted in training, committed myself to extra sessions when the rest of the lads had long packed up and left for home. It was the only way I could keep my sanity. Even on the practice pitch, mind you, I would persecute myself, demanding more than was humanly possible. If I missed the target, even in a five-a-side, I would curse myself out loud and denigrate myself in front of the other players. I was forever in perfectionist mode, reaching for impossible levels of achievement.

I have always been my own severest critic. You know whether you have worked properly or performed to your absolute limit. Every footballer is the same. The next time someone needs to tell me I have had a lousy game will also be the first. I know better than anyone when I have failed to deliver. My conscience tells me. So, in those dark and worrying early days at United, I used to crucify myself. I created monsters in my own mind. There wasn't a week allowed to go by when I didn't put myself on the rack and scrutinize what I considered even a minor failing. It was ridiculous at times and I subjected myself to that kind of ordeal for roughly eighteen months. Complete madness, really. It only ended when, with the chips down and my ankle busted, I determined that as soon as I was fit I would have a vastly different philosophy. Privately, I decided that I would be a hit, or I would be busted as a United player. At the end of that injury-blighted season I notched eight goals in just fourteen first-team appearances. Not a bad return and certainly it reinforced that single-minded conclusion: 'Andy, my boy, it's up to you now. You either show what you are made of or you are history at this club. Forget all the nonsense, prove you have the bottle for it, and be true to yourself.' The following campaign I banged in twenty-five goals and those ominous clouds were shifted from my career. They will never be allowed to return and overshadow me again, I can promise you that.

When I arrived at Old Trafford in the midwinter of the 1994-95 season, nothing seemed too complicated. Not immediately anyway. The goal-flow was still there. I ended up with twelve goals from seventeen games, a very respectable return that included walloping five past Ipswich to establish a Premiership record. I thought I had cracked it. The next season, I promised myself, would be bonanza time. Goals by the bucketful, how could I fail? I would be a driven man, too, inspired by my early success and goaded by the first hint that a few sinister enemies were out there waiting to ambush me. They crept from the football undergrowth at the end of that first half season in a United shirt when we played West Ham in the final game of a championship race which would have tested the nerve of the most strong-minded competitor. It was at Upton Park and it amounted to a ninety-minute title showdown. Back at Anfield, Kenny Dalglish and rivals Blackburn were playing Liverpool. They lost but still won the championship crown and, guess what, I was apparently to blame for it. If we had beaten the Hammers, it would have been our trophy, but more than that – according to certain elements of the media – I had cost United that particular success by missing a couple of goals. You can't allow the facts to spoil a good story, it seems, and accusing a newly acquired, £7 million striker of being the arch blunderer, well, it was the best headline you could have. Obviously, I didn't agree with such damning verdicts, and they all read more like a mischievous indictment to me, but there was another reason for my anger. Everybody had conveniently forgotten that five days earlier, on 10 May 1995, I had volunteered to help United and miss the most important date of my adult life. The birth of my son, Devante. That's right, I had played against Southampton in a 2–1 home victory. I scored as well when, in reality, I should have been in the maternity ward with my girlfriend Shirley. Not too many modern-day footballers would have contemplated such a sacrifice – they would have cried off the game, don't worry about that. Now here was I, the baptismal season just over and the title lost, and I was taking dog's abuse for it. I know now precisely what I should have done. I should have ignored everything and everybody, even the blind loyalty to a club that pays my wages, and been present for the birth of my son. You never know, but that experience might never come my way again. As long as I live I will always regret not being alongside Shirley to see our son come into the world. Because of the person I am proud to be, and because I considered the amount of money United had invested in me, I felt I owed it to them to play.

It was the wrong decision. I know I should have been there, at St Thomas's Hospital in south London, instead of fighting for a championship that was lost, collectively I might add, the following Sunday. Missing the birth of my boy just to play football, jeez, I must have been off my head. Proof of how wrong I had been, if I needed the proof, came with the unwarranted slagging I took on that major weekend for all of us. In that instant, I learned the lessons of where my true loyalties must lie ... with my family, naturally. I wouldn't ever make the same stupid mistake again. That's the emotional reaction finished, now for the facts of the West Ham game just in case somebody out there is still holding me responsible. From what I remember, I hit the post against West Ham and also forced two outstanding saves from their goalkeeper, Ludo Miklosko. Now, as a striker, I always understood the first requirement is to hit the target and then see what happens. I did precisely that, so what the hell was I doing taking all that back-page flak? I'll tell you why – because it was deemed necessary to seek the scapegoat again. And it was convenient and attention-grabbing to single me out as the fall guy, the £7-million flop if you like. I've never harboured any doubts that I did my utmost for United on that day, a belief confirmed by the rest of the players who never even suggested I was guilty of costing them another medal. They appreciate that we are all involved in a team game, where individuals might flourish and be heroic at times, but that any single player should not be hounded if things go wrong. What happened to me back then changed my attitude to a great degree. I swore to put certain people in their place. I leave you to make that judgement, but let me say I am content with what has happened since. Very content.

It did, admittedly, take me some time to justify such a statement. Longer than even I expected. And with quite a few torrid, confidence-jolting experiences along the way. Like the following season, for starters. That was absolutely horrendous. Correction, I was horrendous, and even the huge consolation of winning the Double for the first time could not possibly contain my personal disappointment. For a player of my standard, my performance level was nothing short of terrible. As I have stressed before, I am a footballer who demands so much of himself, and during that depressing period I can unhesitatingly

say I was ashamed of what I was doing on a football field.
Yes, I was that bad. When you are letting yourself down,
you feel the world is on your case. I started to get para-
noid about it. I couldn't eat, sleep, or even live properly. I
was knocking myself mercilessly after every failure and
the grimmest goalmouth stats of my life didn't offer me
any cushy excuse. I still cringe when I think of a measly
thirteen goals from more than forty first-team appearances. People accused me of being unable to cope with the
pressure of United stardom, the old graveyard syndrome
if you like. They suggested I was freezing when the
moment of truth arrived and I had the opportunity of
scoring. They were wrong, dead wrong. My problem was
in being too precise, trying to be the class act too early. I
wanted everyone to look at my finishing and go home
convinced they had seen nothing like the Cole phenomenon before. That I was the top gun. At Newcastle, where I
scored forty-one goals in a season and sixty-eight in just
eighty-four matches, it seemed I simply couldn't miss. I
just caressed the ball into the net, no sweat, mate. In all my
time there, I doubt if I hit more than ten shots with full
power. I was the cracksman who preferred to be cute – it
felt all the sweeter that way. But during my nightmare in
Manchester I became so completely bewildered by what
was happening to me, I didn't know whether to stick,
twist or simply go home. Then Sir Bobby Charlton generously pulled me to one side and whispered in my ear. He
advised: 'You're thinking about it too much. Just relax.
You are trying to make it look good. Forget about the idea
of putting the ball in the perfect spot. Simply hit it, and hit
it as hard as you like. Because if it goes in the net that's all
that really counts.' They were the words of a man who had
been there and done it, and I have never forgotten that
such a respected and influential football statesman went
out of his way to help me.

Others, mostly notorious rather than famous, did the opposite. They tried to pin me to the wall. Every crack seemed to reveal another one. I'm talking of players I used to play alongside, players long retired, and personalities who should have known better. They came from the usual rent-a-quote breed. Perry Groves, my old team-mate at Arsenal, sniped at me in one article – 'I can't believe Cole's gone for £7 million. He couldn't lace Merson's boots' or words to that effect. Cheers, Perry. Malcolm Macdonald, with the Newcastle connection, also jumped on the band-waggon. Then there was that mouthy old favourite, Tommy Docherty; even Alan Hansen, once a top player who really should have known better had a go.

All of them had an appetite for sticking the knife in me and weren't happy until it was dripping in blood. Not one of them had a decent word to offer about me; the whole emphasis was to drag me down and to sensationalize. I appreciate my form was shabby, my contribution as poor as it has ever been, but these people, I felt, were just hell-bent on destroying me. It wounded me even more that all of them were former professionals who well understood the ways of football, yet they were prepared to say such detrimental, hurtful things. It was an outrage. A lot of my contemporaries found the whole business degrading. When I finish playing, there is a firm undertaking here and now that I will never take that route. I know instinctively how a player feels when he misses a chance, or performs poorly, and the last thing they need is some outsider, even an informed one, passing judgement on them in the public arena. It can't be right and it is certainly never fair.

The verbal garbage hurled in my direction was often vicious and very personal. I couldn't comprehend at the time how somebody could be so malicious, putting the boot in when a man was already on the deck, and particularly when they barely knew me. It was all deeply offensive and it gave everybody close to me a really bad time. Throughout it all, I needed to be mentally tough and I never felt as though it would get to me and I would crack. But there were times back then when I felt lower than a snake's belly. My parents were horrified at what was happening to their son, but Shirley and my close friends, along with Paul and Margaret, were top drawer. They shielded me, they protected me from the worst of it. Mates of mine in both London and Nottingham used to get embroiled in pub fights defending my reputation. They just wouldn't tolerate anybody bad-mouthing me, which seemed to be the favourite social pastime for a while. Now I am able to flick through the old scrapbooks, every nasty little comment down there in black and white, and just laugh in the face of my accusers. Because I have answered their jibes in full and the trophies I have accumulated so far are proof of just how wrong and mean-spirited they all were.

They weren't, it has to be accepted, the only people who didn't fancy my chances as my first full season with United drew to a close. In that summer of '95, once the medals had been dished out and champagne quaffed, only one other issue topped the back-page agenda. Where would United dump me next? They ranted that I hadn't scored enough goals, I didn't deserve another chance, and the speculation was endless. I was bound to be sold to Everton, Villa, or Spurs. And that was only in this country. I half remember a couple of clubs from Mars getting a mention! It was a soul-searching time for me and naturally it was upsetting, too. That summer the manager was linked with Alan Shearer. I realized then that if England's captain had signed, instead of disappearing over the horizon to Newcastle, I would have been finished at United. I understood that reality only too well. The exit door was, what shall we say, slightly more than ajar. But the gaffer spoke to me about it, insisting Shearer was not in the frame. That's the job of a manager. He was only trying to put my mind at ease. But I knew the truth. When the transfer initiative for Shearer collapsed, I also knew what I had to do. Put my neck on the block and go for it, otherwise I was history. With so much uncertainty surrounding my future, I couldn't afford another flawed season. This was the moment, buckle down or be busted. I reckoned I was on my last chance. So what happens? I copped for pneumonia, then suffered a broken ankle in a very crude tackle, and I finished up playing just fourteen matches.

The illness was extremely alarming. I don't know where I contracted it or how it developed and attacked me so suddenly. The medical team carried out extensive tests but they couldn't pinpoint the cause of it either. They explained that sometimes pneumonia can be passed through air conditioning and that summer I had been roving the Far East as part of a promotional tour for some of my sponsors. It was something of a mystery, though, and very scary. I couldn't get my head around being laid up with it in July. I figured pneumonia was a problem that plagued mostly the the very young, the elderly or hospital patients, and even then it was a complaint that hit hard when the snow was on the ground. Never, surely, in the summer. With me it struck just three days into the pre-season preparations in 1997. I felt absolutely wrecked, so low and demoralized and very, very weak. I was a helpless case. I couldn't train, in fact I could barely move without being gripped by a mood of lethargy and utter exhaustion. The weight simply peeled off me and pounds and pounds seemed to disappear in a matter of hours. The smallest effort seemed beyond me and I was just sleeping for most of the day. I was in a serious state for a while, there was no doubt about that. I saw the United physio, David Fehvre, and complained that I just couldn't stop coughing. My chest was wracked with pain because of it. I wondered if it might be a chronic bout of hay fever. I was given a course of antibiotics but nothing happened. The illness just got worse. I couldn't run a yard and I felt really ill. That's when the club ordered me to undergo a series of blood tests and scans and very swiftly they told me I had pneumonia. It was a diagnosis that shook me, I was really frightened.

There very rapidly followed a reaction of total and absolute terror when the doctors explained a little bit more. If the disease, they said, attacked my heart and lungs then I might die. It was incredible. I didn't really understand the full impact of it all until that stage. I classed myself as a young, fit guy and now they were telling me I had something that I had only ever associated with old people – not a fit, young professional footballer. Nothing has stopped me in my tracks quite so fast. But the medical team that handled my treatment was brilliant. I didn't even have to go in to hospital for any length of time. They just ordered long-term rest and that meant I was out of the game for around three months. I had intensive physio, plus a course of steroid-based medication, and slowly but surely I recovered. It was a harrowing time and it halted my progress, knocking me back and undermining my ambition to be a success with United. I felt the fates were stacking up against me once more. People started suggesting that because of my illness and injury record I was a little suspect and they dismissed me as a bit of a sicknote. More frustration, more hurt. I started to think whether I would ever be in the position to win over what appeared an army of doubters. But I was determined nothing would drag me down and I shook off that temporary mood of despondency and stuck to my self-declared summer code: Andy, just go for it, because there's no other way now. In early October, I made up my mind I was ready to return. I bobbed into see the manager and told him, very confidently, that I felt fit and prepared for first-team action. I even pushed him a little further, demanding, 'Why am I not in the side by now?' He urged me to play one more game in the reserves to sharpen my reflexes and get myself more combat-ready for the Premiership. Then, he promised, I would be back in his front line. Reluctantly, I accepted the Gaffer's advice. So guess what happens? I play at Anfield in that final workout, half-time is approaching and we are 1–0 up and I get nailed by Neil Ruddock, and suffer a break in my right leg. Cruel, so cruel, you might say, but I have a much stronger word to describe it, only I'm too polite to use it here.

The argument from Ruddock was that he made the honest interception and played the ball. Let's examine that statement. I was two yards in front of him, goal-side at that, and the ball was shielded by my body. I was in an oustanding position to score a goal. Legitimately, there was no way Ruddock could get to the ball in my estima-tion. I was in the box, boot raised to make the strike, and he took me from behind. To add to the injustice, the referee declared it an acceptable challenge and gave Liverpool the advantage in telling them to play on. When I crumpled in the inevitable heap I knew immediately something was wrong, but not that I had a busted leg. United's assistant physio, Rob Swire, gave me some treatment, I tried to jog and that's when the pain shot through my body. Back to the casualty room for a few more soul-destroying months. And the gaffer wasn't too happy, either. Having seen video footage of the challenge, he went absolutely ballis-tic. As you might imagine, I felt just wonderful! There was muggins, left to ponder Ruddock's action. Exactly why did he want to crunch me? Our paths had never before crossed in an aggressive way and there was definitely no history of grudges to settle as far as I was aware. There we were, playing in front of ten men and his dog with nothing at stake, and Ruddock gets himself involved in an incident which puts me out of the game for half a season. Think about it. It was lunacy. But I had seen Ruddock, a fairly robust sort of chap, in an earlier incident while I was at Newcastle. We played Liverpool in a testimonial game and I shuddered then at the sight of Ruddock's elbow coming in contact with Peter Beardsley's face. His cheekbone was left in bits. I couldn't really take in what I was seeing. When I looked across at Ruddock, it didn't seem to have affected him at all. It's not for me to suggest he was parading himself as the hard man, but the whole incident has remained stuck in my memory as if it all happened yesterday.

The Ruddock episode, in which he claimed innocence and also insisted that I had simply fallen awkwardly, had one result. Disastrously, I missed another five months of what I had set aside as my make-or-break season. It should have been disheartening. Earlier on in my career that's the way it probably would have been. This time it was different. I was mean, ready for it, extremely focused and I delivered eight goals in just fourteen matches while the rest of the squad, more usefully employed over the ten month slog, celebrated yet another Premiership title. For me, there was another reward waiting, although I have to concede it came as a major surprise. I was summoned by England to play for them in the prestigious Le Tournoi competition in France. It was hard to figure. So much heartache over being ignored by my country and then, after barely kicking a ball in anger, I got the beckoning finger. It's a weird world, don't you think? But, whatever the people at the highest level of the game believed, there was still that nagging issue of whether I was actually of the calibre to play for United. Time and again it was raised. Incredibly, it was still a question on the lips of the dubious few after I scored twenty-five goals in the season when even that personal total was not enough to deny Arsenal the Double. Once again, I was supposed to be on the move and, yet again, the whole matter hinged on United needing an outstanding striker if they were ever to win the European Cup. Clearly, in the judgement of my persistent critics, I didn't have such qualities. I understood I was always going to attract such speculation; the fee dictated that I could never avoid it. But I'm not the type to shirk responsibility or bow down before an ill-informed minority. If I hadn't considered myself good enough for United, I would never have signed in the first place. Simple as that. Other renowned players had rejected the club because possibly they were overawed by the demands and immense expectation of the place. My view was very different. I wanted to join United to achieve the dreams which might be well nigh impossible to reach anywhere else. So not for a single moment did I think of chucking it and walking away. I always wanted to see it through. Any departure would have been United's decision, not mine. But they granted me time, and provided the all-important support that allowed me to emerge from the nightmare.

What they did, too, was radically change me as a player. They transformed me from base-model striker into a confident and proficient all-rounder. It might have been a whole lot easier, mind, if they hadn't allowed Andrei Kanchelskis and Lee Sharpe to leave the club shortly after I arrived. I think with those two in attack, particularly Andrei, I would have settled much more quickly because of their direct style of play. Hey, look, I'm not attempting to duck out here, but the attacking approach of Kanchelskis was made for me. You didn't have to second guess him. He was fast, direct and delivered the supply which strikers relish and defenders dread. Andrei's crosses were like tracer bullets in bouncing off a fullback's boot or a 'keeper's body, causing chaos and setting up chances. They dropped at your feet on the rebound or they fell to perfection and only needed an angled finish to divert them into the net. Andrei was a route one footballer, therefore his intentions were very easy to read. Yes, it was a blow for me when Kanchelskis, much to the consternation of the club, moved on to Everton. I was used to timing the run into the box, meeting the whipped-in cross, and wrapping up the bits and pieces with almost a tap in. That was the simple way at Newcastle. Now I was playing with Giggs and the emerging Beckham. In many ways it was like re-inventing myself as a footballer, because the one thing you can't do with Beckham and Giggs – as many a defender will tell you – is second guess them. It's taken time, but now I think we have a fantastic understanding between all of us. I couldn't survive on goals alone in this United team, even if I had been prolific from the first day of my arrival. I couldn't be one-dimensional any longer. Change was inevitable and beneficial, even if it meant hours of extra graft in bolting on the missing pieces. I was a very straightforward player when I signed. Now I am a far more complete professional in every aspect of the game. I feel I am miles better as a footballer now than I could ever hope to be at Newcastle. And KK's prophetic words often come back to me. They'll make you a better player.

I have enjoyed the process of development, tough as it has been, almost as much as the satisfaction of doing the business on the pitch. I am very much the all-round player, not just the pure goalscorer managers were content to employ a few years back. I can bring team-mates into the game, do the linking, hold the ball and control it under pressure, drop into the deeper attacking spaces and, yes, I can head the damn thing a whole lot better too. OK, I know what you're muttering . . . well, ain't that what a pro footballer's supposed to do? I take the point, but my answer is that at Newcastle I was never asked to provide such skills to the collective team effort. Up there, they wanted one product from me. Goals, and plenty of them. At United that would never have been enough. You have to be able to play as well as plunder. Put the effort in, reach the higher standard, and your team-mates appreciate you far more. I didn't just become a player, I also became my own man in the process. Whatever people say these days, behind my back or to my face, good or bad, doesn't matter any more. It's true they used to get under my skin, but those days are long gone. I am happy, very content with a God-given talent, and at the stage where I still have an abiding hunger to win so much more. It was irritating, a major aggravation in truth, when the cynical types among us attempted to chip away at that inner conviction. But I have responded to the challenge and I believe I have come through with flying colours. Somehow I doubt if it could get any better. It's a sweet life now.

Yet the season when deep in my heart I knew that I had come good and justified that £7 million was as sour an experience as I have known. Personally I claimed twenty-five goals in the 1997–98 season, spread across Europe and all three domestic competitions. I should have been able to celebrate, but there was no reason for a party. Individually, I was a winner, but United ended up the big-time losers and it was Arsenal who monopolized the sales of end-of-season champagne. I was left with just a hollow success and when it happened my mind went back to a particular game we had blown at Christmas. It was against Coventry. We were 2–1 in front with three minutes to go and we lost it 3–2. That Saturday Shirley picked me up at the Four Seasons Hotel following the coach journey home and I said, 'I hope that's not an omen. If we can only win the championship this time, I want to feel as though I belong to a championship-winning side at this club.' Come the end of May, I had my answer. It was a horrible feeling.

Chapter Five

Two starts, five caps, four men in charge. And just a touch more than four years to collate those telling statistics. Yes, it's my England career, bang up to date until the start of the millennium season. From Graham Taylor, who introduced me to the senior squad, to El Tel, through Eileen's big chum, to King Kev, I've spanned some wildly different approaches to our international football. What's that saying people use ... lie back and think only of England, isn't it? Well, I've been lying back a lot during the 1990s, largely unemployed as far as fulfilling my country's football needs, and puzzling over some very odd situations indeed. Particularly with the first two managers, namely Terry Venables and Glenn Hoddle. They both revealed a very bizarre way of handling their players or, at least, they did in my case. My verbal war with Hoddle, provoked by the man himself I have got to stress, received more than its fair share of back-page publicity when it erupted in November 1998. But there was a much earlier incident with Venables, when the FA wanted everything hush-hush, that was just as weird for me in the way it was handled by the men of power and influence. You could say, if you are being kind, that Venables and Hoddle were two men who had their own way of working and leave it at that. Except I am not in the mood for biting the diplomatic lip right now. Because when they were in charge, they had their own spin doctors and special media mates doing overtime to project the right image and slant on a story. Now it's my turn, with the two likely lads of Lancaster Gate long gone, and Kevin Keegan, the man of the people and the players, very much in control of events. What you see with Kev is exactly what you get.

But with Venables I was never too sure what I was getting, if anything, and where he was coming from. Late in 1994, for instance, I figured in one baffling episode of his international management. I'm still not sure whether it was supposed to be a fix-it telephone call in which I was expected to play dumb, and I would see the benefit later. Whatever, it was a strange, strange affair. So I'll let you be the judge. Earlier that season, let me just remind you, I was having trouble with my calves. They were giving me a certain amount of pain during games, but I was soldiering on, nicking a few goals, and Newcastle appeared perfectly content with my performances. I was fit for action, certainly, and ready for England duty, absolutely. And it was squad announcement time, with Venables about to release his latest twenty-two-strong party. Just before it was revealed, Kevin Keegan was made aware he was due a call from the FA about me. It came, right on cue, from David Davies, now the FA's executive director but who back then acted from time to time as Venables' mouthpiece combined with his more formal role in media relations or something. The understanding was that I would be left out of the squad and the excuse, alibi, or whatever you want to call it, was that I was to be declared injured. I wondered, obviously, what the hell all this intrigue and subterfuge was about. Kevin, as usual being the straight guy, called me into his office while he took the call from FA headquarters. The message delivered in the clearest detail that, firstly, I was not included in the squad and, secondly, what exactly should be said, and not said, in any response to the media. It was like they had it all scripted. Spin doctoring, is that what you call it? I sat there dumbfounded. I couldn't believe what lengths they were prepared to go to in explaining my absence. I was out, surplus to requirements, full stop, that should have been enough. This was nothing less than a smokescreen to get them out of an awkward spot. It was a device, a dupe. What did I do? I went on Sky and told the truth. In fact, I had a right go about what looked to me like a small-minded cover-up. The interview ran something along the lines: 'I can't believe I am not in this squad. I should be. I am playing well and scoring goals. I have had a few problems with my calves, but I know I am in shape and ready to play for my country. There is nothing I would like more.'

That kind of reaction, I suspect, didn't go down too well in the Venables hierarchy. It all went quiet with England for a while. I figured I might be suffering some kind of unwritten punishment for speaking my mind. It didn't trouble me over much. Sure I am patriotic, I want to play for my country, but I don't want there to be a price, and that price to be a code of silence when somebody demands it for no good reason. Suddenly, though, there came a reprieve. Venables named me in a friendly against Uruguay, played me as sub, and when I finally got on I hit the bar. We moved on to the summer Umbro tournament against Japan, Sweden and Brazil which, incidentally, was when a young man named Juninho was discovered by my old captain, Robbo. I had to report to the England camp at the Burnham Beeches Hotel outside London, which I duly did, even though an appointment had been booked for me to see a specialist over my still-sore calf muscles. I spoke to Venables before I went for the check-up and put him completely in the picture. His reaction surprised me. He said he didn't want me to visit the specialist; if I could play at all, he wanted me available for selection. I was straightforward with him, suggesting, 'If they say I am capable of playing right now, then there is nothing I would like better. But I still must go to seek medical advice about it.' Venables frowned at that. The specialist, on the other hand, wouldn't budge. He told me surgery and rehabilitation had to take place immediately. I agonized over the decision, but I always knew I had to follow the specialist's advice. I needed to think long term about my career and whether it might seriously be jeopardized by playing on without an operation.

Venables never made contact with me again. By this time I had arrived at Manchester United and I always felt playing there would enhance my international ambitions. I was scoring goals and playing some decent stuff. It was the season we lost the championship to Blackburn but, that cruel disappointment apart, I was fairly happy with my game. But from Venables not a whisper, just nothing. Did he feel I should have ignored medical advice and sacrificed myself the summer before? As a direct consequence, or that's the way it appeared, I was written off and banished from his plans. There is no other word for it, I was shunned. I had the op, instead of playing for El Tel's England, so that was me done and dusted. Don't mess with the boss, or else, to put it bluntly. But I was left with no regrets. I believe, and still do, that with my future under threat, I had to put my career first, much as I enjoy playing for England. Think of the option: if I had played in the Umbro tournament, in other words played through the summer, and then broken down in pre-season training, there could have been a tasty little reaction at Old Trafford and understandably so. It would have led to trouble on the grand scale. If Terry Venables saw fit to cut me out, then that was a consequence I was prepared to suffer. I took the only decision I had to take. It was a case of heads they win, tails I lose. That kind of situation was getting all too familiar.

But, wait for it, a new dawn. Venners was up the road and Hoddle was appointed the next manager for England. This was it, they said, the golden era. Hey, Coley, I figured, this is when you will enjoy the benefit of a reprieve. Foolish boy! I scanned the text on the given day but, no, I didn't get a sniff. For Hoddle's first few squads I was nowhere. He then picked me intermittently. In for one, out for the next two; it was extremely disconcerting. I was playing well, I should have been a regular candidate, but it just wasn't happening. The greatest disappointment was when I was forced to miss the Wembley game against Chile when Marcelo Salas, who might have joined us at United at one stage, decided it was the night for him to have a bit of fun at our expense. It was to lead to my first little niggle with Hoddle. In the preparations, I pushed myself and really trained hard, and paid for it. Two days before the match, I woke up with my back in spasm. I felt wrecked, both physically and mentally. What a mare! Another opportunity blown. I saw the physio, Alan Smith. He checked me out while Glenn was looking on in the medical room. Hoddle asked what shape I was in; the answer was less than optimistic. The suggestion was that I wouldn't be ready for the England game and it might well be wiser to ship me back to Manchester for treatment. Glenn urged, 'Just keep working on him and see how it goes.' I knew better than anybody how bad it was and told him, 'It's no good. I won't make it.' I packed my bags, went home and watched the game on the box. And soon discovered I was destined for more silence and more time in the wilderness. Maybe I should have volunteered to see the legendary Eileen.

What annoyed me even more was something that happened some months later. It might well be categorized as the first of Glenn's big gaffes in dealing with my situation. It wasn't exactly the worst, but it was bad enough. He claimed that the reason I missed out on so many subsequent England squads, the World Cup, and whatever else he was involved in, was simply because I cried off the Chile game. Not the wisest example of man management and a comment likely to give any self-respecting footballer the raging needle. How can you possibly hold an injury, one collected in preparation for an international fixture by the way, against any player and use it as a justifiable right for ignoring him forever? It wasn't as though I ducked out deliberately on him. I had wanted to play, desperately so. In my heart, though, I knew it wasn't possible. That's not a walk-out, is it? And it was certainly no reason for dumping me. Yet that's what Hoddle did. He dismissed me in little more than a sentence, saying I had missed my chance. Yet other players, many other players, were granted a lot more than one opportunity to prove their worth for England. The chosen few never had to wait long for a recall after any injury, or even that time-honoured excuse of a convenient groin strain when they failed to turn up. It was another kick in the nuts.

I never had any great contact with Hoddle at any time. He was an isolationist in many ways and I never got remotely close to him. I doubt if we had more than five minutes' conversation in all his time in charge. I recall being left utterly confused by one chat. He talked to me about a possible partnership up front with Paul Scholes, as though we were a pair of complete and utter strangers. It was altogether too baffling for me. Hoddle said, 'If you and Scholes get together, you can play this way and that,' and then rattled on about the different technical options we might have as a pair. I mean, the two of us happened to be at the same club, had operated as a strike partnership in the Premiership, and yet Hoddle seemed completely oblivious of what we did at United. He had no knowledge, no awareness, of how close Scholesy and I had already worked as attacking allies. But that conversation, which left me scratching my head in wonderment about the new manager, was about the extent of his real interest in me. Too often I felt like an outsider, unable to build a relationship with the man in charge, because any one-on-one dialogue was so rare it barely existed. I reached the conclusion he didn't want to play me, really, and it was only the pressure of my goals, plus the public demands of being a success with an opinion-swaying club like United, which compelled him to give me any international recognition at all. Too often his reaction appeared to be dismissive of me. The lame excuse that I had been injured against Chile, for instance: hard luck, and that was it, you're history, mate. Certainly between that friendly fixture and England's departure for the World Cup in France, I never figured in a single squad. It was wrong, I felt, a serious injustice in fact to be jettisoned because of a solitary injury without being granted a second chance. If you are returned to the fold, and still fail, then that's fair enough, you can accept your fate. But just being cast aside leaves an understandable grievance and I certainly felt wounded by Hoddle's treatment before the World Cup. Let's not forget that that season I finished as the Premiership's top marksman with twenty-five goals, yet at no point during those months of exile did I ever feel I was going to be in the party for France.

Just twenty-four hours before Hoddle's rejection call came one Friday in May, 1998, my mind was made up anyway. I was at the end of my tether as far as England was concerned. I told my advisor Paul Stretford that I felt so cheesed off, even if the miracle happened and I was selected, I wouldn't be going. Now that's a perilous step to take and a massive decision for any player to consider, but Hoddle's behaviour towards me had been so bad, almost contemptuous, I couldn't possibly turn the other cheek. Then came the phone call. It was short and not very sweet. Hoddle said: 'I just want to touch base with you. I am leaving you out of the squad for the World Cup.' I replied, 'That's fine, I never expected to be on the plane anyway.' Pause. 'Yeah, sure, I know you are bound to be disappointed, but I felt I had to get in touch and talk it through.' I closed the conversation very quickly: 'Fine; don't you worry yourself about it.' Hoddle had, in fact, taken a huge burden off my shoulders because, the way I felt, I would have told him he could hand that precious place to somebody else. I appreciate, of course, that playing in the World Cup Finals is the pinnacle of any footballer's career, but squeezing in when the manager essentially has little faith in you is not the way to go. I would only have been making up the numbers at best and there is nothing worse than entering such an important tournament in the knowledge that you are never really going to be that involved. For such an unfortunate individual, it's a month of tracksuit purgatory, like training for a fight that never comes along. You are only ever a passenger and when the rest are focused and hyped up for the big event, you have to accept you are little more than a waste of space. That was never what I wanted from England.

I didn't harbour any resentment against Hoddle at that stage, mind you. Naturally, there was hurt and an element of damaged pride, but he was doing the job the way he saw fit. That's OK by me. I didn't cause a fuss. I had reconciled myself to the situation. I just accepted that Hoddle believed I wasn't of the required standard to play for my country while he was in charge. You have to hold your hands up in that situation. He was calling the shots and so

I kept my mouth shut. But come November, just a few months after our cruel defeat against Argentine in St Etienne, he deserved to get both barrels from me and this time there was no backing off, no diplomatic silence. He questioned my ability as an international player and, in a kind of a sneering, mocking manner, said I needed six or seven chances to score a single goal. Nothing wrong with that, either, because it was his opinion. But Hoddle's big mistake, in my judgement, was to go to the newspapers with his comments. I don't have a problem with anyone having a go at me, but I ask them to grant me the privilege of doing it to my face, and not behind my back. Why didn't he just pick up the phone and call me first before going to the papers and coming out with all the hard stuff? It was a cheap shot. And, surely, I had the right of reply. If he wanted to exploit the media in fighting his corner, then I figured I was entitled to go the same way. Which, despite some quite prickly criticism in some quarters, is exactly what I did.

The whole business blew up so unexpectedly when I broke the habit of a lifetime and went to collect a morning tabloid. Shirley pestered me to buy one as we prepared for a day out with my son. That's when I first noticed the back-page headline with Hoddle rambling on about me again: 'It could be 12–18 months before Cole is able to perform consistently on the international stage.' I wondered why I was back to being the whipping boy. I hadn't had a barney with Hoddle or said anything to provoke his wrath. We hadn't spoken in ages. Then I read the article closely and, by the time I had got through all the different flaws and criticisms he levelled against me, I was boiling with anger. This was too much. I had had a bellyful of it and knew I must react. It wouldn't have been all that bad if a quarter of it had been true, but none of it made sense. Or added up logically. Six chances to score a goal, for instance. Yes, I agree, I do benefit from a lot of chances during the course of the average game, but I always figured that's why I get paid so much. I am a striker. It's my responsibility, the major focus of my job, to know where to run, to hunt, to have the instinct of being where the opportunities drop. My game is all about having your wits about you. My record, I suggest, is argument enough. In truth, it doesn't matter how many chances come your way because there is only one statistic to be counted at the climax of any season: How many goals did you get? If it's twenty-five, or whatever, that's the job done. Let me remind you also, there is never a single penalty or free kick in my scoring chart. Look at the guy who occasionally notches, say, thirty and invariably it will include around ten pens. Enough said, Glenn?

I know that my critics, and they are not exactly in short supply, condemned me for retaliating in print. But I couldn't possibly agree with their stance. Hoddle never, let me point out, spoke about any other individual in the same way. He also presented certain showboating football reporters with the general excuse to start sniping at me for no other reason than Hoddle seemed to approve it. I was offered as a target and when you are singled out in that way, it's unfair. Hoddle's a man, I am a man, so let's sort it. If you form an opinion about me, don't hide away, just express it. But in the proper way. Talk to me, that's all, and privately. All Hoddle needed to do was pick up a phone, as he had over the World Cup squad, and go through, step by step, what he described as my faults. We might have been able to work things out. I would certainly have been prepared to listen to constructive criticism, particularly if he had presented it to me in the confines of a room or on the training ground. You never know, we might both have benefited from such a discussion. Definitely, I would always have been prepared to thrash it out and see where the argument took us. But putting the whole issue in the public domain, without giving me any advance warning of his view, was totally and shamefully wrong. It left me wide open to a sniping campaign where, if you had accepted every negative point placed in the argument, I shouldn't be collecting a wage packet from the game at all. It was an utter travesty and a distortion of my career record. He was also, if only Hoddle had thought it through, questioning Alex Ferguson, the United coach Brian Kidd and everyone else at Old Trafford who had approved my £7-million signing. They all had faith in me, reckoned I wasn't a bad player, yet Hoddle's assertions, if correct, meant they didn't know their jobs and they were all wrong. So, rightly, I thought it was about time to remove the gag and speak my own mind. It's something I intend doing in the future, too. I accepted that I might upset a few people with my comments, but that was tough. Hoddle had been granted his say, I was determined to have mine. I simply accused him of dealing with the matter wrongly, carelessly and unprofessionally. Everything was off my chest, and I felt happy and contented. If Hoddle had challenged me about it, I would have been ready to speak to him man to man. He never came close. Even when he named me in his squad for the friendly with France during the autumn of '98, he didn't make any personal call to me. And by the time we gathered, he had been sacked after creating more awkward headlines. They exposed once again his lack of sensitivity.

Since his sudden departure, many people have dropped the hand grenade in my lap and asked the question: What was he really like with you? Well, for a start, when he left the England job I had no great emotional feelings of revenge or anything like that. It wasn't as if I was screaming for it to happen. The only lasting ruck I had with him was in trying to protect myself and my professional reputation, that was all. So his resignation, in less than glorious circumstances, didn't have any impact on my life. I just shrugged my shoulders. There was no dancing on the grave of a famous football personality as far as I was concerned. Apart from that somewhat distanced reaction, it's hard for me to be judgmental about him as a manager. I was never allowed that close to be qualified as a real associate of the man, I suppose. He used to distance himself from his players, unlike the approach of his successor, Kevin Keegan. He enjoys being up close and personally involved with his squad. Hoddle lived, as far as I could make out, an ivory-tower existence; everyone was kept at arm's length. I can only repeat that, in all his time in control, I spoke for no more than five minutes with him. How are you supposed to interact and get to know a guy when that's the relationship? He might have talked to one or two of the carefully selected few, but that never included me. He didn't mix socially at meal times, but took his place at the high table with the rest of his staff. KK has a habit of plonking himself down wherever he feels, ready to join in the banter and have a laugh. There was no way of breaking the ice with Hoddle and that's when, I feel, unwanted tension builds up within a squad. No, I never hated the man and, let's be honest, because he kept me at a distance, I managed to avoid any invitations to meet Glenn's guru, dear old Auntie Eileen. The rest of his England staff also didn't exactly get close. Glenn Roeder was the exception. He was always helpful, a listening ear for me in an environment where so many stayed silent. It's weird, isn't it, the way people change when their title moves from player to manager? They seem, in an instant, to forget what they were like themselves in their playing days, laying down demands and petty little laws they would have defied and contravened just a year or two before. They apply different rules and yet, coming from their background, they should really be more understanding and flexible.

When Glenn's appointment was announced in 1996, I think there was a general view in football that it was the right way to go. Most players welcomed it. I certainly did. Players believed he would be massively helpful to the international set-up because he had been there himself and succeeded at the highest level. He was also a footballer of very high technical merit. There wasn't too much Hoddle couldn't do with a ball except maybe win it. He wasn't merely restricted to explaining what he wanted, or chalking it down on a blackboard; this fella could actually demonstrate it and not look a mug. He did, too. On the training ground, I have to concede Hoddle was inventive, interesting, and technically very good. We all listened, and we learned. He knew, too, how he wanted the game to be played and that revolved around changing England's style. It was the Mediterranean way, a controlled passing game, shaped on his own experience of playing abroad. But to make that system work best, it could only function with someone like Paul Gascoigne at the fulcrum of the team. Without him, it was never quite the same, but that's a whole different ball game which I will come to a little later. Gazza can't properly be discussed in a paragraph or two, and neither can KK.

Kevin's arrival in the England job during 1999 was anticipated as an appointment of huge benefit. And not just for me in particular, but for the football nation in general. I, of course, supported it to the hilt. For all his humour, happy demeanour, willingness to spare a minute for anybody who tugs his arm, KK is a tough cookie. Emotional, as we all know, as well. A fact most famously underlined with that gut-wrenching TV interview from Elland Road when Newcastle, by this time minus one Andrew Cole, were being ruthlessly hunted down by my new club, Manchester United. Kevin, swearing he would never back down, came out with the immortal line: 'I would love to beat them, I would really love it.' He looked to be on the point of tears, probably out of sheer frustration. But also there was so much ambition there, so much yearning to give the Geordies what they had demanded for decades, and that compulsive need for it to happen was literally burning deep into his very soul. I felt for him. But you can imagine the reaction within the Old Trafford dressing room. I took some terrible stick. 'Look,' they sniggered, 'your big mate's blown it now, Coley.' What could I say, how could I try and defend him? 'I know, man, but that's not like Kevin.' Privately, I realized he had lost the plot and that, psychologically, Alex Ferguson had got to him. There was no way back for Newcastle from that critical moment. But I don't regard that as a weakness. It is a part of KK's make-up, wearing his heart on his sleeve, and it's an integral part of his character and strength. Once he took on the England job, he carried that formidable desire with him. From that point in his life, his only concern was, what his country wanted, he was prepared to give – if at all possible. For that very reason I always thought when he took on the part-time role, while continuing to lead Fulham to promotion, he was bound to end up at Lancaster Gate sooner rather than later. He just couldn't resist the call from England for very long. He had told so many people down the years that if the offer came, and the timing was right, he wouldn't be able to refuse.

Given the support he deserves, and no matter what the cat-calling of the media, I believe he was always the candidate perfectly cast for the job. Just allow KK the necessary period to put together the team fulfilling his ideals, and I have never felt anything less than England would be grateful for his contribution in the long term. International management is much tougher, and under even greater scrutiny than club management, but this man has never shirked the big decision. Once he accepted the job, he appreciated the inevitable consequence of hurting people, breaking hearts, including mine when I was left out of the squad for the final Group Five qualifier in Poland. With England you are dealing with big names, some of the biggest in fact, and towering personalities. They can't all get into the team and that invariably creates its own sizeable problems. But the most ominous challenge comes under the heading of quality. Have we, despite all the hype and self-congratulation of the Premier League, the genuine quality players to conquer the world? I happen to believe we do possess top performers, but they operate unfortunately in the cocked-thumb era. One day it's up for encouragment, the next it's down in condemnation. You are either a genius, or a clown. We play well, and it's England I am talking about here, and for a few wonderful months we get the big build-up. Then we get together for five days, play a game, play lousy, and instantly the whole bunch of players is written off. It's a cycle of madness in this country and nobody can expect to succeed in this black-and-white world. Player X is world class one minute, a complete prat the next, and so it rolls on. With such instant judgements must follow the ruination of our international ambitions. Not even KK, the supreme optimist, can survive in such an arena of cock-eyed optimists where you must have the perfect performance every time by demand. In his very early days, he must have recognized the symptoms for ultimate disaster in the long term. At one time his players were hailed as a superteam and yet, within a matter of weeks, the same group only deserved to be dumped into the dustbin. It's lunacy.

There must be more patience, shaped around sensible, long-term policies, instead of the panic reaction of shifting one bunch, on the grounds of one poor result, for another bunch who might not be as good. We all want the best team in the world to be wearing the three lions on the shirt, but, equally, I can tell you it's never going to happen by this method. Pick-and-dump methods have never worked. KK, granted a more realistic approach, was born with the leadership qualities, and vitally the courage, to put it right. You have to show absolute faith in a collection of players over three or four years, not three or four weeks. He had occupied the England chair for arguably less time than that when people – envious, nit-picking people – started to question his opinion. I was bewildered. It was crazy and self-defeating to raise such issues so quickly. When Kevin was appointed you could hear the applause in every corner of football. He's THE man, they said, and then a month later they began shaking the statue, attempting to dislodge it from the pedestal. It was frightening and farcical. You have to give everyone a reasonable chance of making a success of the England team because, to borrow a political phrase, boom and bust ideas have no lasting chance. The heads-must-roll opinion, following the slightest setback, is simply counter-productive. And let me promise these impulsive agitators they don't need to try and goad KK into going. If, in two or three years' time, he is not satisfied with the progress being made, he will be the first to acknowledge any failure, and go without any official shove. I'm not suggesting he is a quitter, but I know Kevin pretty well. If he ever reached the conclusion his country would be better off without him, he would opt out before his time was up. If he felt it was right, and England would benefit, that decision would be made by Kevin without the slightest hesitation.

For the moment, though, nerves have to be steady and the resolve for the future unchallenged. When he took over, part way through the qualification programme for the European championship finals, some damage had already been inflicted on us. Kevin was the repairman. When we beat Poland 3–1, with Paul Scholes' hat trick, the whole nation was out and literally dancing in the streets. Next it was Sweden, well-organized and the group leaders, and the mood switched to the other extreme. A draw was rubbish, they screamed, and England found themselves contemptuously dismissed as a shambling, leaderless, tactically-dumb rabble. Nice, that! So it was Bulgaria five days later and more vitriol hurled at the players. The same players, I have to remind you, who only weeks before had been praised like golden-haloed heroes. What a complete joke. When I was growing up, I looked at the England team and it seemed the same names, the same faces stayed in places for ages. Now it's the age of madness. You feel the team is almost being run on the basis of a media feeding frenzy. Everyone has an opinion, and everyone is right. Or so they think. If a player scores a couple of goals before an England squad is due, the clamour is cranked up to get him in the team. Nothing else is considered. Whether that individual is better than what we already possess, doesn't seem to count. It's selection by hysteria. Boys, let me tell you, it won't work. But, give him a chance, and I know a man who can make it work. That man is Kevin Keegan.

Chapter Six

At this point I intend laying down a challenge. It's a difficult subject and it all revolves around that long-running debate about my international appearances or, to be more exact, the lack of them. So here goes . . . now look, big Al, this is nothing personal, but you are the one man on the planet with such power and influence you might just force me to reject the England team and walk away. Forever. I'm talking, of course, about Alan Shearer, the favourite, always-picked, chosen son of all our national managers during the 1990s. By the time you have flicked to this page it might already have happened. I could be history. Because, as I sit down in the summer of 1999 pondering my most important football options, there is but a single question heading the agenda: What chance has any other top striker got with England while old golden boy Shearer is still on the scene? It's an issue which bugs me. Actually, it does more than that. I do believe that his position should have been more open to challenge, given the other options open to the management. I have been affected, but so have four or five other top strikers. All of us had to fight for a single place in England's front line because Shearer, automatically it seemed, was guaranteed the other. That had led to frustration, dejection and even the serious consideration of whether it was all worth the hassle. Raising, inevitably, the subject of whether I actually wanted to play for my country ever again, this question would never have entered my head if I had played for ten years and had fifty caps in the trophy cabinet. Then it would have been shock, horror, and a no, no, no consideration. I am patriotic, too, if you are beginning to doubt my loyalty. But I have been shunted to one side, ignored for long periods and granted barely a handful of appearances, to the point where the issue is not anything of heartbreaking proportions.

I am also in my twenty-eighth year, not getting any younger as they say, and a highly personal question needed to be addressed: Is it worth sticking around any longer? I've never been the type to outstay my welcome and there is ample proof of that at every stage of my career. Hogging a squad place for the sake of it, keeping an aspiring young kid a little further back in the queue, has never been my style either. So, following the triumph of Manchester United's Treble, I did sit down and reach one solid conclusion. It wasn't complicated at all. I accepted then that if it ever got to the stage where I felt I should move over, allowing England to progress as a team, I would willingly do it. Bluntly, I could accept quitting without any manager, including Kevin Keegan, pulling me to one side and whispering the dreaded words in my ear. It wasn't a case of not wishing to carry on if they wanted me, but more that I wouldn't bat an eyelid if they didn't. I had done my fair whack of having boots and travelling the world, yet at one time there was no one more passionate about representing my country than me. It burned me up if I wasn't up there with the best and seriously involved. Progression up the ladder occupied all my thoughts. Now, if I glance at the Teletext and my name fails to appear, I am not exactly devastated. I don't agonize over it any longer. The adrenalin rush now comes with

United, not with my country. I have endured too many disappointments with England; they are not going to plunge me into despair ever again. I have to be honest with myself about that. There is no point in putting on a public appearance, delivering the platitudes and saying the things that please any more. Deep down inside, I have to say I couldn't really care less one way or the other now. But don't misinterpret that sentiment. It doesn't mean I don't care about England being successful, because I do. And I have been encouraged by the talented young breed – players to take us well beyond the millennium – coming through. At my age, and bearing in mind I have hardly been an international regular, I would be duty bound to stand aside and let them through. That's what regularly happens with the other high-profile footballing nations. It's about time it happened here, too. Bring on the kids, give youth a fling, because it is the only way we will reassert ourselves in the global game. In stating this maybe unexpected philosophy, don't misread the message. I have never said, and I am not saying it now, that I didn't scream for an opportunity to play for my country. 'Course I did. Who wouldn't? But you do reach a point of frustration where it's no longer the priority it once was. I know, because I have.

It has always been my fate to be hardly the darling of the nation. Some people would even suggest I have never possessed the quality to play for England. They would rattle on about it being a step too far. Nonsense. I have played in Europe for United against many of the world's finest defenders; footballers from Brazil, Germany, Italy, Spain and Argentina, the finest around, and the very same guys I would be likely to oppose at international level. I never had a problem. If you can do it with your club, why not with your country? In winning the European Cup, my partnership with Dwight Yorke showed just how menacing we can be in challenging the best around. We did, in fact, literally terrorize some of the most famous defenders in the game. If I am capable of that, how can these supposedly well-informed critics suggest I am not good enough for England? That just doesn't add up. I just wanted a consistent opportunity to state my own case on the pitch, the only place where any serious football argument can be settled. All I ever begged was the chance with England to demonstrate to these doubters that they were emphatically wrong. For that, you must have an uninterrupted run of several games to prove your worth. Once that was achieved, you could hold up your hands and accept whatever happened. Even if it meant the exit door. This fatalistic opinion was reached to a great degree because of the Shearer factor I mentioned earlier. Every England manager in my time never looked beyond him, never shuffled the pack and measured the impact of any other combination. It was always Big Al and A.N. Other, the two strikers for England. His name was first on the England teamsheet for five years or more. Other centre-forwards were damned as the famous outsiders, knowing they were having a hell of a time in their club side but it wouldn't make any difference. One place was guaranteed, and that was for Shearer, and the rest of us were left praying to be picked as his partner. The older you get, the more tired you become of such an unfair situation.

While Shearer was around, he was simply granted priority over everyone and every other tactical consideration. He remained the whole focus, the central hub of the England team. I suspect a lot of his rivals were left totally disheartened by this unrealistic way of treating one individual. All of us were forced to accept, regardless of form and success away from the international arena, that once you made the England squad the only way forward was to be Alan's partner. Nobody else was allowed to compete for his place; it appeared sacred and he was the untouchable. That was upsetting, and hardly beneficial for team morale. I have always believed every single member of a football team should be treated as an equal, but Shearer was different from us all. He was privileged. If you are enduring a bad patch, you should be left out in the same way as anyone else, and we all know that Shearer has not always played well. If he had always been the master, performing to a high level and plundering goals, then fine – he had to play for his country. But Shearer was protected and retained his position when his form, both at club and international level, was some way short of what we had come to expect. That would never have been allowed with any other individual and that's what made the situation unjust. Because he was Alan Shearer, famous striker and England captain, that appeared to be enough, the only factors that mattered. He wasn't dealt with on a logical management basis. When other players fell below an expected standard, they were bombed out. In the World Cup that happened and some of the unfortunate players never recovered to reclaim their places. There must never be a rule for one, then different rules for the rest. You can't allow people to get away with it – not even Shearer. It only allows discontent, accusations of favouritism and worse, to creep into the dressing room. There had to be an element of resentment among the other players. It was inevitable. You are supposed to select the best eleven, not shape every possible strategy around the supposed golden boy. There was little point in living in the past and remembering what a glorious Shearer might have achieved a couple of years earlier.

When Shearer suffered his cruciate ligament injury, I recall a mood of virtual panic swept the country. The cry went up: 'Who is going to play up front now?' It was hysterical, it was ridiculous. The suggestion seemed to be that no other centre-forward was ready to replace him, or even fit to lace his boots with England. I felt insulted, and so must a few others. England, I feel, has been blessed with high calibre strikers in recent years. I'm thinking of Ian Wright, Les Ferdinand, Robbie Fowler, Chris Sutton and, more recently, Michael Owen, Emile Heskey, not forgetting yours truly. Nowadays, that sort of thing doesn't bother me too much. It's not as if I have had a major international career, anyway, and so I don't reflect on such disappointment in my private moments. I don't worry or get fussed about it any more. I have never been what you might call the blue-eyed boy. Such is life! My problems with previous England managers are well documented and so also are my various attempts in winning recognition by first being the silent grafter and next the upfront drum-beater. Nothing really changed my position. I played at every level for my country from schools, through the Under 21s to England B and always scored goals and revelled under the coaching influence of Dave Sexton. Only when I reached the senior squad did I ever face a barrier. There, I have never felt part of the happy band whose faces always fit. No matter how well I have played, it seemed I collected a zero rating and little recognition. At Newcastle, I slammed in the goals but mostly I was shunned. I figured the move to Old Trafford would alter everything. Surely, operating for the most feared club in the land would be the ultimate guarantee that England's manager would take notice. There was little change. That, subconsciously, was when the initial disillusionment set in, reinforced later by the debacle of my World Cup exclusion, until now I honestly couldn't care less whether they pick me or not. Think about it. I feel it should never have taken anyone with my goal-scoring record so long to gain a place in the squad and still not be established as a regular five seasons later. Now, being selected or ignored doesn't disturb me for a second. The anguish is over and if England never beckoned again I would not be bothered in the slightest. The end of last season, with three trophies in my lap, was my true moment of satisfaction. With England I always felt the outsider, a figure pushed to the fringes.

Such treatment has left me with the overriding conclusion that I much prefer playing for my club than my country. If it ever came to the crunch – United v England on a football field – I'll tell you something else – back United every time. I remained unconvinced that the general philosophy would change even when Keegan took charge. He, too, was a Shearer disciple, but the critical difference in KK is that he is always prepared to give everybody a reasonable chance. Whether that happened with me was of little consequence, because I have faith in the future of the England side. There are many candidates to be put under scrutiny and I feel the time is right to concentrate on the young lions such as Owen, Fowler and Sutton. They, surely, are the class of 2000. Maybe they, though, will never attain the heights of a player I have idolized for years, the immortal Gazza. I doubt we have ever clapped eyes on a greater creative talent than Paul Gascoigne in the last thirty years. And the fact that we banished him from the 1998 World Cup finals must rank as a crime against the best interests of this footballing nation. I have never been able to understand or reconcile myself with Hoddle's decision to leave him out. He should have been an absolute, stone-bonking cert for France because of his finesse and match-winning flair. In terms of creativity, this fella was a genius and England desperately needed his unique input in midfield. OK, we had David Beckham in there, but he operates wide on the right and carried different responsibilities. Then there was Paul Scholes, another extremely clever player, but he likes to play in the hole higher up the park. We were left with an alarming gap to fill in the vital area of the team and Gazza should have filled it.

His role was always to collect the ball from deep positions, carry it through into offensive areas with a pass or a run, and feed the ammunition to the front men. In France, we just had no one to fulfil that responsibility. There were players to win it, to scuffle, to close down, but what we cried out for was the puppet master. That was Gazza, the most inventive player this country has had in many decades. When on his game, fit, healthy and strong, he was by far the best midfield player in the country. He might never have been ready to be the box-to-box athlete, so common in our game, but he was an individual who didn't need any special discipline: he was the utterly versatile, three-ring performer. You could leave him to get on with his own special business safe in the knowledge he could win any game on his own. What an immense talent. People have a certain image of him, a carefree guy full of booze and recklessly wasting his career. I never accepted that perception. Once again, as so often happens, he might well have been an unfortunate victim of that well-known British hobby of building up the idol only to demolish it. His reputation was forged very early in his life and he had a huge amount of pressure imposed on him when he was very young. He felt there was a way to deal with it and we shouldn't criticize him for the odd madcap escapade. I would certainly never dare to criticize him, because he's an individual, a one-off, a special guy. Whenever he played for England he shed a few tears, endured the wounds, both verbal and physical, but never let his country down. For me, he was the white Brazilian. There's nobody left in the game now who can offer his control and imagination. In truth, there's just nobody in his league and he has been irreplaceable in England's midfield. Even when Gazza was some way short of desired fitness, he was ready to create that moment of absolute magic. They might have knocked him off the park, but nobody slagged him on it. Every footballer appreciated they were in the presence of a player who represented a different dimension to the rest. Some sneered that too many visits to the bar meant he couldn't run any more, that he had lost a yard or two of pace. When you are blessed with Gazza's brain you don't need to rely on pace. Your intelligence provides that missing extra yard. Just remember nothing moves faster out there than the ball itself. Pass it with Gazza's excellence and the opposition swiftly understood he was more deadly than any road runner.

Within Hoddle's system of play, Gascoigne was essential. He had the presence to intimidate the opposition and, of equal importance, he had the stature and composure to be the team's playmaker. In his absence, missing that quality to go past opponents and pick a pass, England lacked a great deal. They had hard workers, the abrasive ball-winners like Paul Ince and David Batty, but they needed the complementary flair of Gazza to make the side function properly. Just consider the World Champions of France. They had a few of what Eric Cantona called the water-carriers but they also had Zinedine Zidane and, to a lesser extent, Youri Djorkaeff. What they would call their footballers of fantasy. Gazza fell into that elevated category, an élite footballer able to go it alone and win the game with an incredible pass or a blinding goal. And with that point in mind, let me transport you back to the World Cup. Gazza's absence was critical and it was fundamental to our eventual failure. When they bombed him out, I knew immediately our chances of success had been weakened considerably. With him around, prompting and inspiring, I am convinced we would have walloped Argentina and at least made the semi-finals. A majority of the England players wanted him with them and that's a fact. They realized his value and, like all pros, they understood an unspoken rule of the game. A good team can always carry someone of Gazza's quality, no matter how fitness-flawed or injury-prone he might have become, for that one pass, that one second of genius. Ever since the game began there have been players reluctant to work as hard as the rest because they felt they were cushioned from the sweat zone by their extraordinary skills. Equally, down the years, team-mates would accept the additional burden, of carrying an individual to some extent, in return for that bit of swashbuckling flair. Gazza fell into that category with the England boys. People, all of them outsiders I might stress, took the opposing, negative view and kept preaching to the world what was supposedly wrong with Gascoigne. They missed the point. We never needed him rampaging around, dripping in perspiration, but we did need him, desperately so. The whole team revolved around his presence. Upstairs, as the thinking man of the side, we just had nobody as sharp as Gazza.

In any case, the focus of his so-called physical deterioration was overblown anyway. I played against him up at Middlesbrough on the way to our Treble, and clearly he hadn't lost that wonderful ability. And for those who have tried to blacken him as a beer-swilling yob, let me add that he was always one of the nicest, funniest blokes in the game. He would do a favour for anyone at any time. The guy would always surrender his time, his money and his support if you needed it. When I made my first start for England in the '99 season, the Wembley game we won 3–0 against the Poles, Gazza sent me a telegram wishing me all the best and declaring, 'This has long been overdue.' And he wasn't even in the squad. I still treasure that little note, now tucked in a drawer at my home. For a fellow professional to go out of his way, to think of you when he

Cole's golden goals

PICTURE SOUVENIR OF STAR STRIKER'S FIRST 26 GOALS

NEWCASTLE JOURNAL

ALLSPORT

Collecting the Golden Shoe on the 25th Anniversary of *Shoot* magazine, in August 1994. *(Right)*

Paul Stretford, me, Martin Edwards and Sir Alex Ferguson on the day
I signed for Manchester United.

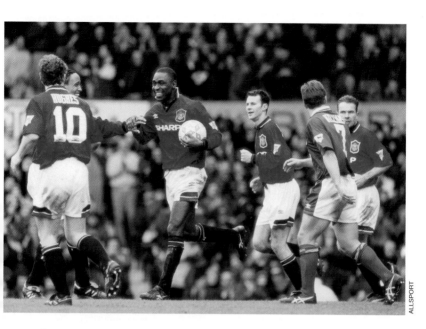

Sometimes the goals came and sometimes they didn't. Celebrating one of my record-breaking five goals in the 9-0 defeat of Ipswich *(above)* and contemplating a no score draw against Spurs *(below)*, in March 1995.

Chilling out in Rome prior to the Juventus v Ajax European Cup Final *(above)* and in the thick of it during one of our huge tussles with rivals Blackburn Rovers *(below)*.

In training with Peter Schmeichel and Ole Gunnar Solskjaer *(above)* and scoring a vital goal for United in our 2-1 win over Chelsea in the FA Cup semi-final in March 1996. My first Double was to follow.

Being welcomed formally to Indonesia during a promotional trip for one of my sponsors.

In Zimbabwe. Showing my skills to the children at the Moshambanzou Hospice *(above)* and then being beaten to the ball by a group of them – all as part of my work for the Venture Kodak Andy Cole Children's Fund.

A proud moment as I'm recalled to the England team by new manager and my former manager, Kevin Keegan. It was a great 3-1 win over Poland in the Euro 2000 qualifier.

must have been really down, was a tremendous gesture. It wasn't as if I was ever close to him in the England squads. Naturally, we would have some banter and he wasn't exactly a character to go unnoticed with his stunts and practical jokes. But that was it. We were team-mates who liked each other rather than being bosom buddies. As another individualist, John Barnes was very similar. So, too, Chris Waddle. And then there was Gary Lineker, admittedly a very different type of footballer, but a single-minded match-winner all the same. They were my favourite England players in the generation before me. I never actually tried to model myself on Lineker, but I was a great admirer of his goal-scoring technique. Like Ian Rush, he was the classic example for all ambitious kids to emulate in the art of making the perfectly timed attacking run. He used to decimate the finest teams and demoralize defenders of the highest class with such quality.

Unfairly, Barnes, another born with instinctive skills, didn't always earn overwhelming applause, particularly on the international stage. Too often, and by too many football folk, he was accused of failing to perform to his potential best when clad in an England shirt. Yet in his heyday, he was unreal, frightening, in that flamboyant way he could control the ball and beat any number of opponents waiting to cut him down. I still drool over that trademark goal against Brazil all those years ago. It must rank as among the greatest goals ever scored anywhere in the world. I loved Waddle as well and he wasn't exactly bombarded with praise either. He should have been, because he was also a special talent whom you could easily compare with any foreign star, but, like Barnsey, he never got the credit he deserved. I suppose we should be accustomed to that by now in this country. Take the case of Matt Le Tissier. He was another very much in the Gascoigne mould, maybe drifting out of games a little more than Paul, but invariably capable of a dynamic impact when he received the ball. Again, because of the persistent bellyaching about work rate, he was roughly treated by England and eventually dumped with the unkind reference of simply being a luxury player. It was all so negative. If you have nine outfield players prepared to run until they drop, then you can afford a Gazza or a Le Tissier; other international teams accommodate their type all the time and benefit from the adventure of it. There should never have been any prolonged debate over Le Tissier – the bottom line is, he should have played for England. And often. Yet, when he failed to score with a header in that Wembley defeat by Italy in 1996, he was dragged off, scapegoated and took the national rap for what was really a collective failure. Injustice on the grand scale yet again. He suffered like me with the international hierarchy and seemed to be forever on the wrong end of a raw deal. Certainly there has to be a comparison in the limited number of opportunities allowed to us both. Matt, in my opinion, should have played many, many times and that is England's loss. For years over here we have bleated and complained that we don't produce such creative, showman-type entertainers, yet when they do appear on the scene we show a bloody-minded urgency to ignore them. Worse still, we take it upon ourselves to pillory them. Players like Gascoigne, Waddle and Le Tissier are born, not made, with their blessed array of skills. We should treasure them.

With such entrenched attitudes, are we ever going to be a major global power in football again? Well, I do think we must be far more progressive, but there is definite encouragement in the developing standards of our youth and Under 21 teams. The stance, particularly in certain areas of the media, that we should always be superior to the rest is a fantasy. We might well have taught football to the world, but many decades ago we were caught and, in some cases, left in the slipstream of a few countries. But now the first promising steps are being taken with the focus on the grassroots of the game, which started with the revolution in the schools of excellence. I am a committed fan of the likes of Emile Heskey and Kieron Dyer, who didn't do any harm to his international ambitions in joining Ruud Gullit at Newcastle. The big fella Heskey, with lesser loyalty, might also have been prised away from Leicester from time to time. Tottenham and a number of Premiership rivals offered substantial money for him in the summer of 1999. He always understood that eventually he must feel the benefit of all that groundwork with Martin O'Neill at Filbert Street. While this pair waited for destiny to beckon, Michael Owen, before he was even twenty, was launched into a spectacular orbit in the World Cup with that fantastic goal against Argentina. As soon as I saw Owen in action for the first time with Liverpool, I realized he had an exceptional future stretching in front of him. Very quickly you could put me down as a committed admirer. But all that myth-creating, heavily hyped stuff about Michael being our very own Ronaldo was complete and utter drivel. It didn't do him any favours either. His name was made with that runaway goal in France, a special goal it was too, but for people to try and create an immediate football profile alongside the Brazilian was just plain nonsense and beyond all reason. Once again, we were in the realms of creating overnight idols. The media clamour served one purpose. They wanted to generate a story that we had the world's best player within our ranks, so Owen, courtesy of just thirty seconds of television fame, was seized upon. Compare his position, his contribution at a global level, with that of Ronaldo, and you must grasp immediately the inequality of the contest at that time. Michael, as he would probably have conceded, knew he was not a patch on the top man. He will become a great player, given luck and his potential, but to measure him with a world legend at such a tender age was just ludicrous. That doesn't mean I belong to the churlish brigade who rattle on about England not possessing any world-ranked players. From my own club I would argue David Beckham, Paul Scholes along with Keane, Stam, Yorke and Ryan Giggs are in that catergory. Unfortunately for us, however, they're not all English. With England, there has been Shearer, Tony Adams and David Seaman and soon they must be joined by Owen. Within these shores, the first reaction is in denigrating our own achievements, and the special players we have, but I see a lot of encouraging and welcoming signs for England in the years ahead. Just so long as the men in charge possess the same vision as our best men on the pitch.

Chapter Seven

They say the wild man is no more. That he's chilled out, that he is a different, quieter, much more mellow person. Calmness itself. And, OK, they might well have a point. But I have stood in the eye of the hurricane. Yes, I have witnessed the game's most legendary cup-chucker in his full, expletive glory. I have seen Sir Alex Ferguson in action. And, let me tell you, I was terrified. I made sure I sat in the most distant corner of the dressing room and attempted to make myself invisible even though I wasn't even the target of his anger. The unfortunate victim on this particular occasion was Paul Ince, who I have to concede is no mean individual with the verbals either. But even he must have shuddered in his boots at the ferocity of the manager's personal attack on him. For me, looking back on the whole scary episode, I think it was the first time I had seen the gaffer losing the plot. It was at Anfield during the tense and important run-in for the championship we lost on the last day of the 1995 season. The bust-up occurred just a few weeks before Blackburn claimed the crown when Liverpool beat us 2–0. We all knew we couldn't afford to surrender any points along the way and there wasn't anyone at United who didn't accept it was a serious setback for us. The accusation levelled at Incey was that he had failed to carry out a specific instruction at a set-piece from the manager and that had allowed Jamie Redknapp to score. The manager, consequently, launched an attack on him that was wild, really wild.

I sat back in an amazed silence and just couldn't believe what I was witnessing. I remember my reaction at the time was that this was so unreal it couldn't be happening. It wasn't exactly a storm in a teacup, more like a war to tilt the world on its axis. The gaffer went absolutely ballistic, just crazy. His eyes rolled and I don't think I have ever seen, before or since, any individual going berserk on such a scale. It was mayhem in that room for a full ten minutes. So much screaming and shouting, the manager knocking cups off the table, laying into Incey with such anger that total anarchy reigned for a while. As someone who had recently arrived from the much more subdued, nice-guy camp of Kevin Keegan, I was left open-mouthed and just a little shaken. Ince, as expected, responded. He's never been the type to lie down and take it. They went at it hammer and tongs and Brian Kidd, mercifully, acted as the referee. He always stepped in. If the manager had singled out any player for what Sparky Hughes called the hair-dryer job, a full, furious, nose-to-nose blast, then Kiddo always intervened. It sometimes got close to being like a boxing match and he would always break it up, with the manager moving in and Kiddo urging: 'Leave it, just leave it for now.' The manager would pause for a second or two and then, if the temper was still blazing, he would roar back. With Incey there was no escape; it was a ceaseless verbal battering. Now you are able to look back on it and just laugh. In fairness, after that first unbelievable experience when I had no warning of what to expect, they were all a bit comical in their way. But that's just Alex Ferguson in the raw, very much the man in charge and never afraid to show the intensity of his feelings. What all those highly charged, emotional tear-ups did reveal to the players was how much success, achievement and United's status in the game meant to him.

After five years in his team, I think the one searing quality I see in him above all others is that the manager is a winner. He has that almost savage belief that he must always finish on top of the pile. It is the most important element of his make-up. He has demanded the supreme contribution from his sides at all times; to play with him you must give nothing less than your best. Every player he brought to United needed to understand that, because it was fundamental to the Ferguson creed. Always, the importance of winning was the first essential he demanded. He had a little mental trick, too, in underlining that desire to the whole squad. When you returned for pre-season, the manager would look every player squarely in the eye and challenge him: 'Do you want it as much as last year, now do you? If you don't, you had better leave right away. There's no place for you here.' Next, would come the crippling punchline when, we all suspected, he opted for the mind games. It was like a ritual. 'I have got four names here,' he would say. 'I am going to place them in the hat because in another ten months' time, when another season is over, they are my men to have fallen short.' They were the first-team players, he adamantly believed, who would have taken their foot off the gas, and not fulfilled their true potential, because their ambition for glory had been satisfied by earlier achievements. The implication was clear: if that were the case, it made them surplus to requirements at United. And the manager, in an almost deliberately threatening manner, would add the final warning words: 'Aye, and I'm usually right about the names I put in that hat, you know.' He never, of course, named those supposedly guilty men at any stage, and my suspicion was always that it was the gaffer employing some quite clever psychology.

He had a well-earned reputation in that department, if you recall. Following the Treble, though, we should all have pulled him and asked him to name the four names. Not a single player could, surely, have let him down in that season. But you never know with him.

So many times I have been asked what represents the manager's greatest strength. Rapidly followed by the next enquiry of why and how has he been so successful. There's no ready-made answer, in truth. Is it man management? Or coaching technique? Maybe his passion for the game? Well, the last suggestion is probably the closest we'll ever get to figuring what made Sir Alex the most outstanding manager of his generation, if only because it comes under the category of the will to win. Which automatically means that he only ever wants winners around him. He certainly had no tolerance for the faint hearted. They were allowed nowhere near him. Swiftly, they were rejected and shoved hurriedly through the door. He has always lived by unbendable rules, knowing precisely what he expected of himself and of his teams. If any players fell below that supremely high standard, they were doomed. Whenever that happened, it was the inevitable signal for another explosion and he would blow his top. Over the last couple of years, as we approached the millennium and there were umpteen trophies to cherish, he started to simmer down. When I arrived, he was just the opposite, a raging inferno. He showed the fierceness and destructive power of a blow torch. I didn't think any manager in the game was capable of behaving in such a manner. Sure, I understood they could lose their tempers, but not go into orbit every time something went wrong. When you saw the manager erupt, as I have explained with the Incey affair, it was a bit nerve-wracking. It was as if he wanted to go to war with the world.

Previously, I had always worked alongside managers

with reasonably high flashpoints. When I saw the gaffer, soon after I joined United, with the thunderclouds gathering around him, I privately thought, 'Now what the hell is happening here?' At first it was the 'hair dryer' routine, accompanied by a screaming, vein-busting yell. He used to go in for that a lot. Now, as I have explained, the manager has quietened down. He still bellows and rages from time to time, but the concession is that it's no longer from a range of one inch and straight in your face. Let's put on record that we are all extremely grateful for such a gesture and change in his lifestyle! Instead, the blast now comes from the opposite side of the room as a clear indication that he intends being more reserved, don't you think? Maybe, getting on in years, he feels the need to be a bit steadier, and if that observation fails to cop me a week's fine, I don't know what will. Actually, I'm joking, boss, honest I am. As a matter of fact, I have felt for some time that when the manager decides to blow his top the team plays better. Usually, I suppose, it's because that blow torch comes out at half time and, singed to our very sporting soul, totally cheesed off as well, we head for the tunnel furiously determined to prove him wrong. Once the game ends, there's normally an apology swiftly followed by an aside in which he suggests that was the way he wanted us to perform in the first place. In other words, just when we thought he might be wrong, he was right again. That is the motivation factor and it invariably comes with management territory. It's just that some are better than others and the one we have happens to be absolute tops at it. I haven't had too many memorable rucks with him. Mostly he leaves me to get on with my business. If he had given me the close-up aggro at any time, I might have ended up giggling, but in one or two shouting matches between us I always knew he had his serious head on. Not that it's happened very often.

Of course, during that doldrums period, I did occasionally feel I was right out of the frame and that possibly the manager didn't fancy me as a first-team player any more. But, without seeking it, the reassurance was always rapidly delivered. 'Don't worry what any other mouthy so-and-so has got to say,' he would tell me. 'I am the manager of this club. You are here as a United player because I want you to be. Nothing else matters, so ignore all the speculation.' In such a spontaneous manner, he lifted my spirit and morale and those little gestures underlined to me that he was never anything less than totally supportive. When Dwight Yorke's arrival seemed imminent in the summer of '98, ballyhooed in most of the papers as it was, he confirmed privately that he would complete the signing soon but I had no need to be alarmed. 'Don't worry – I'm not flogging you to Villa as part of the deal. I wouldn't consider selling you to them. Furthermore, you are not going to any other club either.' He buried my fears right away and not many days later during our summer tour of Scandinavia he publicly made that position very clear. So that was that – and endless weeks of speculation over my career were dead and buried for another season at least. I had felt very concerned about my future during that period, despite scoring twenty-five goals the season before, because there had been such a build-up in the papers about a swop transfer that it almost appeared to be official United policy. Thankfully, it wasn't. Yet I remember Shirley calling me on the mobile at the height of all the transfer activity, asking me if I had been sold to Villa. It had just been on TV, she said, so it must be right. I knew for sure it was bum information, but when that sort of wild talk starts affecting your family's daily life it does become really hard to take. First there is the paragraph on the back page linking United to another centre-forward, whether it be

Gabriel Batistuta or the Chilean guy Salas, and the next one bluntly states you are the one being dumped. Nice, real nice! I felt belittled and insulted that certain sections of the media refused to acknowledge my achievements for the team, but at least the manager and the people at United remained solid and supportive.

I am not saying the manager is an angel because, in the eyes of his players, no manager can be. In making his decisions, they are bound to get hurt. And, without question, in my first five years at the club I have had a few up and downers with him. Mostly they have centred on selection when he has dropped me from the team. When Yorke signed in August 1998, for instance, there was a really weird episode which eventually led me to the gaffer's door. And it wasn't for tea and cakes either. Dwight came on board at United just three days before we were due at West Ham for the opening away game of the season. We didn't train together for the first time until the Friday and then it was only for about thirty minutes. Nothing too involved, just a session of shadow play because time was scarce. Off we go to Upton Park for the match, the two of us up front as anticipated. Then came that dreaded finger. I had got the hook after just seventy minutes. I couldn't take it in. Next game comes up and I am named among the subs. The SAS couldn't have stopped me then and I was straight in to see the gaffer. I demanded to know what was going on. He didn't take long to reply: 'I don't think it is working out. I have yet to be convinced there is a partnership there to build on with you and Dwight.' I was gobsmacked. We had played together for less than one game and, suddenly, I'm getting the message that the pairing appears destined for an early redundancy. It rocked me. I looked in the manager's direction for a more satisfactory reason and nothing came. 'I can't see you two doing it, so I have got to look at my options.' What options? I had believed that for at least another five games that just might be my role. To leave me out of the team, just like that, after barely getting to know Yorke, never mind understand his style of play, was a real kick in the nuts. When someone new is thrust into the side, you reasonably anticipate a settling-in period before any firm decisions are reached. I felt as if I had been mugged. I also felt that with such an instant reaction I might be surplus to requirements and finally on my way out of Old Trafford. It looked alarmingly like the thin end of the wedge.

Just a few days earlier I had been so elated. Now I was on the floor again. Yorkie and I, or so I thought, were to be the dream team, the partnership made in heaven. The manager, remember, had been adamant I wasn't to be sold. Now, trudging out of his office, I was again in a state of utter confusion about my role at United. Just consider the obvious scenario. If you have just bought a striker for £12.6 million, a club record, he's hardly the one to be jettisoned, is he? I had to be the spare part and that's how it proved to be. I was out of the team for two miserable, bleak months during which, on every solitary day, I swore to myself when I got back in, nobody would be able to drop me again. I would play out of my skin – I just wouldn't allow it to happen. But Ole Gunnar Solskjaer was summoned in my place and I well understood what a threat he always represents. Ole played well, too, and I feared the worst when we slammed Charlton 4–1 and he and Yorkie nicked two apiece. I just had to accept the reality. I was clearly powerless at the end of the dialogue with the manager. He promised me I would get my chance but, when you are being dropped, those words sound almost like a death sentence. Any pro, and you can ask any of them, wants to play every game. They don't want to be kicking their heels and I was no different. Patience is not my strong suit either. Soon, though, it was to be Bayern

Munich in the European Cup. Just before the big one I played as a midweek sub against Liverpool and the manager felt I had performed well. His congratulations, gratefully received, were followed by the promise that if I didn't play up front against the Germans, I would definitely be in against Southampton the following weekend. Teddy Sheringham's aerial ability suggested he had to be favourite to tackle Bayern and, what if he had a blinder, how could the manager pull him out of side for the Premiership? But the manager stuck to his undertaking and, though Teddy did extremely well against Bayern, I was granted my chance for the duel with the Saints. We won 3–1. That was the real christening of the partnership with Yorke which subsequently delivered fifty-three goals over the following midwinter months.

There is no denying that with such a prolific return it was damn near impossible for the manager even to consider separating that front two on any kind of permanent basis. But his frankness with me, and the fact that he fulfilled his every word, was important to our relationship. Here was proof that, at the moment he felt it was right for United, he was quite prepared to make the unpopular decision. So what's Sir Alex really like? Well, as you might well imagine, he doesn't mix too freely with his players. He remains very self-disciplined in keeping his distance, possibly in the knowledge that familiarity can often risk contempt as well. Not that you are likely to take liberties with the gaffer. Sometimes you found it very difficult to read him or his mood. One moment he might be joking and joyful, and the next he would be scowling and prowling around like a bear with a sore head. You just never know how to take him. The best advice for anyone is mostly to button the lip and be on your guard. In the past couple of years, though, he seems to have chilled out, but still the players show him enormous respect. You don't reach the manager's position in the football profession without deserving it either. You might, I suppose, say that daily events at United operate under a rule of fear. Yet, in return, he always shows respect to the players; he naturally understands that grown men have to be allowed their space. We are treated in the way, I suspect, that he always insisted on being treated in his playing days. He applies a simple disciplinary code: if you don't step out of line you won't get hurt. Become a little too bold, and there is always the iron fist, whether you are player, training staff, pressman or doorman. That is simply the nature of the beast.

As far as the technical and coaching side is concerned, the manager was rarely involved. That was the domain of Brian Kidd until he surprised us all and left to take charge at Blackburn Rovers. The manager occasionally ventures on to the practice ground to offer the odd word of constructive advice, but the bulk of the preparatory work fell at the feet of the well respected Kiddo. To be honest, the manager's major contribution always comes on match day. He loves the big team meeting; the opposition dossier and detailed planning is a major focus. You can't knock it, mind, considering the number of trophies United have managed to win during the 1990s. He can be in there, for twenty minutes, half an hour, or even longer, drilling us in the tactical side of the forthcoming game. The emphasis is placed on the strengths of the rival team in what they might do at free kicks, corners, how they like to play, their danger men, and that kind of well researched information. Just the opposite of Kevin Keegan, in fact. Kevin's creed was that if his players fulfilled their potential, and played from the heart with passion and commitment, he would back them to win. To him, the opposition didn't count. At Old Trafford, the gaffer has always been big into the spying dossiers and he certainly did his groundwork, particularly before we faced foreign teams in the European competitions. You never went out on the park without being fully briefed on what you could expect. It was systematic, methodical, and a little brain damaging at times, but as part of the United first-team squad you get used to such intensive preparation. The only problem is that when the gaffer speaks about a certain rival player, you feel by the end of his speech that you might well be set to confront the best player ever born! But that's the way of the man; he is meticulous, a planner by nature, and he feels his methods help eliminate the worry factor.

Then, of course, there is the team tinkering. It provoked criticism in the papers and on television and very often the fans were left startled by the United teams that took to the field. Some of it was tactical, but on most occasions I felt it was to keep high-profile players content and happy in the squad. When you are yanked out of any team, it's like a kick where it hurts most. I have yet to meet a player who doesn't want to play every possible game. The boss's comforting words about taking a rest are never of any consolation. If you are playing well, scoring goals, and in the zone, as I describe it, nothing else matters expect being picked on every possible occasion. The manager, for his part, has never stopped trying to make each individual understand the overall merits of the squad system. I'm afraid he is doomed to failure. Not a single United player, from a selfish standpoint of course, has any sympathy with it. You might hear season-long complaints about too much football, maybe fatigue and stress-related injuries, but if a footballer was asked to play seventy games a season to stay in the side he would snatch your hand off. Whenever the form dips, a player has no legitimate griev-ance when he is dropped. But, during the periods when the football is flowing and the form is hot, the shirt is as precious as a wage packet. If a big game is looming, believe me, the footballer has yet to be born who would release it from his grasp. But the manager, inevitably, works within different parameters and must be guided by other priorities. And the man in charge of United since November 1986 has an outstanding record to justify his own well-tested methods. It is a record which is second to none in the modern era, and maybe in any age. His attitude has always centred around winning every possible honour within the game and not many, if any, have eluded him. He has vowed to retire at sixty and, despite a fierce attachment to football, I believe he will not alter that decision. He appreciates he has had a fabulous innings and it's always much more satisfying when you can determine your own time to go. We must never underestimate the pressure that is the daily burden of management. Pressure from outside influences, pressure from the players, pressure from within the boardroom, and pressure from the public never to ease your foot a fraction off the gas; success, in the eyes of the fans, is their lifeblood and it must never be allowed to drain away. In thirteen years, there has been an incredible run of high achievement, but he also experienced the other more unpleasant aspect when people clamoured for his head and wanted him out of the job. Aggro, acrimony that goes with the territory, call it what you will, but there is no question you need a hardened, impenetrable, inner shell to survive in football.

I haven't, I like to think, given the manager too much grief. He has sacrificed me a few times, discarded me from the side when I was convinced I didn't deserve such treatment, and, yes, there has been confrontation. But far less than you would ever have expected having witnessed his early demonstrations on management and player relationships. When we looked like winning our first championship in my time at the club, in 1996 against Nottingham Forest at Old Trafford, he banished me to the bench. We won 5–0 and I didn't make an appearance. I was gutted. In the build-up week to that climactic game he deliberately went out of his way to sound me out. How was I feeling, was I in my best shape, things like that. I told him I was fine, all he had to do was pick me. I suffered the same way when we won the title down by the Riverside at Middlesbrough. Sore-backside Sunday, that's what it was for me, plonked on the touchline and waiting my moment, only this time I at least got on and scored the winner to make it 3–0. He did it to me again during the Treble season, before the final match against Spurs. Once again it was the same ritual. How are you? Just fine, etc, etc. This time I knew what was coming round the corner. Maybe it was supposed to be a none-too-subtle warning. Then it was Sunday, the big game, and the pits for me. I had been dumped again. I don't mind admitting I took it very badly. It was just a matter of personal dignity being undermined. The greater hurt was the professional within me wanting to play so much on the very day the championship crown was secured. I had given so much and it ended, for me, in a few hours of desperately felt disappointment. I suppose on the last occasion, the manager needed to consider his options for the FA Cup Final and, later on, the European Cup Final. So much was on the United agenda in eleven hectic days, but that was not my concern; I felt after figuring in thirty-odd League games I had earned the right to play. I have never understood whether the manager controls the strings in such a way to keep the puppets – that's us – on edge. But all I can say is that I have never believed there could be a second of time to be complacent at United. I have alway appreciated if I didn't play to within a finger-snap of my potential, I would be out on my ear. There are not too many players at this club who can consider themselves totally bomb-proof. Some are admittedly safer than others, but every first-team player has been dropped, rested, or left behind at some point in their career. Jungle law, I suppose it might be called, making certain that only the fittest survive.

And the fittest were always left standing defiantly, surrounded by a silver pot or two at the end of most seasons, not just because of the gaffer, whose importance can never be understated, but also because of a guy called Kiddo, who we all respected with absolute loyalty. He was a great United coach and an outstanding man to boot. Nobody has ever helped, cajoled and nursed me through the traumas on the training field more than Brian. I owe him a great debt and I have got so much time for him. He was always the ear I could bend, particularly when I felt down in the dumps, and the subject never seemed to matter; Kiddo was there to listen anyway. He was comforter, adviser, confidant, protector and coach all rolled into one. If I had needed a minder, he would have volunteered for that as well. Yet when I first arrived at United, he stared me in the face and delivered a home truth that stopped me dead in my tracks. Kiddo, stone faced and deadly serious, told me: 'Don't you come in here thinking you can score forty goals a season and that will keep everybody happy. I'm telling you that might make you feel good, but it won't be good enough for United. You have to be a footballer to survive at this place.' I shook my head in sheer disbelief when he had finished, turned my back and sauntered into another nearby room. I couldn't believe what had been said to me; I thought the man was off his head. I wondered, in truth, what he was on. But within a few, enlightening weeks at the club I fully appreciated that Kiddo was right. Goals, even in gold-wrapped bundles, were not going to be enough, nowhere near enough to be exact, when taken on their own. I had to wise up. I had to change my game, I had to become a more complete player. But Kiddo, hard as nails in one way, also had another side to his nature. When things were horrible, and it seemed the whole world had a fixation for ganging up on me, he was there, strong and defiant and helpful. He used to remind me, 'God has given you a talent. He is not going to take it away from you either. Keep your confidence and you will come through it.' Kiddo believed in me and, just as important, he told me to believe in myself and it would all turn round. For the second time, he was right.

The working relationship between Kiddo and the manager was akin to the good-cop, bad-cop routine. When the gaffer was losing it, Brian would sit down and talk to the players and analyse maybe what had gone wrong during the game. If the manager was flying off the handle and very angry, the message could be a little blurred. Kiddo, subsequently, would take a quiet moment to detail exactly what the manager wanted from us. He would put us right about any conflicting issues and he was always a helpful, understanding type of character. I worked with Kiddo for countless hours, long after the rest of the boys had vanished from the training ground, diligently putting my game back together during the hard times. I well recall how he nursed me through the anxiety, that self-defeating vicious circle of trying too much, by insisting I stopped the habit of always aiming to pass the ball into the net. Just belt it, ordered Kiddo, and the rest, once the luck turns your way, will follow automatically. It wasn't really my style at the time, just to hammer the ball, but when the simple instruction started to bring dividends on the field, my broken confidence was suddenly repaired and it all came flooding back. The world seemed a much cushier place, less menacing and frightening, and I was able to do my job with a clearer mind and with far more impact. Within a few weeks, guess what, not only was I able to clatter the ball into the net with real destructive venom, but when the opportunity demanded I could pass into it as well. A very fundamental psychological trick cured my scoring crisis. Not only that, Kiddo also devoted a lot of out-of-hours time to me and, as a former striker himself, it meant the bond of understanding was even closer. He would tell me that in his playing days he was very much of a rebellious nature himself, that he would cause waves, and I felt I could relate to that kind of man and when he offered any confidential advice I knew it was born out of personal experience and had to be valued. He had lived through the football wars himself.

At one time, in another insight into how he rebuilt my damaged confidence, he compared me to Denis Law, that fabulous, all-time great and a United forward whom Kiddo played alongside in the 1960s. What he emphasized about Denis was that if he missed a chance, and like all of us even the near-genius footballer can do that, it would never deter him from flying into the box time after time after time. In that gutsy way, Brian told me, I reminded him of the Lawman. The huge compliment was gratefully accepted and, crucially, I have got to underline it was offered when I was missing chances by the barrow-load and people were pinning me to the wall with their criticism. Kiddo always praised, never carped, and when he exposed the faults it was always in a positive, objective way. He raised my depleted morale no end and Brian was exceptionally helpful with all the United players, not just me. He was called the Ledge (after legend, of course, earned in winning the European Cup for the club in 1968 when he was just nineteen) and he deserved huge respect from everyone. He was never fancy, or flash, just a simple man who, at the very thought of being reminded of his own playing achievements, would cringe and shy away. I never heard a personal boast from him, not one, but he would defend United with his life; he was a Red through and through. In his eyes, the club was all about the players of today, not those remarkable, glorious giants of the past, and that was something Kiddo stressed to us all.

My name for him was Capello – borrowed, you'll have sussed, from one of his close friends, the Italian coach Fabio Capello. I tried to fix it in his head as a collective compliment from us all, because he was truly valued in the dressing room for his technical knowledge and unyielding support. He toured the foreign clubs, importing their ideas and methods throughout the last few years, until the training and preparation of the United players was the equal of anything perfected abroad. Kiddo was an innovator who was dedicated to fierce commitment and hard work, from both himself and his players. He flogged us to the limit at times, but we understood it was for our long-term benefit. He would, after a strenuous workout always remind us: 'This is money in the bank. You will feel better for it later.' And, naturally, he was proved right. Some of us, pushed to the limit of endurance, might have been out on our feet. Then he would deliver another of his favourite sayings, 'This is fuel in the tank. You need it now – you can't make it up at the end of the season.' That was Kiddo's philosophy through and through, because he believed that condition was so important in the creation of champions. When you reflect on United's trophy successes, they all came down to that physically-demanding charge for the line late in the season when the weak fall away and the powerful stand supreme. We were blessed with great talent and skill in the side, but as we approached March and April we used to blow the opposition away with our stamina and reserves of energy. We steamrollered them out of our path through the virtue of being much fitter; they were on their knees, but we felt as if we could run forever and, if you look back, the fixture records show how we very often beat teams by four and five goals during the all-important run-in phase of the season.

All of us, I don't mind admitting, were heartbroken when he left the club. Not one of us expected it to happen. It was like a thunderbolt striking the whole dressing room. We read the speculation at the time, linking Kiddo with Blackburn and apparently talks with Jack Walker, but we dismissed it all. He wouldn't leave United, never, it wasn't going to happen, just about captured the mood of the first-team players. Then he was gone. It was midway through the Treble season, late autumn down at Tottenham in the Worthington Cup, and the boys knew immediately something was wrong when he was absent from the team meeting. The buzz of alarm, worry as well that a vital cog in the wheel was missing, went round the boys. He had been our protector and the mentor on the training pitch. Nobody messed us about while Kiddo was around. He was a real tough boy, believe me. I have seen him in many a dugout, an uncompromising figure, and no one ever took liberties with him, not rival managers, coaches, or players, not anybody. If they tried it on with his players, they were very rapidly put firmly in their place. Kiddo, even though we succeeded in winning the Treble after he departed, was an essential, vitally important part of our success. What he had laid down in the years before, in the countless, highly rewarding coaching sessions and his readiness to cajole the players through many crises, laid down the platform from which we were able to launch our run for glory. The manager would be in charge, without a doubt, but Kiddo's influence was just as crucial in a different way; he had a daily impact on our progress. And the combination of these two strong personalities in control of United gelled perfectly. The players hated him leaving, it was such a disappointment, and for weeks there was a strange atmosphere about the place without his influence and guidance. Then there was the matter of his replacement. Who would it be? Like the supporters, the players relied heavily on the newspapers for their information and, just like them, we saw the names of Steve Bruce, Alex McLeish and Mark McGhee taking most of the projection. Finally, it turned out to be Steve McClaren. Steve Who? Honest, the boys just hadn't heard of him before the appointment.

Actually, without knowing it at the time, we had been very close to him and not, to be candid, been too impressed. A couple of days before Steve stepped through the dressing-room door we played Derby County at Old Trafford. There was this geezer in a track-suit, bawling and shouting from the Derby dug-out and behaving like a care-in-the-community lunatic. Honestly, he seemed to be off his head. The players on the bench agreed: 'Who's that plonker?' He kept pelting down the stairs to the touchline and giving the County players a right old coating. It was embarrassing. So, just imagine the look on our faces when he was presented as Kiddo's successor and our new first-team coach. Only forty hours before, I, Yorke and Raimond had been giving him some right old abuse. Now, it was, er, sorry Mr McClaren, didn't really mean it, sir! Very quickly, though, I have to report he fitted in with the players and we have all been duly impressed with his contribution and he mixes extremely well with the whole squad. His coaching methods are good, very much on the Kiddo lines I have to say, and Steve is now regarded as very much one of the boys. He didn't take long to get us into the video scene – and I don't mean *Debbie Does Dallas*. He employs examples from American basketball to emphasize the importance of team bonding and competitive focus. The great Michael Jordan and Chicago Bulls also get a regular mention in his talks. But, I think if you speak with Steve, I suspect he appreciated that team bonding and spirit have always been the underlying strength of a United squad which occasionally changes personnel, but never alters in attitude. I have never travelled or played with a better set of boys. Talk about the code of the musketeers, nobody takes liberties with these boys. The whole unit has that formidable strength of togetherness. At United, if one player is ever in trouble, the whole eleven are there to sort it. There is no back biting, cliques have always been taboo, and the collective will is probably the secret of our success. The order from the manager, laid down long ago, is that when we score, the whole side must celebrate to emphasize it is not one man's glory but down to the success of everyone on the field. It might be corny, it might be a cliché, but we have a never-say-die attitude, a belief that no game is ever lost even in the final second, and that has created the most effective winners of the 1990s. No other side, in my opinion, has ever matched us in that area. We are not to be acclaimed as the greats, or eventually the legends, but one day we would all like to be. That sums up the manager – Sir Alex Ferguson – and his team. The best in the business by a long shot.

Chapter Eight

It was all a myth about Eric and me. The myth being that we hated each other's guts, that we despised each other with an absolute passion. We were, they mocked, the double act from hell. You've got the message, it's Monsieur Cantona and me, otherwise referred to so regularly, in a sneering sort of way, as Old Trafford's odd couple. Only one thing wrong with that description, I have got to say, and that's the fact it has no basis in truth. Never had. You know why? I didn't even know the geezer well enough to decide, in the first place, whether we could get on or not. We were just football team-mates, not mates, no more and no less. We played together for a time and I knew him as an incredible United idol and little more than that. Honestly, I didn't really get any closer to Eric than any of the fans who worshipped his every move and believed he was the greatest thing since Pele. What I did appreciate, in an instant, was that he was a fabulous footballer blessed with an immense talent. He arrived at United two seasons before me and by the time he left was rightly regarded as having secured a place among the legends of the club. I wouldn't argue with that because he was a towering figure for United, the catalyst, as the gaffer so rightly described him, for the creation of a highly successful era and, just maybe, THE player of the modern

141

game. Me? Well, I was supposedly the bad guy who just went around annoying him every Saturday of the season. Not true, as it happens, but a good story all the same.

These highly critical wise guys weren't out on the park, but what they could detect in our partnership from afar was just beyond me. I couldn't play with Eric, they crowed, couldn't even get on with him, and it was all because there was a huge barrier in professional respect between the two of us. The body language, according to the cynics, indicated that Eric and I had a major problem, the broadest signal you could have that we were virtually at war out there on the park. Good gossip, bad information. I just haven't a clue to this day where all that garbage came from. Now here are the facts. The two of us never had a single disagreement in the two and a bit seasons we were at United together. I always felt fine, very comfortable with Eric, on or off the park. And, no, I didn't ever feel inferior to him, wasn't scared by him as a footballer or a man, and wasn't intimidated by him in any way. OK, he used to wave his hands in the air, as if disgusted, disgruntled or frustrated with what was going on around him on the pitch. And then there was that well-known, dimissive Gallic shrug if an attacking move broke down. But I don't think I was the only one in a United shirt to receive that sort of treatment; he reacted that way many times and to many different individuals in the team. That was just Cantona, the law unto himself. Eric could have lived in a volcanic crater, an active one too, and felt at home. He just loved the drama of the game and the intensity of competitive football.

It was easy to see why. Eric was such a demanding player, fuelled by a great burning passion to win. He had so much desire it made you tremble. And sometimes that desire was uncontrollable. When I think of Eric, I think of the manager, in that they both had this fierce commitment to winning every game in which they were involved. The manager could, and still can, erupt at half-time and trigger the release valve. Eric, I felt, could never do that, so the rage of frustration bubbled on inside him until something had to give way. Often, in that situation, it might be the nearest team-mate who copped for it. But we weren't the only ones to get scorched; sometimes Eric got burned as well. Many rivals, you see, weren't slow to spot the chink in the Frenchman's armour either. They could see when he was fired up, stoked by the passion of always wanting to be the top man, and they would try to get under his skin. The major opposition tactic, as I saw it, was a determined attempt to wind him up so that notorious fuse would blow. Then, they figured, three parts of the job were done. Before I signed for United, I remember Neil Ruddock trying to goad, even humiliate, Eric by grabbing his famously raised collar and roughly turning it down. When stunts like that failed to work, defenders loved to whack him from behind, mess him about and try to provoke him with a few more dirty tricks. They well understood Cantona could easily be pushed to the limit and then he would blow. I was playing alongside him on that sadly spectacular night at Selhurst Park in which he got sent off, whacked a lippy punter who asked for it, and finished up with a nine-month ban that came very close to driving him out of the English game.

The Crystal Palace boys were having a bit of a niggle at all of us that night, but Eric, predictably, bore the brunt of it. They were piling in from behind and a few naughty, rough-house tackles were very much part of a bruising game. Eric, I suspect, simply waited his opportunity and finally he nailed one of their central defenders, Richard Shaw. It was an act of sheer frustration because of the way a spoiling, ugly match was developing and it looked as though Eric stamped on his tormentor. He just lost his rag, got the red card and there was no arguing – he had to go. What Eric subsequently did to the Palace punter shortly afterwards has been well documented. I'm sure many of you saw it and, fair enough, it looked nasty. But I believe anyone of us, provoked by the same kind of remarks about our family, would have reacted as well. What right has any guy to stand there, just because he has paid the admission money, and give a footballer a serious slagging about something completely unrelated to the match itself? Yet I never thought I would ever see such an episode unfold in front of my eyes. To this day, I find it quite unbelievable. As Eric reached the touchline after the red card, Norman Davies, our kitman at the time, was deputed to escort him to the dressing rooms. I can remember Eric sauntering along the edge of the pitch. Then there was this blur of violent movement and it all went off. Horrified, I watched as Eric jumped the barrier of the stand and aimed that kung-fu lunge at the mouthy Palace punter before he was hustled away. It appeared shocking but, hand on heart, I can't now condemn or blame him for what he did. Eric might well have been a superstar, a man paid to entertain the public and take some criticism in return, but first and foremost he is a human being with the same feelings as the next man. At that vulnerable moment, with his temper already difficult to control, he was subjected to a volley of particularly insulting comments. Self-restraint can only be pushed so far, you know.

Naturally, it was almost impossible for any of the United players, or the Palace boys for that matter, to concentrate on the game after such an incident. It was a case of collective shock, I think, that Eric had actually behaved the way he did. But think of the fan. He must have been daft, brave, or both, even to consider he could take such liberties, because Eric was a powerful man, unbelievably strong. The punter could have challenged an easier opponent, like Mike Tyson for instance. The next day, there was the expected hue and cry and the clamour went up for Cantona to be banned. Some, in their frenzy, were close to calling for his expulsion from the planet! The view was that he was finished as a footballer in this country. The United players generally feared as much. But Eric, typically, rode the controversy, stuck it out, eventually came roaring back to more championship success, and effectively stuck it up his critics once more. He proved a lot of people wrong, but I doubt if he ever won the final argument with the unsporting cynics: that, in effect, we could never work effectively together in the United front line. They thought then, and I don't think the opinion has changed, that Eric didn't want to play with me, although I never felt that for a single moment. The circumstances didn't help me, of course. At the time, I wasn't scoring too often and I was basically fighting for my form and struggling to justify myself. Eric, on the contrary, was the king of Old Trafford. He was flawless, he couldn't do anything wrong. I was scratching and scrambling for my career, weighed down by all kinds of pressures, while Eric was idolized if he did no more than walk on the pitch. I was bound to be seen as the freak in the show, the player guilty of cocking everything up, and I had to live with that somewhat harsh reality like it or not.

Eric could have bad days like the rest of us, but nothing would be said. Nobody dared voice a hint of criticism, or so it seemed. If I missed a half chance, I was hounded for days on end. That was my problem, not Eric's. There was only one person who could put the unfair situation right and that was me.

I didn't have a problem with Eric. He had his own life to lead, his own career to protect, and yet some misguided, ill-informed people constantly attempted to create the conflict between us. The myth mushroomed to such an extent that eventually there was a general belief that Cantona actually hated me. Yet not once did Eric complain that he had a problem with me as his striking partner. If he had, it might well have been an issue which we could have thrashed out together. A powerfully independent man like Eric, I can assure you, wouldn't have stayed silent if he had felt strongly about the situation. He wouldn't have kept it to himself, he would have spoken up. Not once did I hear a murmur from him, not a single derogatory remark. But I had to wait until years after he retired before I was vindicated and that came, would you believe, with a few well-chosen comments from the great man himself. Perfectly timed it was, too. Just a couple of days or so before that fantastic European Cup Final victory over Bayern Munich in Eric's adopted city of Barcelona. He went on public record, in advance of the final, to declare his firm belief that United would win the Cup because of the football power and outstanding pace of Dwight Yorke and, yes, believe me he said it, Andy Cole. When I read those words, a shiver went down my spine. There it was in black and white, the very proof I needed of what Eric Cantona really thought about his old sparring partner. If he had really disliked me the way some people suggested, and if he had despaired of me as a footballer, Eric would never have put his name to such an opinion. If you think somebody is not a player of real calibre, you keep your mouth closed. I knew all along he respected me. At last I had been given the evidence to show the world.

In establishing that point, I do concede it was very difficult for me to adapt and play with someone of Eric's distinctive style. I wasn't familiar with it because the majority of the time I was up the sharp end and playing virtually as a lone striker. I felt isolated. Eric would frequently drop into midfield, stray even deeper to get the ball off the back four or even our goalkeeper Peter Schmeichel, drift wide left or right and roam wherever he wanted. He never really stuck to a recognizable position. In truth, Eric could do exactly what he liked in the United side and, without the natural support of another front partner, I experienced obvious problems in coping with this strange set-up. I was left scampering around, attempting to create space for myself against two centre-backs instead of one designated to marking me. I had to make a lot of runs, most of them ignored I might say, and my scoring opportunities were frustratingly rare. We didn't try to work out a better understanding between the two of us on the training ground. It was pointless. Given Eric's unique situation, that was never really on, because he refused to be tied down to a single role as an orthodox striker playing in tandem with me. You couldn't order someone like him to stick rigidly to playing in the hole behind the front players. He would never stand for that and, anyway, it was, I have to agree, an insult to a footballer of that calibre. Eric could peel off and drill a forty-yard ball forwards to take apart any back four and he caused limitless damage in a split second. He was blessed with that kind of genius. Why, then, try to place him in a tactical straight jacket?

Peter Beardsley, in many ways as gifted as Eric, was a lot more flexible. Even with the attacking freedom that Kevin Keegan granted him at Newcastle, he would make certain that on eight out of ten occasions he was lurking back around the box to give me support. He mostly made sure he was able to get back to the really attacking zones of the pitch when it was necessarry. So, in that way, we had a different kind of partnership from the one I shared with Cantona. Supposedly alike, certainly in the way they prompted and set up their team-mates, Eric and Peter played in vastly different ways. Eric, given a licence by the manager to operate wherever he chose, really belonged to a breed of his own. Because of his stature at United, he had the privilege to do absolutely anything and get away with it, whether it was for the benefit or detriment of the side, and mostly it was to our great advantage. I certainly have no quarrel with the accolades he earned throughout the game. He fully deserved the respect shown him by team-mates and opposition players alike. You can't pretend to hard-bitten fellow pros that you are a great player; you have to prove it 100 per cent and, without a shred of doubt, Eric did that during his five amazing years in English football. There are other fabulous players, perhaps not always equal in ability but who probably shed more sweat beads than Eric ever did. Players such as Pallister, Bruce, Kanchelskis to my mind, when I first arrived, and without doubt the indomitable Ince because he commanded so much admiration from both the players and the masses. But nobody had more charisma and the fans absolutely adored him. It's a cliché I know, but at Old Trafford he was a god. Eric could do no wrong.

Our relationship was more a less on the basis of a nod and a wink. I didn't talk to him that much, really, but it was very much the same with the rest of the players. He was a very plain, simple man in many ways, even if he appeared extremely complicated in some of the things he did in his life, on and off the field. Eric would just slope off after training, barely a word exchanged, and as far as we knew he would be home indoors until he turned up the following morning. There was a lot of fanciful talk about Cantona the poet or the water-colour artist, but I believe those kind of activities were a long way behind him once he was at United. He wasn't the normal kind of footballer, swanking over a big house and a fast car, but the players genuinely liked him even though he was very often a distant, almost remote figure. Inside the dressing room Eric would open up, revelling in the banter and mickey takes. He could mix it with anyone, although he clearly preferred to be a very private individual. The big mystery for all of us was how the most lauded player of the lot could quietly disappear and dodge so much of the attention, commercially as well as with the media. I know there were a few famous TV videos of him, but generally he kept out of the way of the hype and promotional stuff. He wasn't exactly a socialite, either, and I can't remember any of the lads, say, going out to dinner with Eric. There was no one ever that close. But when we were allowed an occasional night on the town, with the gaffer's permission to have a boys' night out, he never missed. Off the pitch, I saw him as a loner but a great guy, and the way he behaved laid down a very obvious message: that he was his own man. You didn't mess about with him whether he was playing football or having a pint.

When you were able to command the respect that Eric had on the field, you could basically do as you wished. It came with the territory. It was the sort of appreciation that wasn't exclusive to his United team-mates because opponents tended to bow in his presence as well. I mean that, too. Eric, they well understood, was a law unto himself. He dominated the whole occasion and consequently was granted as much time and space as he wanted because of the respect he demanded. Take a look at a favourite video now, flick back to Eric in action, and immediately you will see what I am driving at. He was, compared to other players anyway, allowed to do exactly as he wanted because rival markers were very reluctant to get tight on him. They knew his capabilities and it was very like the cap-doffing respect that Beardsley was granted at Newcastle. Defenders worried that these two exceptional footballers would spin away, turn them and leave them for dead before creating panic behind the last line of protection. It's not a lie that many very big names, established stars in their own right, held Cantona in awe. Then, before we could blink or even appreciate what was happening, he was gone. He never breathed a word about his impending departure to any of the other players. At the time, it had been mentioned in certain quarters that Eric was not the same player, that he was losing his edge and also carrying a little more weight than before. Eric must have known what was being muttered behind his back and it couldn't have been very pleasant for someone who previously had known only unqualified praise. Maybe it all preyed on his mind, but who knows, because only Cantona himself could reveal what was really happening to him back then. The first I knew about his overnight vanishing act was when I heard a radio announcement one Sunday lunchtime. By then, as far as I understood later, he was long gone. He only returned for a testimonial match and afterwards I had a brief conversation with him before our 3–3 Champions' League result against Barcelona, where he had gone to live. Apparently, he was around also for the European Cup Final, but none of the players met him. He arrived at United like a shadow and disappeared in much the same way, a legend all the same. I was never privileged to see the likes of Denis Law, Sir Bobby Charlton and George Best at their peak, so it is impossible for me to draw comparisons, but certainly Cantona deserves an exalted place among the most complete foot-ballers of the modern era.

Chapter Nine

No bigheads, no egos, no cliques. It's the unwritten eleventh commandment at United. There is absolutely no tolerance for the so-called star syndrome.

I doubt, even if I play until I'm forty, which is highly unlikely, that I will ever be fortunate enough to play with a more likeable bunch of players. They play the game very much with a musketeer spirit in that it has always been all for one and one for all. If there is a spark of trouble on the pitch it involves everyone in the team, not just the victim. And it's the same ethos with winning, or scoring a goal, in that it is the celebration of the whole group and never a matter of individual glory. All the successful United teams of the 1990s have been constructed around attacking flair and special skills, but a far more significant strength has been the bonding of the players. It has been the huge difference between ourselves and other Premiership sides and, I feel, it has been the fundamental reason why there is such a will to win, such a massive desire for success and a fearsome fighting spirit. I know that you have maybe witnessed all of that in the flesh, but I reckon it's now time to bring such famous characters in the red shirt to life. Players like the Mad Mullah, the Nervous Brothers, the Gannet, Dolly and Daisy, and the Iceman, to name just a few. They have all earned those dressing-room identities for various reasons, but whatever you call them they add up to one unavoidable job description: this lot have been a real class act.

Nobody epitomized that more than the Mad Mullah. If I had christened him that, maybe I wouldn't now be here to tell the tale. Brian Kidd was the person who first used such a nickname for Peter Schmeichel, and it's arguable that he was probably the only guy who would have got away with it. But one thing I can call Peter is the best goalkeeper I have ever played with, or against, and I am convinced I will not come across his like again. He was utterly magnificent in every respect. He was such a dominant figure, physically powerful, decisive, good on the deck or in the air; in truth, he was as flawless as you can get in football. He pulled off saves that other goalkeepers, many of the highest calibre as well, might only dream about. They couldn't even get near to big Pete in terms of professional expertise and near perfection. There was that almost miraculous act against Rapid Vienna in the mid-1990s, and I can't remember their guy's name who pushed Peter to the absolute limit, but I just recall Schmeichel twisting in mid-air, totally changing direction in flight, and putting a header which seemed certain to be a goal over the bar. Up at Newcastle, another searing header from John Barnes was on its way, too, until Smikes flung himself like a maniac and kept it out. Barnesy reckoned it was one of the wonders of the world, and I don't blame him. More recently, can you remember the Zamorano bomb for Inter Milan which looked another certainty to hit the net until Peter defied the belief of about fifty-odd thousand punters inside Old Trafford? It was the one where he spread his own body into a star shape, presenting an awesome barrier to any striker, and I'm still trying to work out why it didn't finish up a goal against. It was a crucial save, like so many from Schmeichel's repertoire, that changed the course and destiny of the game. We went on to beat the Italians 2–0, a result that meant so much on the road to the European Cup Final.

I have no doubt whatsover that the big Dane was the single most important player in United winning so many trophies down the years. And in making that distinction I include Eric Cantona. He rescued the team from defeat more times than I have the ability to count and his saves were of as much benefit as twenty Premiership goals from a top striker. When you have a perfectionist like Schmeichel standing behind you, the last, indomitable barrier, a 'keeper capable of making the most astonishing saves, it creates in any side a mood of impregnability. He was such a key component of the team. There have been many outstanding players at United, all of them valuable in their own way, but Schmeichel was in a different category to any of us. He was so much ahead of any rival, within this country or more probably the world, and that made him very special. It also created an aura of invincibility around him. Even the best strikers in the land needed to be on top form to beat him. His physical size and demeanour were so intimidating, you just never thought you could get anything past him and into the net. To score a goal against him was like winning an Oscar. He was so immense, and his calculation of the angle so astute, that he appeared to blot out any chink there might be in the target. Sometimes I faced him on the practice ground and it was almost as if Peter was in the zone. In a dimension of his own, really, where he had walked out of training with a private vow fixed in his mind that nobody was going to beat him that morning. For him, I am sure, it was an important mental exercise, and a crucial part of his match preparation, but for the rest of us it meant a couple of hours of heartbreak. He would quite literally stop everything that was flung in his direction. Pete, in such a frame of mind, was absolutely phenomenal. When you have seen him like that, from Monday to Friday, you well know it's going to be no sweat come Saturday. We had so much faith in him it was like going to war with a one-man army. This was Superman in a goalkeeper's jersey.

Naturally, it was a huge disappointment to all of us when we discovered he had decided to leave Old Trafford. When you know damn well you have the best goalkeeper in the world on your team, you desperately don't want to lose him. I know a few of the lads voiced their concern, and I'm sure Pete listened, but his mind was made up. We all knew, though, we were losing a very rare talent and a dynamic personality who was of great value to us all inside the dressing room and on the pitch. As we approached a new season in the summer of '99 it was a weird feeling to walk into the ground and find the big man was no longer around. It was as if half the team had packed their bags and walked. We were so used to him moaning and groaning, because Pete, believe me, was the unrivalled king of the bellyachers. Our kitman, Albert, bore the brunt of it and he merited a special bonus for putting up with it or, at the very least, a free ear test every six months. The decibels of complaint poor Albert put up with were beyond all the safety regulations. Pete grumbled about everything, from his boots not being right to having no gloves to no change of kit, and from morning till midnight he was a complete nightmare. I used to laugh until my ribs ached at Pete's antics. That was the barometer with him. If he was moaning before a game, you knew he was going to be ready for anything, but if he was quiet you needed to be a little concerned. You sensed there was something wrong, but that was an extremely rare experience in my time playing with Schmeichel.

As a moaner he was a true professional, very definitely one for the world eleven. He gave us all plenty of unsolicited abuse on the pitch as well. I'm told it took Smikes a few weeks to adjust to life in English football, but his voice was at full volume in no time at all. He used to shout and bellow and give us all major grief, laying down the law and any defensive orders we were prepared to listen to which, I have got to admit, weren't all that many. But I suspect the loud-mouth routine was more to help Pete's concentration than put the rest of us in our places. All the hollering and screaming was intended to get him hyped up, and the louder he bawled, the better we liked it. We knew then he was in the mood to take on the whole of planet football. Then he quit and what a great shame that was. He admitted that he felt the Premiership strain was too much, two or three games a week were tough for a big feller who had been throwing himself around on hard ground for twenty years or more. For him to stay sharp and in competitive shape, he believed he had to work harder and harder throughout the week just to be ready for the weekend game. Pete thought that physically it was getting too tough for him, but there were certainly other factors involving his family's future. It all got a bit too much for him to accept. But, in my opinion, he was still the best goalkeeper in the world when he left and I had no doubt he was well capable of being United's No 1 for at least a couple more years. But that was Smikes, always his own man, and so independent that some people got the wrong idea and felt he was aloof and arrogant. In the later years with the club, I got much closer to him, knew him better as a bloke, and got to like him a lot. I was, in the end, sorry to see him go, very sorry indeed.

I would offer a similar sentiment for Roy Keane, too, our skipper and, despite his much-hyped reputation, very much the nice guy. I haven't got a bad word to say about him. He's a top man. Now that's not exactly what you expected to hear about the Irishman, is it? Bit of an uncontrollable monster, you thought, I suppose. Outsiders tend to think of him as a right nasty so and so. Not true. He's just the opposite. People rub Keano up the wrong way and he defends himself, that's what I say. Nice guy, good laugh, and he wants to win. Badly and always. As a consequence, people might get in the way of such ambition and pay for it. His image is that of being the enforcer, even an intimidating hard case, and it's a fact that Roy will never hold back for anyone. He is what he is. This is a guy who speaks his mind and, if you don't like it, then tough. Even then he's not as bad as people would make him out to be. Admittedly, on the field of play he is a real handful. That's just his will to win. Period. But I do believe opposition teams have always been scared by him. He has such a presence and they fully appreciate what he is capable of doing to them. They know he holds no fear of anything or anyone. He just gets wired into any player prepared to stand in his way. He intends to dominate and you can see him relish the contest when someone, maybe Denis Wise, Patrick Vieira or Emmanuel Petit, fancy their chance at working him over in a midfield battle. That's Keano's chance to be the warrior, the ultra competitor, and I know they are the challenges for which he lives. He just wants to walk off the park knowing he might have a few scars but that he emerged the winner in the end. I have seen him take some terrible whacks, really fearful stick, and there was never a murmur of protest for him. He just waits for the opportunity to dish out the odd reprisal himself. Moaning is for whimps. And, dead right, Roy does bide his time and he will get you in the end, don't worry about that. I remember up at Middlesbrough, one of their young defenders, Robbie Stockdale I think it was, caught him badly and Roy had to quit the game in the first half. Then there was the FA Cup Final when Gary Speed, one of Newcastle's midfield players, wiped him again with a late, lunging tackle. Both times, Keano was gutted, but there was no protest. He accepted his fate and headed for the tunnel. He takes that kind of incident as part of the game. This season, next season, you never know what might happen, but Roy will know when the time is right. That's him. He doesn't take prisoners.

All the exceptional teams of the modern era have needed players of his outstanding combative quality. The first edict, of course, is that even Pele couldn't play without the ball and that has to be won by someone. And that's the speciality of Keano and his breed. He gets it and passes it, which sounds simple but isn't, and that makes him the fulcrum of the United side. Roy wouldn't boast about being a passer who rips defences apart with a single delivery, but his strength has always been with accuracy. He rarely gives possession away, nicks a few goals along the way and gets box to box with the ease of a marathon runner. When his tongue is hanging out, that's when I know I am safe to give him a bit of the verbals. At forty yards' range, abuse is a deadly weapon. 'Hey, Roy,' I might yell at him, 'you only pass it back or square. Any chance of making a goal for us by knocking it forward?' Usually the long-distance taunts come from Dwight Yorke and me. They are just a reprisal or two for the way Roy puts us through hell, bickering and bellyaching with all the players. Our off-the-cuff replies never go down too well with Keano. He snarls in our direction, unloads a few expletives, and then gets back to his moaning ways. You know why? Because he is the one footballer on this earth who reckons he never makes a mistake. The rest of us are mugs, continually messing up the team plan. Not Keano. He is just perfect, he is, or at least he believes he is. Ten out of ten every week, in his dreams, and that's why the rest of us get on his case. There's no malice in it and, mind you, any of Keano's critics always make certain they are back on friendly terms by the time the final whistle sounds! Wonder why? You can be brave with the banter, but it's never wise to push it too far at close quarters with blokes like him. Not when he's frothing at the mouth anyway. There you go, I told you what a nice, affable guy Keano is.

Ryan Giggs is my room-mate on away trips. He is also a footballer very difficult to define. How can you describe him? It's almost impossible to put him in any category because he can do anything, play anywhere. Is he a winger? Or a central midfield player? Even a striker? At any given moment, Ryan has the ability and drive to operate in any of these roles. He is just good at absolutely everything, curse him. When Giggsy is in the mood, he has more destructive power than any other single individual. He just terrifies the opposition. On the other flank, we have David Beckham. When I first arrived at United, he was very much on the fringe of the team; now, I have no hesitation in saying he is truly a world-class player. David has blossomed beyond belief. He has great vision, the quality to strike a pass most ordinary mortals only dream about, and for a goalscorer those crosses are like Christmas coming every Saturday. I have to say, playing in a side with Becks and Giggs is a complete pleasure. Sure, David has a bit of a temper and occasionally we have seen it erupt. The more progress he has made, both in the Premiership and international football, the more he has become a target for the wind-up merchants. That volatile nature, though, makes him what he is, and though he is hardly a physically intimidating sort of guy, we all appreciate he must take steps to protect himself. He won't let the opposition mess him about and David, even with that beanpole frame, can look after himself. After the bother with the Argentinian player, Diego Simeone, in the World Cup, there was a view that David had a short fuse and, if

you provoked him, that was the way to negate and under-
mine his ability. Then he had to endure and survive the
most unbelievably crude taunting from the terraces and
the way he coped with it amazed me. I think a lot of other
players of a less deteremined character might well have
cracked. It was ridiculous to hold David solely responsible
for what happened in the finals in France. And though he
was condemned across the nation for his so-called stupidity, the way Becks coped showed that he has a very strong
mentality. No matter how outrageous the attacks made on
him, he refused to show a hint of weakness, and the
United players made certain he always received the right
support.

Then we have the Dutchman, and Jaap Stam, as the fans
so often sing, is a very fine man and a defender of the
highest calibre. For his first few months at Old Trafford,
Jaap was the archetypal quiet man; he played, did the
business and said little. But once he had settled and established his territory, he started to emerge from the shell and
become a very dominant personality, a genuine defensive
leader. He began to voice an opinion, organizing people at
the back during the game, and that had to be beneficial to
the side. Once Jaap started expressing himself we knew he
had settled in properly and he rapidly became very much
a cult figure for the supporters. His first season was excellent and you could see immediately that he is a class
player, even though the intellectually challenged had written him off after no more than his first three matches at
United. Some of the criticism was brutally based, as usual,
around the argument that he had cost too much. A waste
of money, they ranted on. Once he had collected three
major trophies in just under ten months, the money debate
didn't seem too important any more, did it? And we
didn't hear too much either from the Italians who sneered
that he was too slow. When I first heard that stuff, I

wondered what game they had been watching. It was clearly another example of the dirty tricks campaigns we have become so used to in the Champions' League. In fact, Jaap is a very powerful runner, very quick as well, and it would be a nightmare for me if I had to play against him every week. He reads the game well, intercepts with such formidable power, and there is no hiding place when big Jaap hunts you down.

He was almost instantly an idol of the fans, but there is a largely unsung hero for the players within the United dressing room and that is Paul Scholes. In my humble opinion, he is another class act, blessed with a superb temperament and untouched by the most demanding occasion; Scholesy, in fact, has the knack of being able to raise his game the greater the opposition, and with both his club and country has demonstrated already how unconcerned he is by the biggest names. He can be a nasty little so-and-so as well sometimes. In my opinion, I think there are times when he could be even nastier. But you have to examine the overall player before jumping to conclusions. The little fella scores important goals, ghosting through from deep positions on late runs to support the strikers in the box and, sure, he will get wired in and mix it. But the abrasive streak is complemented by real quality. For me, he is a quieter, lower-profile Beckham in the ability he possesses and the passes and imagination he shows. This lad really has all-round vision. Becks just loves the limelight, Paul doesn't and is quite forthright in making certain it never invades his front door. He has chosen, and it costs big money to make such a decision, to walk away from the commercial world of endorsements, advertizing and sponsorship, which is pretty remarkable and very rare for a prominent name at United. He must be the most under-exploited footballer United have ever had in recent times and that's been because of Paul's deliberate decision in preferring his well-guarded privacy to an extra few quid in the bank. I don't think I have ever come across such an accomplished player untouched by fame. He plays his football and disappears off home; he trains and he's gone before you know it. At United you are supposedly celebrity material but Scholesy would run a mile to escape the glitzy side of the football business. Honestly, though, I just don't how he gets away with it at a club of such global proportions as United. If I'm quiet, Paul's invisible.

But he can be quite lippy among the players and it was Scholesy who came up with a fabulous nickname for two of his team-mates. He called them the Nervous Brothers. No particular prize, I have to say, for guessing their identity, Gary and Phil Neville, but it brought the house down when he said it. He says they deserve it because as soon as anything happens, well, they just panic. Paul, of course, has known the two brothers since their schoolboys days and was able to get away with such a mickey-take better than the rest of us. Actually, I can have a laugh here at their expense, too, because Gary and Phil must be the two oldest footballers I have ever played with. They are both twenty-odd going on fifty. At least, with their attitude, views and outlook, that's the way they appear. The way they are, they need a pipe and slippers more than a win bonus any day. Gary, arguably, is the worst of the two in this respect. He has an opinion on anything and everything, politics, football, stocks and shares, you name it, and, if you take his word for it, he has never been wrong in his life. Listen to him for five minutes and he will have you believe he has done everything, seen everything, and experienced things you couldn't ever expect to see. He can be impossible.When you tell him to stay cool, or just to back off a little, he still goes on and on. I've had less grief on Hyde Park Corner on a Sunday morning when the preachers start giving it big time. Gary takes himself so seriously, he ends up being funny. Scholesy and Nicky Butt encourage him, quietly chipping in and then reeling him in, and Gary always takes the bait. Most footballers are quite laid back and the world to them is not a serious place, but Gary has always been extremely mature. His die was always cast as a leader and there is absolutely no denying that Gary must be regarded as captaincy material. I don't think anyone in the United camp would ever dispute he deserved such recognition because he has devoted every element of his life to being a professional footballer. Nobody could have given more. He didn't have the natural gifts, but single-minded application and a phenomenal work rate have been the assets to get Gary to the top in his career. And I do mean the pinnacle, too, because I have yet to see a better defensive full-back in the country. His strength in the tackle, and his powers of recovery, definitely allowed Beckham to operate with a freer approach in front of him. David knows the back door is locked and bolted most of the time. The other Neville, Phil, has always had more natural qualities than his brother but in outlook they are almost a mirror image with the same maturity. Phil is a magnificent athlete, able to run all day. He can fulfil a number of team responsibilities, too, at full-back, as a wing-back or in central midfield, where his inbuilt stamina means he can cover any area of the field. Neither of them are ball jugglers, mind, and that's why Scholesy, blessed with instant control and awareness, thinks he has a licence to poke a bit of good-natured fun at them.

But the resident dressing-room comedian, I suppose, is the role mostly played by Nicky Butt. That, and his ability to eat. Correction, his ability to devour anything, and everything, placed in front of him. For years there has been all this talk about the European food mountain. I have the solution. Butty's the man for the job. If they gave caps for eating, he would have a hundred at least in the trophy cupboard. He is the planet gannet, and that's what we call him (oh, by the way, Giggsy can't be far behind him). If you sit next to him on the bus, he always tells you he is starvin' (that's inner Manchester dialect, I am reliably informed, for being hungry). The same in the team talk, the same at half-time, the same just after he's eaten a Chinese banquet for ten on his own. Nicky, though, is a bundle of laughs, the joker in the pack who maintains the squad morale in good times and bad. On the pitch, the character changes dramatically. There he is a warrior, another Keano, a player who can take the hit, dust himself down and wait for the reprisal opportunity. Oh, he will do you, no danger, and one of the finest examples I can recall was against Chelsea. It was the FA Cup tie when we went on the rampage, scored five, only to ease off the pedal and it finished at 5–3. There was an early incident where Roberto di Matteo went straight through Butty, a tackle which would have kept many lesser men on the floor. Our old mate, Sparky Hughes, standing nearby, immediately said, 'You deserved that, Nicky.' There was a glower and then Butty was off. Not so long afterwards, Sparky dawdled on the ball a bit too long than was good for him. Like a piranha, or even a shoal of them, Nicky went in, dumped him in a heap and delivered the ball perfectly for Ryan Giggs. He released it, I popped it in the net, and it was 4–0. Now that's how you inflict revenge on a football field. Hurt and hit, that's the name of the game. Like the captain, Nicky will challenge anybody and with those two and Scholes we have three midfield players who are frightened of no team on earth.

They might, on second thoughts, try to get out of the way of Henning Berg if they have any sense, particularly on the training pitch. Now Henning's a lovely Norwegian geezer, but there was a lesson with him you needed to learn early: don't get in his way. I think they invented the phrase about not taking prisoners especially for him. He has always played a highly physical game and will wipe you out, friend or foe, with barely a backward glance. He has always prepared for the big games by playing to the same tempo in training, so anyone risks being clobbered, and I remember Dwight Yorke being taken apart by Henning just after he arrived. Yorkie couldn't believe what happened to him. One second he was showboating on the ball, the next he was in a groaning heap on the deck. Henning had just smashed him and almost launched him into orbit. There was only one thing missing and that was a calling card declaring, 'You have just been visited by Mr Berg. Have a nice day – in hospital.' Like the rest of us, Yorkie soon knew it was wise to be careful when in the centre-back territory of his new team-mate. Henning doesn't do it out of any sense of malice or a desire to hurt people, and we all appreciate that was Henning playing his natural game, but he has taken a bit of ribbing about being the animal even his own club-mates must fear. Ronny Johnsen, his fellow country-man, couldn't be more different in playing the same posi-tion. He quickly proved with United that he wasn't out of place in the Premiership as a quick, strong, determined defender but more of the interceptor type. With Stam, he established a very handy partnership during the Treble campaign. Ronny almost as rapidly became known as the Iceman. It wasn't for his coolness under pressure, I hasten to add, but because he seemed to be a permanent resident of the treatment room. The perpetual request from Ronny, before a game, after a game, the end of training, at almost any time, is: 'Get me some ice – more ice, please.' He needs it on any given occasion and, apparently, for every part of his torso. No offence, Ronny, a quality player who you're always glad to have alongside you.

Someone who invaded from the opposite side of the world is Yorkie, my football soulmate, as the media very swiftly started to describe him. The first thing I recognized about Dwight was that, after playing with him on a regular basis, I realized he was an even better footballer than I thought he was in opposition. He earned rave reviews long before he joined United, but with us he was able to explore the full range of his game because of the standard of players around him. Footwork, natural balance and upper body strength are the three qualities which first come to mind in assessing Yorkie's game, but, in truth, he's got everything a striker needs to be successful. Our partnership quickly slid into gear because, while basically being asked to do the same attacking job, we prefer to do it differently in the positions we take up. I enjoy being 'up top', operating high up the field in and around the penalty box, while Dwight chooses to drop off, picking up the ball from midfield or even deeper and developing the linking play. Once you have that sort ot movement, you will inevitably hurt rival teams. Big, muscular centre-halves like a more static game and are not too happy when lured out of the defensive line. Forwards, let's be honest, are normally quicker than the men who mark them, at least on the turn, and if you spin off them and escape, there is nothing left to prevent the hit on goal. The understanding created with Dwight (and it developed very rapidly between the two of us) allows us to make runs into areas where the heavy mob don't like to go. In that way, we have been able to create a great deal of space for our team-mates. In simple terms, we proved to be a perfect foil and, given reasonable opportunities in the future, I feel the partnership is destined to get stronger. If United fans recall, during the most productive part of our first season together when the goals were flying in, it was because the rest of the team chose to knock the ball early to us. The longer that went on, the sharper the pairing became. We rapidly became the best of mates off the pitch as well; I assume this is because we both hail from a Caribbean background. Culturally, although I was raised in England and Dwight in Tobago, we share a lot in common. Accepted, he does smile a bit more often than me, but I've got more into practice with him around. Dwight seems to believe a laugh is a reason for living in the first place. He possibly does it even in his sleep and that broad grin barely disappears for more than a minute in any day. He even plays his football with a beaming smile. When he misses a chance, and any other player would be tearing his hair out, you don't get a grimace, only a grin. If somebody whacks him, there is the initial reaction to the pain and then a laugh. He is a one-off – I can't think of another player like him in this way. You can't help but like the guy because of his friendly traits and we quickly became the closest of mates. I remembered my own isolation, the life of the hermit, and I didn't want anyone else to suffer the same way. I realized I could help him settle in very quickly. Just scan the record and there is ample proof of that with twenty-nine goals in his first season and thirteen in Europe against some of the best defenders in the game. It had a fantastic impact on the United team and very swiftly muzzled the moaners who said he cost the club too much.

One player who didn't cost much at all and has been an incredible player is Denis Irwin. For sheer consistency as a first-team player during the 1990s there has been nobody like him. I can't remember him having a solitary lousy game during my time and I don't think any left-back in the country has come close to matching Denis's week-in, week-out standard of play. You never witness him getting a chasing. Why? Well, Denis has a fair amount of pace still left, and the old head to get himself out of trouble, but the key point is that he always had his covering angles just right. Such a quality footballer, with the added bonus that he rarely gets injured.

Ole Gunnar Solskjaer is of a different generation, who plays as an attacker, not a defender, but has the same dedication and loyalty as Irwin; he might also offer the club something like the Irishman's value for money in the years ahead. Already he has demonstrated that he is a quite phenomenal striker and, as someone who is hired in the same trade, I really admired Ole's finishing technique which is based around two very quick feet and a knack of shaping his body for the perfect hit at that decisive moment. I realized very early on that I needed to perform to the highest level to keep him out of the side. I hope that underlines the respect I have for him. Major clubs such as Spurs and Everton have also realized his value in the Premiership, but he stayed loyal to Old Trafford. Why would he do that? Because he's a determined little Norwegian so-and-so who remains convinced he can be a regular at United, I suspect. It's an attitude to be admired and it certainly makes sure I can't allow my level of performance to slip back by a fraction, otherwise he will be in there.

At all clubs, not everyone sees eye to eye. Well, that's the same for me and my rival striker, Teddy Sherringham, with whom I have had to joust for a place from time to time. As this book goes to print we have hardly spoken a word to each other for close on two years. It gives a whole new meaning to silent partners, I reckon. We had a disagreement during a game against Bolton Wanderers in the season they were relegated in 1998. They had just scored a goal when the ruck first started. I don't really remember what had happened, whether I had given the ball away or something like that, but at the re-start Teddy turned to me and said: 'That was your fault.' I couldn't believe what I was hearing. There are two facts I feel I must emphasize right now: number one, is that I have a disposition where I can get along with all my team-mates and always give 100 per cent whenever I walk across the white line; number two, I cannot tolerate somebody accusing me of showing a lack of team responsibility in a game. I wasn't prepared to back down when it happened and we naturally exchanged very strong words. It was a barney that began on the park, continued off the park, and, sadly and realistically, I considered the only way to handle it was not to seek any further confrontation. Instead it's been *omertà* – the vow of silence. If we play together we put the disagreement to one side and give everything for the team cause and we would never allow the situation to come between us in a football sense. There has been no lasting animosity except that away from the action of the pitch we just don't talk. But that doesn't mean the gag must stay in place and prevent me from an assessment of Sheringham the player. He is not shy to suggest he has vastly improved with age and I am not going to disagree. Teddy has changed from the Millwall days when he and Tony Cascarino used to be a couple of handy target men whom the Lions would batter the ball towards until it screamed for mercy. Since then he has developed into a clever link player as well as a goalscorer, retaining – as we have all been grateful to applaud at times – that aerial power. So, as a footballer, I have undoubted respect for him, a creator able to bring other influential players into the game and he was, for quite a long time, an important partner for Alan Shearer in the England side. Teddy obviously made vital, goal-scoring contributions to United's victories at Wembley in the FA Cup and over in Barcelona when we lifted the European Cup. Professionally we stand together – privately we remain apart. It's better that way.

So often Teddy needed to bite his lip and stay patient

during the glories of last season and I can well understand his frustrations. Less prominent figures like Wes Brown, David May, Mark Wilson and Jonathan Greening also had to show they were behind the collective cause in stepping into the first-team gaps when they were required to, to help more senior players to rest. Jesper Blomqvist, another Scandinavian and a willing deputy for Giggsy out on the left, needed to show a lot of courage as a valued squad player in his first season as he hid the pain of a long-standing foot complaint. But their time will come, I am sure of that. The era of Dolly and Daisy, christened by the gaffer, has long gone, but what an era it was; the era, in truth, that did so much to help United break the cycle of failure and a fair amount of heartbreak in securing the first Premiership title in 1993. Take a bow, of course, Steve Bruce and Gary Pallister. They were an awesome pairing and they helped me enormously, both on and off the park. They were, after all, the bedrock of United's breakthrough as a significant force, capable of winning trophies year after year. During the hard, uncomfortable times, Brucie regularly reassured me, and was always available to give encouragement for a deflated player like me at that time. Pally was exactly the same. I remember we all went on an arranged night out and, yes, we did get a bit pissed. Pally, half-cut but talking the truth as we are all supposed to do when we have had too much drink, leaned over and said to me, 'Don't worry about all the aggro and criticism at the minute. Think of this – the cream always rises to the top.' He didn't have to be that generous, but he was never anything less than that to me. They were tremendous defenders, too. Certainly, I would never have been brave enough to address them as Dolly and Daisy. By the way, which one was which?

In that side was the flying machine, Andrei Kanchelskis, out on the right, and I've already mentioned that his sudden departure had an immediate impact on me at United. Somebody who wanted to have an even more immediate influence on my arrival was Paul Ince. I had first got to know him in the England squad and after that we chatted to each other countless times on the telephone. Persistently, he kept telling me: 'Fergie wants you down here, you know.' He suggested, I don't know whether he was having a laugh or not, I put in a transfer request and the manager would 'come and get you right away'. I told him flatly I couldn't do that. 'They would lynch me in Newcastle if I ever dreamt of doing such a thing,' I warned Incey. It didn't stop him pressing me on the subject, though. Paul was some guy and when I landed at United I realized also that he was a player of rare calibre. The only disappointment was that I didn't have longer playing in the same United team. He had tremendous power, great physical reserves of energy and an absolutely crazy work rate. In that midfield holding role, where he was such an intimidating tackler, there were few in the game who could match him. I arrived in the January and Paul was long gone in the July. It was a hurried departure which puzzled me at the time and still does. I recall a conversation we had after losing the title at West Ham in 1995. He nudged me, trying to loosen a mood of understandable gloom, and promised: 'Don't you worry, we will win it by ten points next season.' We still had the FA Cup to play for, although we lost that as well, but Incey seemed so focused on his future at United. He was as gutted as anybody that the final rewards had been wrenched from our grasp. Also, for a man who is naturally a brash person and always full of bravado, they weren't the words of a footballer who didn't want to stay at Old Trafford any longer. But a month or two later, he had been sold to Inter Milan. We all missed him.

Then there was Sparky, and believe me he was a frightening man, who also didn't survive that same summer at United. What can you say about THE man? Well, I suppose you start with the acknowledgement that off the park Mark Hughes was the nicest guy you could ever meet; on it he was nothing short of an uncontrollable monster. He scared the life out of me with his sheer intensity to compete and, think about it, I was actually on the same side. The opposition's first request must have been a change of underpants at half-time. In that first season, I still shudder at the experience of playing alongside him against Arsenal. I made the mistake of not going on a decoy run to help take the cover away, and he just stood there, glaring and going off his head, and literally took me apart in about ten seconds flat. I thought right away that I just couldn't play with this guy. He seemed like my worst nightmare and I was totally in awe of him. I didn't think I could handle it. He wasn't just a United legend, he had also put himself around at Barcelona and Bayern Munich, and I felt simply out of his league, maybe not even deserving of his company on the pitch, for a little while. The feeling didn't last long. You only have to flick the memory switch and recall all those unbelievably spectacular goals he created out of almost nothing to win major games for United. I don't think I have ever seen a stronger footballer in my life than Sparky. When you fizzed the ball up front, even though he was seemingly ambushed by two or three defenders, it stuck to him as if it were controlled by super-glue. In that period he was, without any shadow of doubt, a world class forward with a novel experimentation in role reversal. He was a rogue animal and he figured if the centre-back was going to kick him at some time, he would get in first and flatten the unfortunate soul standing in the wrong shirt, which he did regularly. He looked after me like I was a ten-year-old at first. The protection amounted to having nothing less than a personal minder on the pitch. Defenders just wouldn't dare take liberties with me because they knew Sparky would move in and batter them. He is the only striker I have ever seen who would smash a big, hefty, scowling centre-back into oblivion and then stroll away as if it were the most natural thing in the world. And he played that kind of physical game from the age of eighteen without suffering too many injuries. Quite a phenomenon really and certainly the material of legend. Almost as soon as I arrived, there was talk of Mark leaving and that was a huge disappointment for me. I wouldn't have minded in the slightest sitting out most of the remaining months of that season watching Cantona and Hughes doing their bit. I could have learned such a lot and, frankly, the notion of actually being out there to replace him is as scary as it gets. Another United player to be admired in that era was Paul Parker, mostly injured in my time at the club. The other lads told me, though, that as a man marker he was unreal. He put the best in his back pocket and was exceptionally quick and very powerful in the air for a small guy. They were the magnificent chaps whose football heritage we inherited and now we have the men to take Manchester United beyond the millennium. All of them have my respect.

Chapter Ten

Some players love the headlines, the hype and the self-glorification that is, and always has been, a part of modern football. A great action shot on the back page, a ten-minute slot on a TV talk show, or doing the rounds of the celeb dinners, that's all yours, man, if you want it. To be honest, I never have. I have been completely indifferent to a great deal of the razzamatazz of the game and, yes, I have suffered for it. I can describe my personal experience in only one way. For a time, and it was, in fact, a very long time, I was surrounded by a persecution culture. The media and I just didn't get on. They pointed their microphones, or sharpened pens, and I was supposed to reel back, alarmed, intimidated and, necessarily respectful, just bow to their wishes. The demand was for me to answer all their questions. I chose not to. The result, immediate and long term, was that I had to endure the media's vitriol, their contempt and their ridicule. That was the deal. I hadn't played the media game, so I took their criticism, whether I deserved it or not, in buckets. Nice, isn't it? When I said no, politely but firmly, that I didn't want to answer question X, I was castigated as a miserable, sullen git. But that was the nice part. If I missed what the media deemed a goal chance, well, that was party time. They were in. It was what they had been waiting for.

Grab a handy spear, lads, and go for it. I was slaughtered, time and time again. Now, like any other human being on this planet, I get hurt by criticism. When there is some justification you have to swallow hard and take it. But when you know there is a hidden agenda then it is an entirely different matter. I became the favourite back-page scapegoat and it went on for years.

It started with the Press and then the rest caught up until television and radio seemed to be just as bad. It was the brotherhood of bad news. They were all on my case for a while, sniping here, dropping a little bit of poison there. I have no doubts, it amounted to a vendetta. But I have always been blessed with great willpower and a huge determination that maybe, I have to concede, is close to being bloody minded. They weren't going to win, I was committed to that, and I think I have now seen off the accusers and smear merchants, seen them off with flying colours, too. One of the fundamental reasons the whole, twisted campaign started against me was that I wouldn't give myself up to the media. I wouldn't yield to their game plan. I just didn't, in truth, ever want to be summoned for what the media believed must be a mandatory interview every time I scored a goal, or didn't, as the case may be. It was never what I was about. First and foremost, my focus was to play football and play it well. For a while that just wasn't enough, for the Press in particular. I had to make my stand, rough and uncomfortable as it proved to be, so I wouldn't be gobbled up, like so many footballers are, before being spat out the other side. The way, for instance, the media perceive me now, compared to a couple of years ago, is totally different. The whole business has been turned round completely. You haven't had a bigger U-turn than this one even in politics. It's amazing what twenty-five goals in a season, followed by another twenty-four the next and a successful partnership with Dwight Yorke, can do for your image. Turn you into a media star, that's exactly what it can do. Believe me. I am that man.

Let me tell you about George Best, for instance. I think those defenders he used to send the wrong way must have done a runner with his memory. He certainly seems a mite confused about modern matters. Back in 1997, if you recall, we lost to Borussia Dortmund in a European Cup semi-final. The manager always maintained we should have won it over the two legs and maybe he's right that we might well have lifted the famous trophy a little earlier than we did. The fact is we blew a few chances, and I was no more guilty than anyone else. Eric Cantona, in fact, had a fabulous opportunity when the great German defender Jurgen Koller ended up on his backside, right on the goal line, and Eric was left with an unprotected target right in front of him from an unmissable few yards range. But anything in football, when the tension is gripping every nerve, is missable, even for Eric, and he missed it. Either corner of the net was beckoning, instead he slammed the ball straight at Helmer. When Besty completed his breakdown on the game, that deep analysis stuff, and it appeared in a certain national newspaper some thirty-six hours later, there was not really a mention of Eric's miss. Now that was a surprise. I don't know how good George's view was at the time. Some had him at Old Trafford, others suggested he was in a city-centre hotel keeping an eye on the action. No matter, I had to take the panning, and I did. Besty slaughtered me, questioning whether United could ever win the big European trophy until they brought in a top striker. It was the usual, well-trotted-out line and it bugged me. It seemed like a fashion statement in that it was the trendy thing to say at the time, like kick Coley because it makes a neat headline. Maybe it was what the newspapers wanted to hear, and I suppose they pay their money and make their choice. OK, water under the bridge, let bygones be bygones; I had to get on with my life anyway. Then we come to the Treble season and Besty's earning a crust with the headlines again. Only this time, his argument was that in Dwight Yorke and me United suddenly had a partnership worth fifty goals in a season (hey, Georgie boy, you weren't wrong!), and we could deliver the European Cup (right again) back to Old Trafford. You see what I mean about Press perception and not being the fall guy any more? It depends very much on the angle you're coming from, I feel.

So, dead on, I had a hate-hate relationship with most of the media boys. They accused me of being sullen, unsmiling, and worse, all insults aimed to get under my skin to taunt me and make me angry. Why? Well, my view is it was because I was never prepared to give them the story they wanted. I didn't feel I should be compelled to do that. Some players revel in the publicity and I have no beef with that. When I dug in and refused to join the circus, the retaliation initially took the form of my having cost United too much money. I was the target for a few sneering comments. Then came the heavier stuff. According to the Press, I was a waste of space because I couldn't play, couldn't pass, couldn't score, and so a stand-off developed. I said earlier it was a relationship based on hate, but that's too potent a word. Intense dislike of the media was a more appropriate way of measuring my feelings at the time, and I can't answer for them obviously, but I believed the whole campaign against me was based on a serious injustice. And that's where they lost my respect. They singled me out, and when the bad mouthing was at its height I genuinely felt I was being persecuted. The way I grew up and approached football, it was a sport to be enjoyed; it wasn't life and death. But from the way certain people started writing about me, I was given a very different impression. Not only was football the only priority that mattered to them but, a great deal worse, unless I started to perform I was going to curl up and die! It was taking personal criticism to the point of lunacy. Such an inflammatory, undeserved campaign gets to you and it gets to your family as well. They might just be walking down the street, popping into the supermarket, or having a quiet pint somewhere, and people would start jumping down their throat just because they had a connection with me. Too often it was unpleasant, occasionally it became nasty. So hurtful, in fact, you had to ask yourself: is this their love for football – or is it war? Hell, it was only a game, for pity's sake. Not many months earlier, up at Newcastle, I had been applauded as one of the best centre-forwards in Europe. Almost overnight, I was being damned as something close to the worst player on the planet. In Italy, a front player can be bought for, say, £15 million, stay at one club for no more than a season and then be off-loaded. They don't suddenly describe the individual as useless or a wastrel, someone to be dumped and despised, and he is allowed to get on with his career minus the hullabaloo you get in this country if a player has a poor season. In England, unless you are an instant hit, the pressure for the quick-fix star is immense. I often spoke to Paul Ince, Roy Keane and Gary Pallister, all expensive buys, about it and they admitted they experienced similar settling-in problems coping with a massive transfer fee.

They, too, understood the media trick of suggesting that the underlying criticism always came from the fans and they were just an echo chamber for it. Oh yeah, right! But very definitely wrong because it was they, for their own ends of filling television programmes or back pages, who stirred it up and stoked the flames. Not once have the supporters turned against me at Old Trafford, yet the paid critics never stopped attacking me from all angles. Harry Harris, who in my opinion couldn't tell a football from a water melon, of the *Daily Mirror*, and the *Star*'s Lee Clayton, were very prominent in leading the attack with the so-called sword of truth. Harris, apart from all the other claptrap he was responsible for creating, had a go over the Glenn Hoddle affair. He said I had no right of reply when the England coach took a swipe at me. But, surely, everyone has the right to an opinion, particularly when defending yourself from more hurtful comments from the man in charge. Clayton, as well, came boxing out of very much the same corner, arguing I had no platform to challenge Hoddle because 'I couldn't hit a cow's arse with a banjo'. Are we talking percussion here, or being a persecutor? Since then I have had a chat with Lee and he has apologized for his agricultural dig at me. We discussed my football in detail and now he sees me in a different light and there is mutual respect between us. I actually think he's quite a nice guy. Obviously, like any reasonable pressman, he has to pass a comment on what he sees out on the pitch because that's his job. As long as such comments are objective, not snide and written for effect, I have no problem with it. My own position, though, remains that you should always try to see the best in a player, rather than the worst. Point the accusing finger at a team because it is, after all, a team game, but be more protective of the individual. That doesn't mean, if I blow three chances, nothing critical can be said and the observer has to stay muzzled. But, equally, don't think of shoving me into the next cell to a mass murderer. I am only playing football, remember.

There have been some really sad people out there and some, I might add, have had a serious effect on me. It was very difficult to accept the drivel that was supposed to be opinion. And the men behind the headlines possessed so much power and influence, which made their campaign far worse than it first appeared. They could alter lives and jeopardize careers, shaping my reputation with the public by delivering all the negative, black propaganda material. Often, they would change the whole perspective of a football match until it bore no relation to the truth, or the game I had just played in. It was the art of mind bending – or should it be the evil of such practices? In the face of it, I had to stand alone and it was very rocky at times, but I reckon I coped pretty well, steering my way through the bad times. I wouldn't want anyone else to endure what I was forced to survive. I can hold my head up high and I have the mentality now to look the world in the eye and say: 'If you are going to try and shoot me down again, then go ahead and be my guest. I am strong enough to deflect anything. I feel bullet proof.' What I did was shut myself off, close down my mind to the incessant insults, and become a stronger person in the process. The more I was slaughtered in the papers, the more it hardened my conviction that eventually I would prove them all wrong. What, I ask you, can they say about me now. I've won the Treble, put my name in the history books at United as part of one of the most successful teams of all time, and believe I have contributed as much as any individual to the collective achievement. Surely, I have swept away the soured opinions about me and even my worst enemy can't suggest I haven't deserved the recognition or that I haven't played a major role in it all. People close to me don't have to defend me any longer; I can protect myself.

One phase is over, that period of doubt and despair and wicked undermining of my position in the game. I have reached the stage where, at the age of twenty-eight just a couple of months before the Millennium, I am moving towards the peak of my career. I am a more rounded footballer, a more complete performer than ever before, and I have brought a great deal more variation to my game. The improvement has been for my own benefit, naturally, but also for the betterment of the whole side. There was always room for that progress, admittedly, but it needed perseverance, a lot of sweat and a good deal of overtime hours to get there. The odd cynic is still bound to take a swipe when a goal chance goes missing, but the torment is over. The pieces have fallen into place and I know exactly what I am capable of doing in the Premiership and beyond. From this much firmer platform, I knew, too, that my philosophy had to alter almost as radically. It did. I decided, in the summer of 1998, that from that point I was always going to speak my mind. There was no purpose any longer in beating around the bush and fobbing people off. It had to be straight-talking Coley and for anybody who did not like it, well, tough. It brought early dividends. I started to read interviews about me and they, very subtly, were written with a far more positive slant. I wasn't an object of vilification any longer, I was a guy who played football not badly, and a nice bloke at that. People began looking beyond the old perception of me and all because I deliberately changed my public persona and stopped biting on my tongue. Diplomacy went out of the window and I started to express myself, forcibly if necessary. Kevin Keegan always preached to me that you can't get hurt by telling the truth. Along the way some people might, I concede, be hurt, but such is life. I couldn't go on any longer just mumbling platitudes so an ego or two wouldn't be jolted. I'm up front now, I speak my mind, and immediately I was able to leave behind the pariah state.

All it takes is for somebody to sit down for ten minutes with me, not to do me any favours but to consider the person beneath the public representation, and they see a different character completely. They are able to under-

The fight for European glory. Celebrating the first goal of my hat-trick against Feyenoord in November 1997 *(right)* and trying out my Italian against Inter Milan in the Champions League quarter-final, March 1999 *(below)*.

ALLSPORT

ALLSPORT

After scoring the winner against Spurs to clinch us the 1999 title, I get hold of the Premiership trophy again, and my son Devante.

With my striking partner Dwight Yorke, the first job complete.

Enjoying Wembley at the 1999 FA Cup Final with Dwight Yorke and Gary Neville, having beaten Newcastle United 2-0. *(Left)*

In the team photo *(below)* and back in the Wembley dressing room with Paul Scholes, Ryan Giggs and Peter Schmeichel *(bottom)*.

With my partner Shirley and the League and Cup Double.

My partnership with Dwight Yorke takes us to the European Cup Final. Dwight breaks through the defence (above) and I race round in support to put the ball in the net and claim a famous victory over Juventus.

With Dwight and the European Cup. The Treble was won.

With my partner and Nicky Butt and his partner Shelley (and the trophy).

Time to relax after the Treble, on holiday with Shirley and friends in Jamaica.

Me and my old mate Chris Kiwomya, now of QPR.

Here I am celebrating my mother's birthday with the rest of the family.

From the family album at Devante's christening, (left to right) Dad, Shirley, me, Mum and Devante.

With my Grandad, such an important figure in my life, who knew the value of listening.

With my second mum – Shirley's mum, second from the left (standing) and Shirley's family.

stand very quickly that I was the victim, a victim of a totally distorted image. For a long time the perception, certainly for a year or two after leaving Newcastle, was that I was a rock-bottom failure. So, it seemed, that was how the media protrayed me *en masse*. And that was why I was seen as this famous flop who would never be of any value to a club with the stature of Manchester United. To walk through that barrier, effectively to flatten it, has given me a great deal of personal satisfaction. I have an impressive career-long, goal-scoring record, along with my achievements at club level, such as three Premiership championships, two winning FA Cup medals, the European Cup, of course, Charity Shield victories and a Division One title at Newcastle. That's not too bad for a failure with two left feet who never could play, is it? There have been other indvidual awards, too, and I have a cabinet of career souvenirs which only needs a sideways glance in the evening to indicate the successful path I have taken. But, although they are a great comfort, you don't need any glittering proof in the shape of medals to provide the feel-good factor, just as long as the evidence of your worth is locked into your head. And with me, despite the media battering of the 1990s, there are no lingering doubts whatsoever. I might not be Pele, but I'm a thousand-times better player than all those tabloids would have led you to believe.

Chapter Eleven

I'm a goalscorer, born not bred. The job I do, I do thanks to one fundamental quality – pure instinct. I haven't analysed it, I can't explain it, I just do it. It is no more complicated than that, and people who try and search deeper into what exactly makes a successful Premiership striker are off their heads. Let me give an illustration. Do you remember that goal I scored against Tottenham on Sunday, 16 May 1999, the one which effectively completed the formalities of earning another championship trophy for Manchester United? Well, maybe you don't, so here's the action replay. It was the forty-eighth minute, the score was one apiece, and the ball came floating over. I didn't really think about my immediate course of action, didn't have a clue really. I simply took the first touch, allowed the ball to bounce again, and just nudged it over the advancing goalkeeper, Ian Walker. Neat as you like. Ask me at any time now to sit down, carefully consider the whole sequence and finish up with the question: How did you do that? and, to be honest, I would have to answer that I really haven't the faintest idea. Just to underline the point, the BBC asked me to repeat it for a special BBC Sport advertisement. I found it tough, very tough. There was no pressure, only specially constructed metal-framed figures in front of me to represent the Spurs defenders and 'keeper, and it should have been a doddle. All that was demanded of me was that I must go through the same physical motions as I had in scoring the goal. It amounted to nothing more than a demonstration, but I found it so difficult to repeat the goal exactly. I felt as if I were miming and I couldn't get it locked into my mind. I had that notorious killer on my back for any goalscorer – too much time. When I scored the actual goal, in fact, I also thought I had plenty of time, but that wasn't true. See the playback and I had a precious second, maybe even a split second. Subconsciously, I knew that, too. And that, in a strange way, made certain I was clinical with the finish. It was pure instinct. For instance, if I received the same kind of opportunity again, with the ball floating over in the same arc, next time I might well cushion it and belt it in one movement. You never know precisely what you are going to do as a striker, at any given moment, and, for the boys out there thinking of being the big-time hitmen of the future, don't let anybody kid you otherwise.

But there are many, what shall we say, benefits in kind for the player who is able to put the ball in the net on a regular basis. For a few brief months at Newcastle, I even had the mouth-watering notion that such a talent might be enough to secure me a thirty-grand super car. Instead, I ended up with a consolation prize – a tie, a very fancy tie admittedly, but still a tie. It was the late summer of 1994, and for the first time the Premiership season was beckoning for all of us at St James's, and the excitement and anticipation of everyone was high. My hunger, naturally, was for goals, plenty of them too, at the very highest level of the game. I felt it was my destiny. Just before the season kicked off, Douglas Hall, one of the club's flamboyant directors, turned up at a pre-season game wearing an incredible, hand-painted Versace tie. I took one look, Douglas could see I was impressed, and I told him I would be very grateful if he could get me one. Instantly, we struck a deal. If I managed to score more than twenty goals in the forthcoming season, Douglas promised, then I could have a whole boxload of them, enough for every day of the year. As the games rolled by, it very quickly became apparent that twenty was going to be a doddle. I might even get past that target by Christmas time. Anyway, they must have been impressed by my handiwork in the boardroom because, right out of the blue, Douglas increased the stakes to a serious degree. 'Right,' he told me. 'If you beat Newcastle's goal-scoring record, I'll buy you that car you have always wanted.' Deal done, I thought, and that car – a BMW three series M special – was as good as in the garage. Still the goals were thundering in the net and in February I smacked in a hat trick at Oldham, and I was on a roll. So the banter went on with Douglas. What kind of wheels I wanted on the dream machine, for instance, the colour of the leather seats, the high-tech CD I was looking for, and he seemed ready to wave the cheque book. Then, one Friday night, we travelled to an away match and Kevin Keegan followed on behind in his own car. When the team coach pulled up at the hotel, KK went absolutely ballistic with me about the wager over my promised car. Apparently, somebody had been on the phone to tip him off. Now he was angry, seriously angry, and he demanded to know if what he had heard about the bet was true. ' 'Course it is,' I answered. 'Right,' snorted KK, 'unless Douglas is ready to buy every player in the team the same car, you can forget it. You're not getting one either.' Here, understandably, he was preaching the theme about teamwork and, although I was annoyed about losing the car, I recognized and sympathized with the message. Anyway, I did get the record and, yes, I did get the car, only I paid for it out of my own pocket. Incidentally, I was also presented with the tie I first wanted, which was a nice touch from Douglas.

So what makes an outstanding goalscorer, what constitutes the make-up of a feared predator in football? Well, you can list all the necessary assets you like, but there is only one that truly counts and that's the one I've already tried to emphasize: you are born to the trade. I can't think of a single case where the beneficial secrets of the striker's job can be instilled into just anybody. Sure, you can practise and sharpen the technical side, the repeat therapy of hitting the ball for hours, but the original gift must be there in the first place. You have either got it, or you haven't. From the age of six or seven, when I first started to play football on a proper level, I was able to score goals. It just happened, I felt the buzz of satisfaction in executing the finish, and that was it; I was hooked. There was never any hankering to play at full-back or centre-back, but only where the real action was bound to be. My life was meant to be spent in the penalty area. And in fulfilling my responsibility as team finisher, I have never really thought seriously about what it takes to do it. The basic requirement is to get yourself into a handy goalmouth position, hopefully minus any marker, where you figure the ball is going to drop. Then you pull the trigger. Nothing high falutin' about that, is there? And most of my goals, throughout a career at all the various levels of the game, have been delivered in that very natural way. I've only ever come unstuck when I started to think too deeply about the job, trying to make the goals look pretty or classy. It was a fatal obsession. I rapidly reverted to my proven philosophy that if you make the danger zone and simply hit the target you have a chance. If the 'keeper then makes the save, so be it, because that's part of the game. A goal roughly every 1.80 games, and that's my record, seems to underline the point that I must have been doing something right. I suppose to the outsider, when a top finisher takes up a position in the box and the ball suddenly falls to his feet, it looks like an act of magic. In reality, it just means that that particular individual is blessed with the knack, the uncanny habit of always being in the right place to reap the greatest reward. You just can't teach it. None of us know, or understand even, why it happens. It just does.

That, obviously, doesn't mean you can laze about, safe in the knowledge that the gift you were born with will always bail you out. No way. It is still critical for any striker with a wage packet at stake to practise, and then practise some more. I have spent many overtime hours on the training pitch, long after my team-mates have packed their bags and left, seeking that element of perfection which inevitably eludes us all. The main work focus, clearly, must be on the very act of finishing. So you keep banging away, striking balls at different heights or angles, close in or long range, and that's very much a part of the mental as well as technical part of football. It is meant to create an inner belief that, no matter how the ball arrives in the box, you can conquer the moment of truth and finish with deadly effect. The other obvious preparation for a front player is laying down an understanding with your playing partner, especially in England where the 4–4–2 formation remains the Premiership favourite. And once again it comes down to instinct. With Peter Beardsley, for instance, he had a second sense, knowing the run I would make or the position I would take up. Very quickly, a similar understanding was established with Dwight Yorke. Two potential goalscorers obviously are of little team value if they are always hogging the same attacking space. As I have said, you go where you figure the ball will drop, but if your partner is already in that position then you might act as a decoy or make a run for the far post if he's at the opposite side of the box. I know in the past they tested forwards like Kevin Keegan and

John Toshack, who were brilliant together at Liverpool, to see if it was a telepathic understanding. Predictably, they discovered it didn't go that far, but you do certainly need to be on the same wavelength if any partnership is to function properly and effectively.

Then, and this is the part I like best, you can get out there and terrorize the life out of goalkeepers. Give 'em hell as long as possible, that's what I say. It's the one bloodsport that should never be banned. I was once asked which 'keepers I considered the toughest to beat. They were slightly taken aback by the reply. None, I told them. It's still true. I have no respect for them. Not Shilton, or Banks, or Jennings, or Zoff, Yashin, Schmeichel, Seaman, and any more you care to name among the global greats, because they all come the same to me. Off the park, they might all be fabulous company and smashing guys, but on it I have one overwhelming motive, and that's to kill them. Destroy 'em, dismantle 'em, turn them into quivering wrecks if I can, and I mean to do that at every given opportunity. That's what it is all about – me and them. Some, admittedly, have deservedly been recognized as outstanding performers, a few even acknowledged as legends, but I have never really come across a goalkeeper where I figured it was impossible to score against him. Not even Schmeichel. When I played against him during my days at Newcastle, the record was two goals in three games, and in my opinion he was absolutely the top man. At that time, like anybody else in a 'keeper's jersey, he was my worst enemy and when I am out on the pitch I have no regard for any of his breed. I don't mean that in a nasty, sneering or demeaning way. It's just that they are out there with one purpose, trying to stop me doing what I really enjoy in scoring goals, and so I put them in the catgory of being a non-person. And, no, I have never asked them what they actually think of me. But I doubt if there is one 'keeper I have ever faced who would be able to turn round and say I haven't scored at least one goal against him. That feels good; it allows me to sleep at night. Once a game kicks off, my approach to them is as if they don't exist. The whole, unswerving focus is on beating them, smashing in goals galore if possible. It happens, and this is an admission that hurts in the making, that sometimes they have an absolute stormer and for ninety minutes appear impregnable. Now that does leave me just ever so slightly cheesed off. Worst still, is when they make a stupendous save and some comic then blames the supposedly offending striker for missing a chance.

Some forwards study the style and methods of goalkeepers they have to take on very closely with in-depth videos and breakdown dossiers. I don't bother. Because I have yet to come across a 'keeper, either in this country or abroad, with enough in his locker to faze me. It is never in my mind to worry whether they have little idiosyncracies to exploit; for me they are just there to be blitzed and buried if at all possible. Like other forwards, I know that 'keepers have a reputation for being suspect in the corners. The other vulnerable area, of course, is down by their feet. If you can fizz in a shot around that area, it is always very difficult for them to react in time and get down to retrieve the ball before it flies in the net. But, inside that box, with tension as high as the expectations on the terraces, you are definitely not whispering to yourself, 'Go on, then, hit it down by the geezer's feet.' The thought processes, I'm afraid, don't work that perfectly in times of duress. You just try to seek out the target and take it from there. If the shot happens to scream past the big goalie's feet then, believe me, more times than not it has got to be a fluke. The striker who could guarantee that every time has yet to be created and when it happens it will need to be a robot working on microchips, not the buzz of penalty-area mischief. Scoring might be all about technical efficiency and strong nerves, but I regard it as more of an art form. And an art that is being threatened more and more by the men I hate: the goalkeepers. They are improving dramatically, season on season, and certainly goals are treasures that are harder to come by. The big fellas are now quicker, more agile, in much improved physical shape, and I reckon their coach on all the best angles must be Pythagoros. They are quite amazing in their capacity to shut off scoring space in the box, able to move over yards of ground very rapidly. Schmeichel, for a massive, barn door of a man, was a master at it, and he was a pioneer in that highly effective method of standing up to the raiding forward and making himself appear even bigger than he was. It may be they hold that position only for a split second longer, but it crucially makes all the difference. The striker has to make up his own mind on what to do next while, in the past, a falling, committed goalkeeper would do it for him. Then there is that effectively modern invention of the trailing leg. How many apparently certain goals are stopped with that kind of blocking manoeuvre these days? About 100 per cent more than happened twenty years ago, I would suggest.

Even in my brief time in football, both the collective strength of defences and the individual prowess of goalkeepers have improved immensely. When I was at Newcastle, I used to stroke the ball into the corner of the net, no power but just a calmly made passing movement, and they were flying in week after week. That, I assure you, just wouldn't be possible nowadays. In such a brief period of football history, things have moved on at a dramatic rate. Up there at St James's, in our first season in the Premiership, I rattled in forty-one goals, a personal record which secured me the Golden Boot Award. It was, looking back, a quite phenomenal experience. How did I manage to score so many goals? To be honest, I can only state the obvious – by having almost countless chances created for me. If I had scored all the goals I could have done, those from genuine opportunities and not merely half chances, I would have been notching up well over fifty. The potential for causing such havoc was because of Newcastle's tactical set-up at the time. It was football played without any fear. Rival teams didn't really know how to combat a bunch of footballers who played with such a cavalier and free spirit. We never worried about the boys at the back; it was a case of blowing the bugle and galloping over the hill with the rest of the cavalry. Lovely, it was. Chances in every game came by the barrow-load and a fair percentage fell to me. I have serious doubts whether such a free-scoring situation, little more than five or six years later, would be at all possible. I know Robbie Fowler, another fantastic finisher, has declared that he feels thirty Premiership goals in a season represents a realistic target for the top men. All I can say is, if any individual manages that they should erect a statue of him. Because, if you added in the inevitable spin-off goals from domestic cup competitions and possibly Europe, we would be talking in the realms of forty goals in a single campaign. For someone to even get close to that must be regarded as quite incredible. In less than half a decade, the technical progress of the modern game has increased to such a degree I only see such targets as little short of the impossible.

The only record, though, that I will really fix in the mind is the one when I finish playing. There it's going to be, graphically stated and in black and white, the number of goals in my career. Nobody will be able to take that figure away and that's what drives me on all the time. Right now, I absolutely haven't a clue, unless somebody generously puts the score sheet in front of me, how many goals I have scored so far. But by the time I retire, and this is not meant to sound conceited or flash, I feel comfortable that I will be proud of a record to compare me with the best. At this stage, it's a fact that I have a goals-to-games ratio much better than one-in-two, usually taken as the measure of a pretty good striker. As for anything else, I am not really too concerned. Frequently, people ask me which I consider to be my best ever goal. It's hard to recall, really, because, ahem, there are just too many to mention! I scored a memorable one against Chelsea in 1994 at St James's Park that I cherish without ever claiming it was the one to top anything else. There is a reason I regard it as special: at the time I was carrying the football stigma of supposedly not having a left foot, only one to swing or stand on. But on this particular occasion a long ball came whistling over the top of the last man and I was poised and ready. I allowed it to bounce just once, then smeared my boot through it and the shot disappeared at a million miles an hour into the top corner from the edge of the Chelsea box. It was struck with that reputedly dodgy left foot and I leapt to the heavens in celebration and, maybe because of the rarity of such a strike at the time, I haven't forgotten it. The people at the BBC must have liked it too, because it was voted *Match of the Day* goal of the month. Back then, I loved the elegantly stroked finish, just to impress people more than anything. And also to see a big, ambling 'keeper, maybe on all fours, scrambling across the goalmouth to try and save a goal he already knew was beyond him. There I go again, revelling in a campaign of cruelty to 'keepers, but I can't help it. I love humiliating the big guys and the knowledge that through sheer precision and the quality of strike you can cajole, no, almost nurse the ball into the net gives you a brilliant feeling. Then there has to be the almost indescribable enjoyment of scoring goals in front of a passionate crowd of people. I can't really explain it, except that there is a huge adrenalin rush and a tremendous feeling of satisfaction. I have never known a buzz like it.

Because all my goals mean so much to me, even when they are a scrappy, scruffy little effort from no more than two feet out, is probably why I can't put my finger on the best. I really do enjoy them all so much. But there's probably a more fundamental reason why I am no memory man in isolating the details of so many of my goals. It is that once the ball is buried in the net, and the grin of celebration has faded in a few seconds, I deliberately wipe everything about it from my mind. The great Argentinian forward Gabrielle Batistuta summed it up for me when he said: 'You score the goal, you celebrate, and you forget it. Then you go to score the next one.' I understand fully that philosophy because it is exactly the way I feel about my job, in both purpose and payment. I'm not the type, either, who scurries off home to scan a game, or my own achievments, on tape. I'll watch the television highlights for ten minutes but my agent has got ten times the videos of my games that I have. I don't even possess one to remind me of the five goals against Ipswich in 1995, which still stands as an individual Premiership record as I put this chapter together. In truth, I don't remember too much about it either except that we trounced them 9–0. So, as I sit here drumming the desk and racking my brains, I just about recall the first one. Ryan Giggs hit the byline, crossed a useful ball and I managed to stick it in, I think. Sorry the detail's a bit sparse. Then there was the header, maybe it was the fourth one, and I climbed at the far post before the ball was diverted into the net off one of their markers. Oh yeah, then there was a rebound that came clattering out of the box and I whacked it back in. See, surprised myself there, in remembering so much about my record. Maybe certain footballers would be word perfect on what happened next, and would have watched the famous five maybe a hundred times over, but that's not me. Which reminds me, I must get a tape of it some time, because it's not very often that you score that many for Man United in a single game and end up as a Premiership stat. Well, is it? I wonder if it might ever be equalled, or even surpassed. Doubt it somehow with the way those mean-streak defenders have improved.

Just a year before that particular feat, I had won the Golden Boot Award and I had to collect it at Old Trafford, which ever since I have looked back on as something of an omen in my career. I ended the season with thirty-one League goals and ten more from other competitions. No one else even got close. Actually, that's not quite correct because some Welsh geezer did, but he was playing every week against the local sheep farmers, I think. Hey, and that's supposed to be a joke if any of you taffys get round to reading this. Then there was the small matter of eclipsing another goal-scoring record held for so long by that giant of Geordie football history, Jackie Milburn. What was it, seventy-eight goals in two seasons? When I managed it, I didn't suddenly think to myself: 'Oh yeah, you're a bit of a boy now.' Maybe, though, when I reflect on my career in a few years' time it will have far more impact and mean a lot more to me. Most likely, too, I will be able to dwell on the great finishers, who have been my contemporary rivals, and the fabulous scorers of the recent past whom I have only been able watch from the archives. The two who immediately come to mind are Robbie Fowler and Alan Shearer, both outstanding in their roles and yet very different in their approach. Fowler has been the latter-day Ian Rush at Liverpool, a genuinely high-class technician who just loves putting the ball away in the corners. Then Shearer, almost the opposite while still remaining deadly effective. I watched him score countless goals but none revealed the guile and cunning of Fowler. The England skipper always opted for power, ferocious, blistering power at that, and when he was on the top of his game he hit everything so early. 'Keepers couldn't react to him before the ball was screaming off the walls of their net. Michael Owen, a good bit younger and therefore with more time to develop and learn, proved himself a finisher at the highest level very quickly. He wasn't in the Fowler mould, either, because Robbie could be so dead-eyed and clinically efficient. Dennis Bergkamp, of Arsenal and Holland, showed that cuteness, too. He also represented the forward you have to be these days to earn a wage packet at Premiership level; not just a footballer with outstanding expertise in the art of finishing, but more a complete, well-rounded player capable of doing more than one job.

Not like Gerd Muller, in fact, even though he was rightfully a legend during Germany's dominant years two or three decades ago. Obviously, I have only ever watched him play on tape, but what a fascinating forward he was. The original pocket rocket, I think you might call him, and he was good, very, very cunning to be fair. He, too, hit everything early and he didn't miss, but what about those 'keepers he faced? In his day they were, well, they were nothing less than shocking. I appreciate it was the era of Gordon Banks and Pat Jennings, and they were absolutely fabulous, but some of those foreign geezers old Gerd took apart were a liability. More recently, the foreigners I have admired as much as anybody have been from South America and playing in Italy. Batistuta, of Fiorentina and sometimes floated as a target for Manchester United, has been sensational. He hits the ball so hard it ends up pleading for mercy and there is certainly little element of sophistication in the way he has built a terrifying reputation as a goalscorer. Just belt it as hard as you like, take the 'keeper's hand with you if necessary, but make sure you hit the target. Then a goal was almost a guaranteed return. What a brute in the box was the big man from Buenos Aries. The Chilean Marcello Salas was different, but still deadly. His first touch killed you and his control was excellent, shifting the ball very quickly. At Wembley, for example, the goal against England was a classic. Cushion it on the thigh for one touch, put it in the net, cool as you like, for the second touch. Little wonder the Italians hijacked him as well. Closer to home they also took Ian Rush from Anfield, even if his brief reign at Juventus was not exactly the most contented period of his career. Rushy was phenomenal, his finishing skills almost unreal at times. He always seemed so calm, so serene, while there was bedlam going on all around him. This bloke was merciless, he never gave a 'keeper a chance, did he? Coldly, he measured the precise area where he was going to put the ball and then, quite frankly, he just didn't miss. Never much power, just finesse. You need ice in your veins when defenders are at the point of panic, and it's more like pinball than football, but I try to copy the well-proven Rush method. There's one message flying round the brain that always must be obeyed: hit the target and hit the corners if you possibly can. That way, if the 'keeper stretches to make the stop, almost inevitably there will be a loose ball from the parry for someone else to punish. It's all about seizing on the scraps and top strikers have relied on such a diet for years. Gary Lineker was able to do that as well as most, although his formidable strength was always to play on the shoulder of the last man and use sheer pace to cause serious damage. I never focused on particular football heroes when I was growing up, but Lineker was a player I watched very closely. Trevor Francis, though he played at my local club, Forest, never was. He was an excellent footballer but never appeared to me as a straightforward, goal-pinching striker.

Maybe the likes of Francis heralded the more diversified role of the footballer in the 1990s. Sure, I still get most satisfaction out of bulging the net, but I have grown to accept, and willingly appreciate, that you need more than goal-scoring instincts to make a living at the top level. I know I was put in a category early: he scores goals and misses chances, which was hardly representative or a fair description of the player I developed into at Old Trafford. It was dismissive, and too often I didn't get the credit I believe I deserved in being much more of a team performer than in my earlier years. At one time I was a right greedy sod, a hit-and-run merchant, don't worry about that. If I had the ball, while a team-mate was in a better goal-scoring position, it was hard luck because I was going to unload the shot anyway. I have learned and realized there can be just as much professional pleasure in setting up a colleague for the winning hit. Which, I suppose, brings me to the topic of the full-time creators who can also score. Gustavo Poyet, of Chelsea, should need no introduction. Rarely could you find a midfield player with so much potency in the penalty box, either with head or boot. From him, fifteen goals a season are never much of a problem as long as he stays fit and healthy. My club-mate David Beckham, thanks to those explosive free kicks, can deliver something similar, and we also have Paul Scholes bombing out of the shadows to get a few more. Robbie Earle at Wimbledon is another decidedly dangerous customer with those blindside runs from deep positions. Players of this sort are invaluable because modern teams can't simply place all their faith and reliance in the recognized hit men. If they are marked out of it, you need other players to contribute with goals from all kinds of positions. That has been the making of the champions of the 1990.

At the same time, we all must be committed and determined to be better players. Sometimes the level of personal achievement, mind you, must be measured relatively. Like, for instance, with my renowned ability for heading the ball. Actually, I think not. Now I have made some significant progress in the aerial part of the game, but when I compare myself with someone like Peter Withe, the old Aston Villa and England centre-forward, I wonder why I bothered. He coached me for a time at the national school of excellence and, if you don't remember him as an exceptionally good player, then let me remind you that big Pete could head the ball further than most of us can kick it. Every time, the cross, free kick or corner, would impact squarely on his forehead and leave it with the acceleration of a ballistic missile. How he achieved such staggering power with his head was beyond me. Wyn Davies, a Welsh international who played just before Withe, was very similar and used to divert the ball with the thunderous effort of a mule's kick. And then there was Andy Gray, now of Sky Television but once a footballer who regularly put his head where the rest of us place our feet. Maybe, Andy, that goes some way to explaining your current views on the game! Only an opinion, and only fair when we have to listen to so many of yours. Before Andy decides to go to town on my heading ability, let me hastily point out I rely more obviously on other assets. If the ball is at a reasonable height, my instinct dictates I pull it down and seek control on the ground. My faith is placed in acceleration and quick feet and if you want my personal theory on heading the ball it is very brief. They tell you to head the ball across the 'keeper from the direction in which it has already travelled. Why do that, I argue, when there is a much shorter route by angling it down, which probably explains why they are unlikely ever to compare me to Messrs Withe, Davies and Gray. Oh, yeah, and another thing about the goalscoring arts, I have only ever taken one penalty in my professional life. Point two, I have only ever missed one penalty in my professional life. It happened at Coventry, just before I left Newcastle, and Peter Beardsley, the regular penalty taker, was unfortunately out of the side. It was a lousy, scrappy, goalless bore of a game and, when we got the penalty award, the rest of the lads ducked for cover, not before, I might add, volunteering me very loudly for the spot kick. So I turned round and replied: 'OK, sod it, I'll have a go.' Seconds later, the words almost choked me when big Steve Ogrizovic made the save. Worse was to follow. When I got back to the dressing room, the damning, collective question was delivered: 'Why the hell, Andy, did you take the pen because, let's face it, you weren't having a very good game, anyway, were you?' Nice one, chaps. From that moment I vowed never to take another penalty and I haven't. The specialists, like Denis Irwin, Steve Bruce, have, naturally enough, moved in with my blessing. I don't think I have ever seen Denis miss, not even in training, and Brucie was amazing; he took penalties like a proper centre-forward, not a brickwall of a centre-back. But that was before Eric Cantona, typically, stole his glory. I have watched the Frenchman take penalties and, in the process, make the goalkeeper look like a complete buffoon. He took them almost as if the act of scoring was in slow motion, but Eric's accuracy was such that, with the 'keeper desperately scuttling across his territory, the ball would run an inch or two beyond his flailing grasp and enter the net. It was a joy to watch, but, then again, did it constitute more public cruelty to that great unprotected species, the goalkeepers? You decide, but I don't care. Winning goals and compassion don't go together.

Chapter Twelve

In roughly a million seconds my life changed utterly and completely and forever. It was Barcelona and bliss. Nothing would ever be the same again. I had won the most historic Treble of all time, sharing in a Manchester United achievement unlikely ever to be repeated because of the growing intensity and increasing demands of the modern game. All of it, the magnificent entity of Premiership, FA Cup and European Cup, the greatest prize in club football if you like, done and dusted in just eleven days. It left me gobsmacked, it left me numb, it left me tearful, it left me drunk, and through all those conflicting emotions it left me with one unconquerable feeling: as long as I live I'll never know anything like it ever again. And to this day I know I won't. That's how moving and special it was for me. From the very minute Sir Alex Ferguson told me I was dropped for the final championship game, through the blur of being the sub who scored the title-winning goal in beating Tottenham, to the walk-over that was our Wembley victory against Newcastle, and then aboard Concorde and the epic, quivering, goosepimply night that was the Nou Camp and the sheer piracy of beating Bayern Munich. Tell me it's true, mate, because even now it's so difficult to absorb it all, take it in, and think we managed what so many of the experts declared was, frankly, the impossible. But then I'm the proud owner of three precious medals and they are, I suppose, the only proof necessary to show me fantasy can occasionally become fact. There are, of course, the scrapbook pictures and the glorious memories, too, but it would take a video tape, running non-stop from the 16 May to the 26th, for me to relive every moment of the most exciting phase of my career.

It wouldn't be too bad, either, watching it all flashing by on the balcony of that five-star Spanish hotel where we stayed before the Champions' League Final. It was set on a rocky bluff above the resort of Sitges, with the Mediterranean spread below us, and we all might well have been enjoying a holiday instead of preparing for the most important game we're ever likely to play. But then, on reflection, maybe that was the whole idea. Put us in a prison, locked away from the rest of the world as we were for three days, but make sure there is an element of paradise about it. So we chilled out, removed from the daily whirl of media hype, distanced from the tension and expectation of thousands of fans. And we ended up so relaxed and laid back that we were almost falling over by the time they had us in the lobby, boots and kit packed, and ready for a bit more action with those rather impertinent, err, cocksure chaps from Munich. We knew very well what they had been saying about us. The propaganda machine had been working well. You know the stuff about the Germans playing the English at football, the Germans score, and the English, they laughed, end up heading home with nothing. Again. We took it all, we swallowed hard, and we said nothing. The cheap talk never penetrated the United camp because every player kept himself deliberately calm and focused about what we needed to do. We knew it was a massive game. It was the European Cup Final, for pity's sake, and you might never get the chance of appearing in it again. More than that, though, it was THE game which would determine whether United could secure the greatest, most monumental Treble of all. As someone cornily put it at the time, it was our three steps to heaven. Did we have the nerve to make it? Actually, in truth, we strolled it. The only thing that really bugged me was waiting for it all to happen; no nerves, no nightmares, and certainly no fear, only the sheer frustration of wanting to get the final job done.

The mood was almost like the preparation for a third-round Milk Cup tie at some Division Three club. We didn't do anything special; a rest in the afternoon, then listening to the gaffer's pre-match talk-in which seems to get longer and longer as the seasons go by. He always digs into his dossier for any of our European games, detailing the strengths and weaknesses of the opposition, focusing on different players, and providing us with a general breakdown. For my benefit, the basic instruction was all about Sam Kuffour, the big fella at the back for Bayern. The manager told me to play him in the same way as I had at Old Trafford in the earlier home leg during the qualifying phase. If I moved him around, was the advice, Kuffour wouldn't stand a chance against me. So what happens? On the biggest night of all, he didn't even mark me, but that's football planning for you. The last word of the team talk was that if Dwight Yorke and I kept busy, kept mobile and kept our heads down, we would win it. Then we all piled on the bus and hit the nearby motorway for the stadium. I tell you, it was unreal. It was like a trip to the beach with Spanish music playing on the coach's stereo system. There was the odd bit of banter, too, but – boy, oh boy – were the troops relaxed. To a ridiculous degree, I would say. If anybody was feeling uptight and screwed-up it didn't show at all. History beckoned and we almost treated it with a yawn. Then there it was, the rising splendour of the

Nou Camp, some battleground that, I'll tell you, and all of it encircled by an absolute mass of red. How could we fail? As the police outriders nudged us through the masses, the United support was beyond belief, simply colossal. Thirty thousand tickets, that's what they suggested we had as the allocation. Double it, then add the number you first thought of, and you might be close. Even then, the importance and impending drama of such a massive occasion didn't even penetrate. It was as if we were in a dream. Maybe we were. And maybe we didn't wake up until the last two minutes of a contest that was surely beyond the imagination of anybody but the gods of the game.

I slouched about the dressing room for a while. Normally, I'm not the type who does the familiar, booted-and-suited tour of the pitch. This time, though, I was tempted up those calf-testing, concrete steps and, suddenly, there I was in that fabulous arena, a huge canyon of a place, but never too daunting, just inspiring. I looked around, thousands upon thousands starting to gather on those towering terraces, and that's when it hit me for the first time. Not quite butterflies, or even the panic of big-match nerves, but certainly the realization of what we were really all about and the immensity of the next ninety minutes of football. Back down below we all clattered into a changing room of calm, matter-of-fact, do-the-job blokes all gathered in near silence with one purpose on their minds. It was time, and we all quietly understood, to get the serious head on. No hollering, no pantomime passion or macho stuff for the sake of it, but we moved again like an army platoon for those steeply slanted steps up to the pitch. And wham! I couldn't believe what was awaiting us, not just a cacophony of noise, a wall of it, in fact, but so much eye-blinding colour and, then, the brain-bashing numbers; it seemed as though the whole planet was there to watch the game and they had all turned up in United red. I've never witnessed anything like it in my life. Never will again, most probably. There was only one reaction in my case. Goosepimples, from the top of my head to the end of my big toe, they just covered me. Along with a shudder down the spine that might well have raised a sizeable measurement on the Richter scale. And I'm not supposed to be the emotional type. But, in that instant, I understood, no matter what happened to be part of the future and without any shadow of doubt, that this was the most significant night of my life in football. Nothing could ever compare. Whatever fate had in store in the years ahead, even reaching a European Cup Final again, for instance, would not be able to compete. It couldn't even come close. This was the first time, the best time. I felt as though my heart was going to explode under the intensity of the whole experience. There was first a rumbling noise, then a roar, then an explosion on a deafening scale as our fans backed their team like never before. At Old Trafford we regularly have 55,000 in the ground and, embarrassingly, I have heard them drowned out by a mere 5,000 from the opposition. But this was something else. This was the hard core. And did they make a racket. It blew my mind, it blew me away.

Maybe that's why most of the match with Bayern is no more than a blur in my mind, so many incidents and yet so little I can recall. I know we were a bit scruffy in the first twenty minutes, fighting for the ball and then surrendering it, and we certainly needed to remove the nerves and anxiety from the collective system. Chances were few and the Bayern game plan was obvious. They tried to be cute and play us on the break. The punishment was endured early, very early. Only six minutes had gone when Ronny Johnsen, harshly in my judgement, was penalized for a challenge on that incredible hulk, Carsten Jancker. The free kick was on the edge of the box, to the right as Peter Schmeichel looked at it and lined up the protective wall. We thought we were set up, we thought we had it right, it should have been no bother. Mario Basler struck it low and skidding round the wall. Actually, in truth, he didn't – he scuffed it and, with a bobble and bounce and then another bobble, the half-hit shot somehow found its misdirected way past everyone into the bottom left-hand corner of Smikes' net. What an absolute bummer and I can still feel every agonizing moment as if it were yesterday. I looked round like the rest, our faces filled with horror, not because of the goal particularly but because we couldn't believe it had actually happened. There was no deflection, no fluky reason for the Germans to score. The accusing looks were directed at big Pete, who stared back and said: 'I just couldn't see it.' I think that pissed off a lot of the chaps. If our goalkeeper, the best in the world at that, couldn't see the strike, he was left with one option. He should have adjusted the wall until he could. And when it went in, creeping across the line, we just couldn't believe it because it was a badly delivered free kick anyway.

From such a demoralizing, disappointing beginning it looked a long way back. All Bayern needed to do was construct two lines of defensive barriers and sit back, which they did. We were in the unenviable position of chasing the game, with all the risk that strategy carries, and we almost paid for our natural ambition more than once. The man for whom we reserved another name but was actually called Jancker hit the bar on another counterattack. Their sub, Mehmet Scholl, hadn't been on long, either, when he whacked the woodwork. I don't think we played anywhere near our potential all the way through the match. We needed a partner for Nicky Butt in midfield and, with Roy Keane and Paul Scholes both under suspension, we didn't have one. Well, we had David Beckham, and he was brilliant in the central role, but we lost so much of the normal attacking supply when we didn't have him out wide. There he would have really stretched the Germans, bombed them into oblivion, if you will pardon the phraseology. Instead, we had Ryan Giggs out of position on that flank with Jesper Blomqvist, nursing a foot injury for a while anyway, on the other. The inevitable juggling act was a serious blow, a real handicap, because Becks is a pivotal player who can switch the play as well as loading in those dangerous crosses. There had been plenty of speculation about who was going to fill the gap in midfield. Mention had been made of Johnsen, or Giggs, but we all knew after the FA Cup Final it was going to be Becks. He secured his place at Wembley when he gave a top-drawer performance as Keano's deputy after the skipper was forced off by injury against Newcastle. That's what confirmed everything for the manager. But for much of the contest with Bayern, for all Beckham's heroic efforts, we were living on the edge and we knew it. Time, and patience, were running out in equal measure as the last two minutes of normal time approached.

We needed an act of desperation, we needed a miracle, we needed some sort of intervention from above. To my dying day, I'll swear we were granted all three. First came the corner. Suddenly, we could see Schmeichel, the stand-in captain, lumbering up the park and heading for the Bayern box. By this time I was back on the bench, subbed with about ten minutes to go, and I was part of a collective groan that was hardly the sound of approval. The last time Pete made such a desperate move he had busted his hamstring against Arsenal. This time there was no pain, only ecstasy. That great lump of a Dane – see, now he's gone I can say what I like! – got the faintest touch on Becks' corner, it spun through the Bayern defence and the Germans couldn't get a clearance on it. Giggs completely shanked what he thought was going to be a strike on goal and Teddy Sheringham, summoned to replace me, spun on the loose ball and diverted it into the net. It was the finest, most exquisitely scuffed equalizer I am ever likely to see. Absolutely brilliant, Ted, it was, even if we are still not speaking. The gaffer, in making those late substitutions, was looking for no more than a goal to take us into extra time. There it was, the miracle had happened, and he had been granted his wish. The whole bench erupted, it was a place of total anarchy and madness, with the boss going absolutely berserk. Why not? Two minutes left, we should have been doomed, it should all have been over, and yet here we had the salvation of a second chance at lifting that famous tin pot. I expected the full-time whistle at any time but, from the Bayern kick-off, we almost immediately seized another corner. Once more, Becks was the delivery man, stroking the ball into a jostling, jousting mass of bodies. Another United touch, this time a flick from Sheringham, and ... well, here I have to make a confession: I just didn't see the winning goal. Not until some weeks later anyway. And then it was on a video. The mob on the touchline, in other words the management and my team-mates, were still creating havoc and I had the worst obstructed view in the history of the game.

But this, I can vouch from television replays, is what happened. As I said, Teddy got the flick and the ball arrowed across the Bayern box and was possibly going wide and into touch. Instinctively, inspirationally, and looking as though it was the most natural thing in the world, Ole Gunnar Solskjaer, another sub, jabbed out a leg and the greatest goal I never saw screamed into the net. That ball from Teddy, as I witnessed later, was flying across at such pace, Ole had no right even to get close, but he did. That, I swear, was the talked-about intervention from above; God blessed us that night, no doubt about it.

Little wonder the directors and the manager mentioned afterwards about the late Sir Matt Busby, such a legend after winning United their first European Cup, smiling down on us from the heavens. It certainly felt like that, once, of course, we had gathered our senses, which took most of us several weeks. At the moment of triumph it felt as if nothing else mattered, even the earth tilting on its axis. Everyone, wearing sponsored boots, tracksuits or lounge suits, was on the pitch. Complete and utter bedlam, it was. Ole, the hero, naturally hurdled the hoardings and headed for United's delirious fans. We all followed. He was just about at the corner flag when we caught him, a breathless bunch of crazed humanity roaring down the pitchside track for fully sixty yards. I am surprised the referee, the Italian Pierluigi Collina, didn't take out his little black book and yellow-card the lot of us. Yes, the mayhem was that bad. I have never experienced a football moment like it and I don't think I ever will in my lifetime. Nobody seemed to give a damn about the re-start and within five or ten seconds the final whistle sounded and, fantastically, we were the champions of Europe. Not to mention the greatest Treble team in history.

But that particular achievement didn't even register with me at such a moment of exhilaration. It was mind blowing. I might as well have been on Planet Zog. You tried to think, but couldn't think, knowing only that the European Cup, the great prize you had seen so many teams play for and win on television as a kid, was now yours for a year at least. It left me almost in a zombie state, wandering around the pitch in a daze close to disbelief. How could we have won it, how the hell did we win it? I couldn't absorb it, not in a few minutes, not even in the party-time hours that followed, and not for many of the summer days which followed. My memory is of the German players, strutting their stuff not too long before, now flat out on the pitch, staring into space or sobbing their eyes out. Then I noticed some guys erecting the presentation stage. The Bayern lads, clearly out of it, couldn't have cared less; come to think of it, neither could we. All of them in tears, the Germans picked up their medals, aware they had felt like winners and now they were just a bunch of losers. They took it bad, real bad, as well they would. Then big Pete was up on the podium, his massive fists wrapped around the handles of the Cup, brandishing it like a war souvenir for the fans. Deliberately, I stayed at the back. You can scan any picture of the presentation ceremony and you won't see my face. Why? Simply because I took a step back, I wanted to remember every second of this moment of history, I wanted to be a witness to it all. The whole staggering experience, I felt, should be locked away in my mind and this was the only way of doing it. I could see the look of pride and elation on the faces of my team-mates and a celebration that was close to hysteria. That mental picture is never going to fade.

Next came that grand, manic, three-ringed circus of the parade around the pitch and that's when I let my hair down and began to go berserk like the rest. We tossed the Cup around, hugged it and loved it, and generally behaved like a bunch of four-years-olds. It was pure playground behaviour but, why not, it might be something we are never blessed to enjoy again. Smikes grabbed me, and you don't get free of him unless he chooses to let you go, and we rolled around on the grass, laughing, screaming and hollering like a couple of madmen. Yorkie joined in, but we didn't mind because the world was welcome to this particular party and obviously that included an invite to the loyal fans. David May, one of our ringleaders, seized the huge trophy as we approached the greatest mass of supporters. 'Ssshh,' he urged and about twenty thousand punters were reduced to an amazing silence, and for a split second we had that proverbial moment when you might hear a pin drop. Then Maysie lifted the Cup skywards and the bellow of noise from those terraces was quite unbelievable, huge waves of it filling the stadium again. All of us, around twenty of the United players, I would guess, went through the same ritual, with the same thunderous, deafening response, and finally I had rested my hands on the great prize for the first time. It was passed around and I sauntered off with Steve McClaren, the coach. We ended up beneath the now almost deserted seats of the Bayern end and Steve said: 'Turn around and look at that, Coley.' We stood there for at least five minutes, marvelling at the swirling, sweating, leaping and jumping mob of United's followers down the other end. We were on the pitch for what seemed an eternity, but then nobody wanted to leave. It was one of those occasions you pray will last forever. Lorraine, my sister, gave me a wave, Shirley, my girlfriend, blew a kiss, and all my mates were up there having a ball. You could see the look of elation, their faces were glowing.

When, eventually, they dragged us off to the dressing room, there was another incredible sight waiting for us. I think you would call it a champagne lake and the lads were quite content to drown themselves in it. None of us had had anything to eat and the old bubbly went straight to the head. I wished I had been close to a camcorder because the video would have been a bestseller in the Megastore, no doubt about it. Most of us were half-cut by the time we staggered out of the Nou Camp. Maybe that's one of the reasons why it took us forever to get away. Departure time must have been at least two hours after the match finished. The old mobile just never stopped ringing as I plonked myself on the bus. My two mates, Marcelle and Clive, my parents in Nottingham, loads of other friends, all called in with their congratulations. Eventually, the team coach got underway, although some of the boys might not have noticed because we were all steaming by then, and we headed for the big bash. Up to the hotel room, bags dropped, turn on heel and back to the party, which rocked on from there. They say Keano didn't quit until 9.30 next morning and that wouldn't surprise me. Those Irish boys, I can tell you, are Super League when it comes to enjoying themselves. When they talk about pushing the boat out, it's the whole damn fleet that goes to sea. So, inevitably, when somebody tried to shut the bar, and close down the disco, at three in the morning it wasn't the most diplomatic of discussions. There was a barney, the chaps just wouldn't tolerate any friendly persuasion, and we carried on laughing, and joking, and drinking until around five, what you might call a respectable hour to end a party. There was food laid on, a few buffet tables buckling under the weight of the stuff, and barely a crumb was consumed. Wonder why? The chairman made a speech, so did the manager – as people in authority always seem to do – you know, a right load of old bollocks. Sorry, chairman, I'm only joking. However he did redeem himself when he jumped on the table and started dancing with the biggest Cuban you've ever seen – cigar that is, not woman. The booze was still flowing so we danced with the Cup, and then danced some more, posed for the madcap photos, and then just about managed to find the lift before crashing out. Next morning, hell, was I rough. I wasn't alone in my agony either. Some of the wives and girlfriends headed for the shops. They could have had any kind of plastic they wanted off me, just so long as they promised to leave me alone. I ended up standing in the shower for a good thirty minutes. The hangover Niagara, they call it, and for me it was partly the cure.

We had flown out to Spain on Concorde. Most of us could have managed without an aircraft on the way back. We were flying anyway. How much can a footballer drink? Endless supplies, it seemed, as long as you have won the European Cup. Those air stewardesses should have been sponosored by Nike for running up and down the aisle carrying trays of drinks. When we landed back in Manchester, the estimate was that 500,000 people would be waiting at the civic welcome. Actually, there looked to be twice as many to me, but that might have been down to the booze. Seriously, for the cynics who regularly suggest United's fans don't hail from their home city, there was the ultimate argument lining the streets. Six deep, growing in size all the time in the journey from the airport to the heart of the city, I'm told at least a million fans showed up, if not more. I didn't even know that many lived in the place, never mind supported us. The formalities were completed with a few speeches, followed by a long wait on the open-topped bus, at a sports arena in the city centre. That little interlude, I have to say, seemed a complete waste of time, but maybe I am being a bit too churlish. It would have been better, following the civic parade, if they had allowed the players just to get on with the party. But very quickly we were split up, packed off home, and suddenly there was a huge feeling of anticlimax. We knew we wouldn't be seeing each other for a few weeks and, after the greatest moment of our lives, we just headed off like ships in the night. But, let's be honest, we had just been through an incredible twenty-hour whirl of emotion and achievement, a day in my career that can never be surpassed.

Twelve days earlier, mind you, I hadn't been all that chuffed. It was Sunday, 16 May, the start of our glorious charge for the Treble, and I found myself out of the team for the big one. Again. The manager named me as sub for the climactic game with Tottenham when we just had to win to hold off the persistent challenge from Arsenal. In truth, I half expected to be on the bench because, in his usual way, the gaffer had dropped a few hints early in the week that United players have come to read without too much difficulty. I got the familiar patter about how I was feeling, and I told him I was fine, and he patted me on the back and went on his way, muttering something about 'you not being yourself'. I knew what that meant. I'm able to read the manager like a book in such situations. I remember calling Paul Stretford and telling him that I wouldn't be playing against Spurs. 'Don't be stupid,' he replied. 'You have got to play – you have to win this game to be champions again.' I reaffirmed my view. I mentioned it to Dwight Yorke and, like the others, he raised an eyebrow and was surprised. But I understood the signals from the manager, and they were coming loud and clear. It was like deciphering a code. Yorkie insisted: 'You have to play. What about your goals? And this is the big one for the title.' Come the morning of the match, Albert, the kit manager, gave me the expected tug on the arm. I was wanted in the gaffer's office. Immediately, he told me I was being left out because he wanted to play Teddy Sheringham. What a ball-acher! I had played so many Premiership games, helped to get the team into pole position, and then came the final fixture, the chance to nail it, and I was out. As players always say, it was a bombshell. I was desperate to be in that United team and I suppose the management considerations were about the FA Cup and the European Cup finals looming in the next few days. But such reasoning was no consolation to me; not when there was a championship to be won. I told the manager: 'I'm well gutted. This is the last game of the season and I just want to play in it.' But he was unmoved. I would play at Wembley, he promised, and, yes, he knew exactly how I felt about the situation. There was no point arguing. I just walked out of the office, devastated. I strolled over to the lads and said: 'Hey, don't worry about me, just go out there and win the championship.' Inside I was in turmoil. I rang Shirley, then Paul. Neither could believe the decision, but I attempted to cushion the blow by admitting, whether I genuinely felt it or not, that in the previous two games I hadn't shaped up too well. Shirley told me not to worry – it would all come good. Paul's final remark: 'When you do get on – and you will – just go out and show 'em.' I put the mobile away and started to get ready.

Once the game started, we took control early and Spurs found it a struggle to cope with our attacking play. The tempo was good, so, too, was the confidence, and the ball was pinged around. A goal seemed certain and the deserved reward almost came via a bit of a fluke. Their 'keeper, Ian Walker, an old buddy of mine from our days at Lilleshall, tried to whack a clearance out of the box. It clattered against Yorkie, thudded against the Tottenham post, and rebounded straight into the grateful hands of Walker. I shuddered; it didn't look as though it was going to be our day, an opinion very rapidly enforced when Les Ferdinand put Tottenham ahead. I'm still trying to figure how it happened. Big Les competed for a ball with Ronny Johnsen and, as they met, it looped twenty feet in the air, dropped like a bouncing bomb and by some mysterious means finished in our net. As though it had been synchronized to add more doom and gloom, we heard that Arsenal had also taken the lead at Highbury. 'No, please, no,' I quietly murmured to myself. The mood of edginess, if not quite despondency, swept along the bench and even the manager looked extremely worried. Half-time was creeping closer, when Paul Scholes and Sheringham linked to feed the ball wide to David Beckham. He drifted in from the line, menacing as he always is in that position, and whipped in a fabulous shot, full of bend, dip and God knows what else, and it flew over Walker's groping fingers into the top corner. It was 1–1 and we had managed to strike back for equality at the perfect psychological moment. No more despair, just anticipation of what we now had within our grasp.

The whistle went and, instead of a dreary, collective shuffle to the changing room, we headed off with a positive stride. I had no sooner got through the door than the manager beckoned: 'Get yourself ready, you're going on.' He then walked across to Teddy and informed him that he was going to be subbed. It was a tough decision for him to accept, obviously, being taken off at half-time against his former club. But the gaffer explained it was for tactical reasons because we needed to chase the game and I might just nick a goal to get us home. There was, perhaps understandably, an element of anxiety in my mind, but after the rejection of a few hours earlier I was definitely fired up. Tottenham, contrary to the popular theory that they would do anything to prevent hated enemy Arsenal winning another title, certainly didn't appear to be ready to lie down and let us win. Their manager, George Graham, ex-Highbury and all that, seemed in similar mood. So, if we were going to pull it off, we would have to do it against the most demanding odds. I can still hear that resounding cheer rippling round the ground when I ran out. Expectation was high. I had to deliver, and I did, with what I suspect was my first touch of the game. A ball was knocked into the danger area and it was only half cleared. Gary Neville was waiting, taking two touches as I first made the run to go short for him, before I spun out for the long one. He just clipped it over in an arc that fooled most of the Spurs defenders. In all honesty, it appeared to be dropping too far away from me, but I stretched a boot and the miracle happened. I just caught the ball on the end of my toe, but there wasn't enough control and it took an awkward bounce. So I was forced to take another touch in an attempt to keep it up and help the momentum of the move. From the corner of my eye, I detected Walker easing off his line. He had made up my mind, granted me one option, and I took it. All I could do was help the ball forward, lifting it over his stranded head, and with one more bounce it was in the net.

I didn't need a second glance. I was off, screaming towards the touchline bench and the United subs. At half-time I had warned Jaap Stam that if I managed to notch, I would race in his direction for a little celebration. So what does the big Dutchman do – he just stands there like a big dummy, never budges from his position, and makes me look a dummy as well. That's mates for you. The other players were more up for the carnival. They pounced on me and I was submerged by a scrum of bodies. They almost put me in intensive care. It was wild, man, really wild, and so was the rest of the match. We, naturally, ended up living on our nerves, a half clearance here, a heart-pounding scramble there, and Spurs trying like bears to drag us back. Arsenal couldn't have done any more if they had been on the park, honest they couldn't. When the whistle sounded, it was like the Seventh Cavalry coming over the hill, and we had survived the first ordeal, reached and grabbed the first big prize. When normality resumed, I found myself wandering around the pitch, accepting the fans' plaudits, with my son Devante clasped in my arms. I almost pleaded with him to drape the championship medal around his neck. He didn't want to know, he was completely unmoved and just brushed it aside. So much for his old man's achievements. Little Devante was totally underwhelmed by the whole affair, a cool little guy. But it was an occasion that naturally meant so much to the United players. We had been hurt the year before when Arsenal swept past us and took the Double; the pain had to be banished and now, to some degree, it had. For me, in particular, there was a lot of emotional feeling to unburden because there had been something personal, something bitter-sweet about Arsenal's triumph. That season, remember, I slammed in twenty-five goals and finished without a medal to show for my efforts. I needed a reward, that tangible piece of metal, to underline a second campaign of twenty-four goals, only this time with the recognition of Premiership Champion to go with it. So there were tears, nothing unusual in that, and the party, nothing unusual in that either, as I was to discover in the next eleven days.

We all headed off to a sumptuous, newly opened hotel in Worsley, in some fine bit of coutryside within a few miles of Old Trafford, and wined and dined the night away with family and friends. We broke up late, and rose not too early on the Monday morning, when I had promised Shirley we would go out to lunch for a more intimate celebration. Our nice little date was unceremoni-ously interrupted by a call on the mobile: 'Where the hell are you?' It was that bachelor free, Dwight Yorke. 'We are all in Mulligan's having a drink – are you copping out?' Nobody had mentioned a thing to me about an ongoing, round-the-clock drink up, but the rest of the players were having the time of their lives in a well-known bar. Yorkie's final request, not very polite I have to admit, was: 'Now get your arse down here.' As you would expect, for a minute or two, matters became a little bit brittle with Shirley. The chaps were out on the town, I wasn't, and, you know, championships don't turn up like buses – two and three at a time. You can imagine the spiel. I couldn't duck out on this one, otherwise I would be in for terrible abuse as the whimp of the dressing room. Shirley relented and I was let off the leash. I arrived at the bar. The chaps, clearly, had been enjoying themselves and, as for me, sober as the time-honoured judge, it looked like a game of catch-up. There was United's strolling minstrel in attendance, the guy who makes up all the terrace songs about the players, and, glasses well charged, we went through the whole repertoire. Two bars later, not the musical kind either, we were all well blathered. That's when the incident happened with Keano, that handbags at ten paces which received so much unwarranted publicity and then amounted to nothing, with the police taking no action. But Tuesday, that's when the real aggro began.

It was back to training, that dreaded day you have to face after enjoying yourself, and no time off for good behaviour in the remainder of a week focused totally on our preparations for Wembley. This was payback time after two days on the booze and it was extremely hard work, uncomfortable, too, because all the cameras crews were down there following the Keano episode. It was a full-blown media circus and, with banging headaches and weary limbs, we were in no fit state to talk to the nation; all we all wanted was to get off home and go to bed. But Steve McClaren – aren't these coaches wonderful? – showed the necessary compassion and let us off lightly in what was little more than a muscle-loosening workout. Next morning, and with the countdown closing in on Wembley, I received what by now was a familiar summons from the gaffer. He asked, and I was getting very used to this question, whether I felt OK. He barely paused to listen to my reply before observing that he felt I had looked tired in the Spurs game. 'Tired?' I groaned. 'I only played the second half – no way am I tired.' But that didn't deflect him and he said I needed to do a bit of extra training. It seemed a bit weird. After all, I had been involved in something close to fifty games and yet I was still expected to do more physical work. But, no matter, I got out there and did it. More than anything, though, that request from the gaffer planted an element of doubt in my mind about a place in the Cup Final. There was a great deal of speculation about the team line-up, but not one of us knew whether we would be playing as we headed for London. There wasn't even a hint come breakfast on the Saturday morning with just a few hours to go. I sloped off to my room and was watching TV at about 10.30 when I could hear doors slamming in the hotel corridor. I shoved my nose out and there was the manager with Jim Ryan and Stevie Mac, his coach, beside him. 'In you go,' he barked at me, 'and shut the door behind you.' A few tense minutes later and he returned. He walked into my room and almost in mid-stride said: 'I am going to play you for sixty minutes, maybe seventy at most. I know it's your old team out there and that's why you are in. I am going to play you up front with Ole.' And then: 'Are you happy with that?' Actually, I was raving mad, delighted, because with the European Cup Final looming I had feared I might not play at all. The room-by-room call continued until the manager, tough job done, disappeared. Nicky Butt, rooming opposite me, banged on my door. He was so down. 'I'm not even sub,' he said. 'They say they can't risk me because of Barcelona.' Nicky must have suspected as much, because we were without both Keane and Scholes for the big one with the Germans through suspension, but it wasn't much of a consolation for him. For me, though, there was a feeling of relief. I well understood I might have been rested, too, in avoiding the risk of injury.

Dwight Yorke was on the bench, our match-winning partnership temporarily out of action, when we finally squared up to Newcastle after the usual pomp and splendour of Wembley had been completed. Within a matter of a couple of minutes, Keane was seriously hurt in a late, lunging tackle by Gary Speed. You could see even the Irishman, for all his incredible courage and ability to endure pain, wasn't going to last much longer. He didn't, and Teddy Sheringham was waved on as David Beckham slipped into his favoured role in central midfield as Roy's replacement. Ninety-six seconds later, Scholesy angled in a great pass and Teddy was celebrating the first goal of the Final. From that moment, and not wanting to twist the knife on the Geordie fans, it was all over; we strolled it, and Newcastle, frankly, just weren't capable of giving us a game. The whole contest became a one-sided bore and if it had been a boxing match they would have stopped it. Their only player on the day, Didi Hamann, went off injured at half-time and we wrapped up the result very clinically when Scholes, released by Sheringham, stole in for the second goal. Roy Keane led us up those famous steps and the second trophy of the Treble was destined for the Old Trafford boardroom.

Ten months earlier, the marathon slog of the Premiership campaign had begun with two unimpressive results which cost me my first-team place for several weeks. We struggled against Leicester in the game that kicked off our season on 15 August. Only the inspired intervention of a Beckham free kick three minutes into stoppage time salvaged a point after Emile Heskey and Tony Cottee left us two goals adrift. It wasn't much better a week later, particularly for me when I was subbed after just seventy minutes of a partnership with Dwight Yorke, signed for that record £12.6 million only a couple of days before. But while the scoresheet against West Ham remained blank, Becks did score a few points for himself in handling a tirade of abuse and obscenity with remarkable dignity. That stupid and misguided reaction to England's World Cup exit lasted quite a long time, but David, with the help of his United team-mates, never flinched and performed with his usual skill and influence. He played an effective part in our first League victory of the season, but it was

Yorkie, in his home debut, who claimed the headlines with two goals. Ole Solskjaer slammed in the other two as Premiership newcomers Charlton were rolled over. No bother against Coventry, either, as Dwight scored again, but that success was soon overshadowed by a 3–0 walloping inflicted by Arsenal at Highbury. I wasn't even on the bench for that game, but towards the end of September I shared in the two-goal win over Liverpool, doing not bad as a sub for Solskjaer, which I later discovered impressed the manager. It was the turning point for me and after our draw in Germany against Bayern Munich in the Champions' League qualifier, I returned to the first team alongside Yorke at Southampton. I scored, so did Dwight, and we romped to a 3–0 win, with Jordi Cruyff claiming the other goal. Wimbledon copped for it, 5–1, in the next fixture and I grabbed the first and last goals. A draw at Derby and a bit of a carnival at Everton, where we won 4–1, and we climbed to second in the table, just a point behind Aston Villa at the end of October.

November was a month of mixed rewards. We battered the Danes of Brondby by five goals while drawing dismally with Newcastle and losing, to the amazement of most people, at Sheffield Wednesday while nicking two victories against Blackburn and Leeds United, both of them finishing up 3–2. I managed just a single League goal during that switchback period but we still were relentlessly in pursuit of Villa, both of us having won eight games as we approached the demands of midwinter. When we played them at Villa Park on 5 December, Paul Scholes seized the lead, but Julian Joachim's equalizer saved them from defeat. At Tottenham it ended up 2–2 and then Chelsea, clearly one of the heavily-tipped title candidates, also denied us at Old Trafford when Gianfranco Zola chipped Schmeichel with about seven minutes to go. Worse, though, was that devastating result against Bryan Robson's

Middlesbrough just six days before Christmas. Nicky Butt and Scholesy scored, but only after Boro had taken a three-goal lead. We couldn't claw the other one back and by the turn of the year we had slipped back into fourth place despite a morale-rousing victory against struggling Forest and a goalless result with Chelsea at Stamford Bridge. But the defeat by Robbo's mob on 19 December proved to be our date with destiny; we never lost again in the Premiership and it was that team consistency which made certain we ended up champions. I notched two, while Yorke and Solskjaer swept in the others, in a 4–1 clattering of West Ham at home. Two more, accompanied by a brace from Dwight, came my way in a 6–2 thrashing of Leicester at Filbert Street. And while enjoying FA Cup victories over Middlesbrough and Liverpool, an agonizer that one, we beat Charlton away and for the first time took over at the top of the Premiership. In February we tightened the grip with four victories and a 1–1 draw with a resolute Arsenal, which didn't quite avenge the earlier humiliation in London but kept us in control. The great memory of that period, though, was the 8–1 demolition of Forest at their ground when Ole Solskjaer arrived as a seventy-second minute sub and proceeded to smash in four goals of his own. It was a fantastic performance and left me in the shade even though I scored twice.

The title lead had grown. We were now four points clear of Chelsea, seven ahead of Arsenal, and Villa appeared to be in freefall following a disastrous run; we had 57 points, they had 44, and it had been an incredible slide by the long-time leaders. In March, two tough European games with Inter Milan, plus an FA Cup replay when we beat Chelsea at Stamford Bridge, were the fixtures which might have sidetracked us, but we still achieved victories over Newcastle on Tyneside and Everton at home. Still four points clear, the two treasured goals at St James's Park added to the personal record that provided the feel-good factor. April, as the boss always declares, is crunch time in the championship, when contenders make the decisive break or wilt under the fixture pressure. There was our replay epic with Arsenal, when Ryan Giggs took us through to the FA Cup semi-final with that fabulous individual goal, not to mention the mighty confrontations with Juventus at home and away when I claimed the winner in the Stadio delle Alpi six minutes from time. With such focus on Europe and Wembley, it wasn't exactly surprising we finished the month a point behind new leaders Arsenal after two draws with Wimbledon and Leeds. We knew it would go all the way down to the wire, and it might well feel like barbed wire in the end, but the whole United team definitely believed that our destiny was there to be claimed with both hands. A firmer grip was established with a May-day victory over Villa when Becks thrashed in another of his spectacular free kicks from twenty-five yards without even the barrier of a defensive wall in front of him. It should have got even better at Anfield five days later. With twenty minutes left, we were on cruise control until Jesper Blomqvist, harshly in our view, was adjudged to have given away a penalty, which Jamie Redknapp put away, and then the referee David Elleray somehow thought nice guy Denis Irwin had to go for two yellow cards. Even worse, Paul Ince, seen by so many United fans as something of a renegade in the colours of Liverpool, snatched an equalizer in the final seconds. The title ground was recovered with Yorkie's only goal at the Riverside against Middlesbrough, our ambitions blunted slightly by Blackburn's obdurate, goalless draw at Ewood Park, before the game that meant so much to me on a personal level, the win over Tottenham, sealed the fifth Premiership title of the 1990. The first step to be followed by the giant leap.

Chapter Thirteen

When you have walked down a dusty African street and seen children, some no more than three or four, with no food, barely any clothes, and a bus shelter for a home, it strikes you as deplorable and shameful. But when you see also that they have full-blown Aids, there is another conclusion. It can be described as nothing less than a criminal outrage. And I witnessed all of that within a fortnight or so of winning the Treble. I was shaken to the core, numbed and bloody angry that I could experience two different worlds, as if they belonged in a separate universe, inside such a short period of time. I went to Zimbabwe on a brief charity mission, squeezed into a summer playing for England and a two-week family holiday in the Caribbean. I had never been before, but I will be going back. Definitely. Because what happened on that whistle-stop weekend in June 1999 left me with some serious and concentrated thoughts on what I might do once I decide chasing a ball around the Premiership is no longer for me. There is a very different life waiting, a much more demanding one, too, when the football career is over. I don't want to sound holier than thou, but if I can help a few people with some charity work, that could well be the road for me. I was asked to go to Harare because I fitted the role as, I suppose, the celebrity frontman for a money-raising campaign called Venture Kodak Ariel Foundation, an idea where big business and the rest of us might join together commercially to help the less fortunate. No doubt I received the call because I play for Manchester United, a very high-profile club, and because I am a black footballer. Whatever the motives involved, I am glad I accepted the invitation. From this trip we have now formed the Venture Kodak Andy Cole Children's Foundation, which I hope will go on to become a collector of charitable funds for the benefit of all sorts of kids with many different problems.

The day I arrived in Zimbabwe, I saw those kids, and they are numbered in thousands not hundreds, trying to survive in absolute squalor. Their living conditions, if that's how they can be described, were appalling. They had nothing to eat most days. Their diet came from rifling through waste bins on the street and grabbing at somebody else's chuck-aways in the gutter. And they sheltered from the night anywhere they could. On the Sunday morning I was awoken in my luxury hotel room to go and see how these unfortunate kids were surviving for myself. It was an horrendous scene, and you just couldn't comprehend such a situation with the new millennium a matter of months away, because, not a mile or two down the road from such unbelievable poverty and deprivation, other people were living in mansions, big, flash pads that wouldn't have looked out of place in uppercrust Cheshire. The first kids we came across – a group of lads aged between ten and fourteen – were living in a hole in the ground next to a mosiquito-infested river. They said they lived there because it was at least dry. Then we travelled a short distance to the bus depot. The bus park was deserted as the sun was not yet up and as I walked through it I could feel how cold it was. Our guide directed me to a box-like structure on stilts. He explained it was where people buy their bus tickets from the vendors who duck underneath the box and then open a door with a grill in it through which the ticket is exchanged for money. The box part was only two foot by two foot with probably just enough room for the ticket seller to move his shoulders right to left, but not much else. Next our guide banged loudly on the box and shouted some instructions. The door gradually opened and cardboard and paper fell to the floor. Emerging into the glare of the camera was a young boy of no more than nine. I thought, 'how could he sleep in such a contained space?' But as all the paper and cardboard was removed from that two foot by two foot, wooden box we found two more boys! One of them was no older than four. Such children of the streets, no more than urchins really, hadn't got a chance in life, and I thought of my own son, Devante, back home. He was of a similar age to some of these children and yet their lifestyles were not just eight thousand miles apart; more like eight centuries. He will benefit from every possible advantage, while they had been abandoned without even hope to help them through. When you witness such scenes on the TV news, or in documentaries, they barely sink in. But when you see the same thing close up, right in your face, it is very different. You reel back in sheer disbelief at the shock of it all. 'This is almost the twenty-first century, man, this can't be real,' I thought to myself. And yet the ultimate horror was that many of them are HIV positive or even have full-blown Aids. Here, we are talking of kids who were just three or four years of age, with a number of others even younger. I don't really want to go into detail about how they contracted such a terrible disease, but some of the stories I heard out there were truly horrific. Since the summer trip, a lot of other people have become aware of this desperately sad situation and have begun helping out. Annie Lennox is, among others, now in the forefront in raising money and I'll continue to do my bit. The cash was directed to helping the kids immediately with food, blankets and the other basics of living, while more long-term finance continues to be re-directed so that local hostels were refurbished to provide proper accommodation. For me it was a huge culture shock, but for the African kids I met out there it seemed to be just as big an experience. Manchester United, I am now aware, has a massive following in Zimbabwe and for them actually to meet one of the club players appeared to be of great importance. All I can say now is that if my presence helped them in some way, then fine, and I will be back to see them again in the near future. It might well lead to a radical change in what I want to do as well in the years to come. Because, after that initial experience of trying to help, I believe that charity work is an aspect for me to explore when I do finish with football.

Such plans, I hasten to add, are very much on hold for a few seasons to come. I've been winding people up, those closest to me in truth, that I always intended quitting the game when I reached thirty, which is not too far away as I write this book. But that's all it ever was, a wind-up, a joke. I would like to think that I have a career as a frontline footballer until I am at least thirty-five. I've kept a close watch on the way Ian Wright, for instance, dealt with his sporting retirement. He made a decision to go at a certain age, announced it publicly, and then got on with playing out the last few months of his career. It was the right way. He was even prepared to drop down a division and join Nottingham Forest on loan from West Ham to make sure he was able to enjoy his football right until the end. I would consider such a move, too, when the moment comes, but I wouldn't dream of steadily descending down the football ladder year after year just to get a game. That's sad, man, really sad. And it's no way for any accomplished performer to bow out, is it? You have to fix in your mind what you want, when you will go, and where you might be heading once the retirement decision has been taken. For me, the time has now arrived to consider the options quite seriously. I was born in 1971, remember, and outside the game I haven't got too many other interests. Recently, I have talked to Steve McClaren, the first-team coach at United, about my aims in the years ahead and I appreciated from our discussion that I must get my head around the problem very quickly. I haven't found it easy, admittedly. I'm the type of guy who has fulfilled most of my ambitions by living day to day; it's been the unwritten code of my whole existence. And football has been the one focus of my life for such a long time, coming up to fifteen years as a pro, that I don't find it easy to consider anything beyond the comforting walls of a dressing room and a regular wage packet from kicking a ball, which is the normal pattern of most players. Outside all that there is a certain fear. You know you might last until that magical thirty-five, if you're lucky, but after that, well, there is a lot of living still to do. And how are you going to live it? That's where the apprehension creeps in, the worry of another thirty years of self-fulfilment, of wondering if there is another job you can do successfully, or even if you can hold one down properly. Hopefully, by the time I reach the end, I should be financially secure, independent enough to go and pursue other interests like charity work. Unless, of course, the investment brokers have scarpered with all my dosh! (another joke, fellas, before you dive in with the writs). But still, even if you are fortunate enough to have plenty of the folding stuff in the bank, you have to enter that zone of doubt and answer the question: What do I do now – now it's all over?

Particularly when you stand in my position as a footballer determined to turn his back on the game and walk away. When I can't play, I won't stay, has always been my motto. I can't see it changing in the next five years or so, either. So many players, once they sling the boots in the corner cupboard forever, hang around, almost begging for a job, any old job, as long as they remain on the staff. Why? For most it's simple – they haven't an option. Also, they are very reluctant to abandon a cosy world where they have started, succeeded and prospered for probably close on twenty years. They are comfortable, they enjoy the banter and camaraderie of the training ground, it's a familiar workplace, and out there is something entirely different where the ability to beat a man, make a pass, or score a goal doesn't matter a damn. That's why they are just a little scared. Maybe I am, too, but you have to confront such fear and get on with it. When it's over for me, it's over. I'll be happy to fade into the background. I don't have any desire to be a coach, even less to be a manager. It has always been said that football is the most selfish profession in the world and I am not going to disagree with such a suggestion. For instance, when you are dropped from a team, your club-mates might offer a word or two of sympathy but, deep down, nobody will go to war for you; as long as they are in the side, that is all that primarily matters. In management you have to carry that jungle-law principle even further. The men in charge rely almost on a pure animal instinct for their success. If they don't, they are well aware that the nice guys simply don't survive. Hand on heart, I wouldn't want to play any part in that kind of ball game. In life we have all told the occupational half-truth, but as a manager the half-truth becomes a code of conduct and you couldn't possibly do the job without telling a porky or two. You get a young player, for instance, and to keep things sweet, to avoid the real issue, you trot out a few white lies. Sure, you think he's half decent, and of course he will make it, or at least that's what you say, but beneath the blarney and the bluster, you know he hasn't a cat-in-hell's chance of being a pro. Dead straight, I couldn't do such a thing. I couldn't look some bright-eyed, ambitious kid in the eye and give him all that kidology; I think it must be an extremely difficult and lonely existence in the role of manager. To me honesty is an important trait in a person. Why, then, say one thing and mean something else? Because, as a manager, dodging the truth is in most cases the only expedient way of getting the job to run as smoothly as possible. Then there is that ruthless, singled-minded streak which is another essential. When that moment arrives and you have to bomb out a player, well knowing the impact it must have on his family, his whole way of life, as well as the career of the individual concerned, you are behaving almost like an executioner. One day that certain player has a hefty wage packet, maybe the next he knows he is history, and there is only one man he sees to carry the blame – the boss. It's only natural. And that kind of baggage in any occupation is just not for me. I would hate to have the destiny of any individual resting in my hands. You are welcome to all of that, because, in my opinion, it is a responsibility not worth swopping for all the gold and glory in the game. The solitary concern of any manager is the team, fundamentally because the success of that unit protects his job, and anything or anybody which gets in the way has to be sacrificed, fairly if possible but brutally if necessary. As I pointed out earlier, in football you have acquaintances and not friends.

You also, more importantly, have to have that fire in the belly, an inner force for all successful sportsmen and women, which drives you on and keeps you going at the highest level for as long as is physically possible. My target is another seven or eight seasons of top-level football. I have heard tough old pros suggest that if you go beyond the mid-thirties barrier, you can hardly get out of bed in the morning because the aches and pains are so bad. I wouldn't want to continue until it all turned into a game of torture, even though we all appreciate that the financial rewards from football, particularly at Premiership level, are quite fantastic. Some influential people have even suggested it should all be controlled with a wage-capping system. I'm afraid that would never work properly, because clubs with the financial clout will always be tempted to move in and shift heaven and earth in terms of hard cash, to sign the best players. I have no problem, anyway, with the salaries being demanded by the star performers. OK, you might say he would say that, wouldn't he, but I believe the arrival of 'Johnny' Bosman, and the judgement he won in Belgium over the transfer regulations, was the best thing to happen in our business for years. Until that legal precedent, the clubs had all the power and players could be manipulated. Now we have, like workers in any other industry, a greater measure of control over our careers. In other sporting arenas, in America for example, where there is the same kind of TV investment, the wages paid to the big names of basketball, baseball and gridiron make even our wages appear like spending money. For instance, I play for one of the biggest clubs in the world, no let me correct that the richest sporting club in the world, yet my salary pales into insignificance compared to the salaries star players at the Chicago Bulls or the star quarter-backs in the NFL. Our earnings, compared to golfers and tennis players, are strictly football league and not premier league. That doesn't mean to say that I don't think we get paid well, but when you put it into perspective and consider the popularity of the team I play for, the trophies we have won, the shortness of a footballer's career, I feel we have a right to expect higher salaries and bigger contracts. That said, the money I have earned has enabled me to fulfil one of my ambitions. When

I was a young, hard-up kid in Nottingham with nothing in my pocket I always wanted a Porsche. Back then it was one of the goals I set myself. Eventually, after a while at Manchester United I treated myself to one and I must say it didn't disappoint - a beautiful piece of machinery that I was lucky enough to be able to afford. Like most men I suppose, cars have always held an appeal for me and I have enjoyed my fair share of expensive grown up toys.

Another way in which I have been fortunate to earn money, has been my through my commercial activities. My face, name and autograph have been used to promote countless projects from football boots to kids' lollipops. Along the way I have learned how to work in many different areas: filming a TV commercial, doing a fashion shoot, making a promotional appearance or doing a press day to promote a company's products. I have to say that, at first, I didn't always enjoy these occasions, but as I have got older and done more and more I have genuinely learnt to enjoy my responsibilities and my role as a figurehead helping promote products and services. I've been to some fantastic places doing promotions and filming and met some wonderful people who, in the main, have a love of and interest in football. In terms of places, I went on a week's promotional tour of Asia, visiting Japan, Indonesia, Malaysia and Singapore. For someone like me who enjoys shopping I can highly recommend Singapore. In terms of laughs, I had a great time making a TV commercial for a sports brand - which I will not mention, as they no longer sponsor me (nothing in life comes for free). The idea was to portray what I would have been had I not worn these products and made it as a footballer. My career path, they decided, was that I would work in a fish and chip shop. Cheers, lads. It was my first real go at acting and after obvious early nerves I really enjoyed the experience and had a good laugh at the same time.

Probably the most unusual commercial project I have been involved in was making a record. I have a real love of music all types but especially, soul, hip hop and garage. I have a friend who sends me real hard core import music on vinyl and I have a couple of mixing decks set up at home. I quite often spend the afternoon practising my mixing technique and was offered a gig at a night club. I really fancied doing it, but decided against it as I don't believe the night club scene is a great environment for a professional footballer.

Anyway, back to the record. I was talking with my agent one day and he asked if I fancied making a record. I thought he was joking at first, but I thought what the hell, it's something I would find interesting and also could have some fun doing. Never for one minute did I have aspirations of becoming a pop star, in fact, the mere thought of appearing on *Top of the Pops* left me bolting for the bathroom with a nervous stomach if you know what I mean. Amazingly WEA records also thought it was a good plan or more specifically a soccer-mad American lady named Barbara Charone who is head of the publicity department, thought it was a great idea. So that was it, an agreement was reached and the record was made. The first step was meeting the producers and writers, to discuss their ideas. Eventually we agreed on a rap record using a sample from the Gap Band record *Outstanding*. Then there was the photo shoot for the sleeve cover and publicity shoots. Eventually the day of recording came and I was more nervous than I had ever been running out at any stadium, no matter how important the match was. But the producers, engineers and everybody involved with the project helped tremendously: they settled me down and actually encouraged me.

Having recorded the track, we made a video in and around Manchester and featured two of the lads from Sky's

Dream Team. Once again it was great fun and very interesting seeing how a different industry from the one I am used to operates. Unfortunately the single was not a huge hit or perhaps that should be fortunately, but that was never my aim anyway. I have achieved what I set out to do and have no regrets about doing it. Of course there are people in the media, with their holier than thou attitudes, who tried to turn it into a nightmare. These people really do annoy me, they are so negative about everything. Making the record gave me the opportunity to work with a fantastic singer – Shena McSween – who I hope gets the breaks and goes on to be a big star. Perhaps from my point of view it was a good thing the record career didn't take off as I have always shunned the notion of being projected as a big name. I like my own space too much for that, to be the quiet guy, to keep my own company. I don't welcome intrusion into my private life, although I accept if you play for a club of United's stature, you have to accommodate well-meaning people, the loyal fans, and be polite about their understandable attentions. I suppose it means you step away from your real self at times. There is a public person, the one that has all the virtues of Goody Two Shoes, and then there is the guy your mates know. The real bloke.

I have two particular mates who know me like their brother. They are both from Nottingham and they are both social workers, so let me introduce Marcel Reid and Clive Sherland. I have other close friends scattered around the country, mainly in London, but these two guys are the ones I speak to and socialize with a lot. What do we do together? Chill out, naturally, and occasionally get smashed together when the football allows. They are the people with the golden arm, people to talk to about the closest secrets, and people to protect me. Many times they have done precisely that. Marcel and Clive, peaceable men I assure you, were among the friends who were ready to defend my reputation in all too many threatened punch-ups when others have been out of order and started slagging me off. I am very close to them and from time to time we take the occasional trip to London for a night out. I have found that Manchester is pretty much starved of the kind of recreational scene I enjoy, and there's another reason. Down in London you can hide, you can be anonymous, you can have fun without being hassled. In the capital I can be ordinary guy Andy instead of Andy Cole, Manchester United footballer. It does make a huge difference to an enjoyable weekend. I am not saying people shouldn't have heroes and make a fuss of them. I have two special ones of my own. One is Nelson Mandela, such an outstanding world figure and rightly respected by people of all races. To suffer the indignities and deprivation of almost three decades in prison and still emerge full of humility and without any bitterness was absolutely remarkable. If there was one man I could choose to meet, it would be this great South African states-man. The other guy I admire, and admittedly his impact has been very different, is Marvin Gaye, the American soul singer. I love his music because I believe it has spanned the generations and still remains very popular. Of course, I am into hip hop and garage, and all the other new-generation stuff, but at home I love to listen to certain sounds of the 1960s when I relax away from the game. Soon, though, such moments might become rarer, particu-larly when I finish with football and start focusing seri-ously on other important matters, like those kids in Zimbabwe. In the meantime, I pray I can deliver a few more goals, give the fans another trophy or two, and keep playing to my personal philosophy that I'm not involved in a war, only a game. Hope you all see it my way. And thanks for the good times.

Career Statistics

ARSENAL

Apprentice to March 1992

1 League Game, 0 Goals; 1 CS

League Division One 1990/91

v Sheffield United	League		W4–1

Charity Shield 1991

v Tottenham Hotspur		D0–0

FULHAM (on loan)

September 1991 to November 1991: 13 League Games, 3 Goals

League Division Three 1991/2

v Swansea City (h)	League		W3–0
v Stoke City (a)	League	1 goal	D2–2
v Bury (a)	League		L1–3
v Leyton Orient (h)	League		W2–1
v AFC Bournemouth (a)	League		D0–0
v Brentford (h)	League		L0–1
v Bradford City (a)	League		W4–3
v Bolton Wanderers (a)	League	1 goal	W3–0
v Preston North End (h)	League		W1–0
v Hull City (h)	League		D0–0
v Huddersfield Town (a)	League		L1–3
v Hartlepool United (a)	League		L0–2
v Stockport County (h)	League	1 goal	L1–2

BRISTOL CITY

March 1992 to March 1993

1991/2: 12 League Games, 8 Goals
1992/3: 29 League Games, 12 Goals; 1 FAC; 3 LC (4); 4 AIC (1)

League Division Two 1991/2

v Cambridge (h)	League	L1–2
v Wolverhampton W. (h)	League	W2–0

v Sunderland (a)	League	1 goal	W3–1
v Oxford United (h)	League		D1–1
v Tranmere Rovers (a)	League	1 goal	D2–2
v Leicester City (h)	League	1 goal	W2–1
v Middlesbrough (h)	League	1 goal	D1–1
v Millwall (a)	League	1 goal	W3–2
v Ipswich Town (h)	League	1 goal	W2–1
v Portsmouth (a)	League		L0–1
v Derby County (h)	League		L1–2
v Watford (a)	League	2 goals	L2–3

League Division One 1992/3

v Portsmouth (h)	League	1 goal	D3–3
v Luton Town (a)	League	1 goal	W 3–0
v Sunderland (h)	League		D0–0
v West Ham United (h)	League		L1–5
v Tranmere Rovers (a)	League		L0–3
v Charlton Athletic (h)	League		W2–0
v Cambridge United (a)	League	1 goal	L1–2
v Leicester City (h)	League	1 goal	W2–1
v Brentford (a)	League	1 goal	L1–5
v Millwall (a)	League	1 goal	L1–4
v Birmingham City (h)	League	1 goal	W3–0
v Grimsby Town (a)	League	1 goal	L1–2
v Swindon Town (h)	League		D2–2
v Notts County (h)	League		W1–0
v Watford (a)	League		D0–0
v Bristol Rovers (a)	League		L0–4
v Peterborough United (h)	League		L0–1
v Oxford United (h)	League		D1–1
v Wolverhampton W. (a)	League		D0–0
v Newcastle United (h)	League		L1–2
v Barnsley (a)	League	1 goal	L1–2
v West Ham United (a)	League		L0–2
v Luton Town (h)	League		D0–0
v Portsmouth (a)	League		W3–2
v Southend United (a)	League	1 goal	D1–1
v Sunderland (a)	League		D0–0
v Charlton Athletic (a)	League	1 goal	L1–2
v Tranmere Rovers (h)	League	1 goal	L1–3
v Millwall (h)	League		L0–1

FA Cup

v Luton Town (a)	3rd round		L0–2

League Cup

v Cardiff City (a)	1st round 1st leg		W2–1
v Cardiff City (h)	1st round 2nd leg	3 goals	W5–1
v Sheffield United (a)	2nd round 2nd leg	1 goal	L1–4

Anglo–Italian Cup

v Watford (h)			W1–0
v Cosenza (h)			L0–2
v Piza (a)			L3–4
v Cremenese (a)		1 goal	D2–2

NEWCASTLE UNITED

March 1993 to January 1995

1992/3: 12 League Games, 12 Goals
1993/4: 40 League Games, 34 Goals; 3 FAC (6); 2LC (6)
1994/5: 18 League Games, 9 Goals; 1 FAC; 5LC (2); 3 UEFAC (4)

League Division One 1992/3

v Swindon (a)	League		L1–2
v Notts County (h)	League	1 goal	W4–0
v Watford (a)	League		L0–1
v Birmingham (h)	League	1 goal	D2–2
v Cambridge (a)	League	1 goal	W3–0
v Barnsley (h)	League	3 goal	W6–0
v Wolves (a)	League		L0–1
v Millwall (a)	League	1 goal	W2–1
v Sunderland (h)	League		W1–0
v Grimsby (a)	League	1 goal	W2–0
v Oxford (h)	League	1 goal	W2–1
v Leicester (h)	League	3 goals	W7–1

Premiership 1993/4

v Tottenham (h)	League		L0–1
v Coventry (a)	League		L1–2
v Manchester United (a)	League	1 goal	D1–1
v Everton (h)	League		W1–0
v Blackburn (h)	League	1 goal	D1–1
v Ipswich Town (a)	League	1 goal	D1–1
v Sheff Wed (h)	League	2 goals	W4–2
v Swindon Town (a)	League		D2–2
v West Ham United (h)	League	2 goals	W2–0
v Aston Villa (a)	League	1 goal	W2–0
v QPR (h)	League		L1–2
v Southampton (a)	League	1 goal	L1–2
v Wimbledon (h)	League	1 goal	W4–0
v Oldham Athletic (a)	League	2 goals	W3–1
v Liverpool (h)	League	3 goals	W3–0
v Sheffield United (h)	League	1 goal	W4–0
v Arsenal (a)	League		L1–2
v Tottenham (h)	League		W2–1
v Manchester United (h)	League	1 goal	D1–1
v Everton (a)	League	1 goal	W2–1
v Leeds United (h)	League	1 goal	D1–1
v Chelsea (a)	League		L0–1
v Manchester City (h)	League	2 goals	W2–0
v Norwich City (a)	League	1 goal	W2–1
v QPR (a)	League		W2–1
v Southampton (h)	League	1 goal	L1–2
v Coventry (h)	League	3 goals	W4–0
v Sheffield Wed. (a)	League	1 goal	W1–0
v Swindon (h)	League		W7–1
v West Ham United (a)	League	1 goal	W4–2
v Ipswich (h)	League	1 goal	W2–0

v Norwich City (h)	League	1 goal	W3–0
v Leeds United (a)	League	1 goal	D1–1
v Chelsea (h)	League		D0–0
v Manchester City (a)	League		L1–2
v Liverpool (a)	League	1 goal	W2–0
v Oldham Athletic (h)	League		W5–2
v Aston Villa (h)	League	1 goal	W5–1
v Sheffield United (a)	League		L0–2
v Arsenal (h)	League	1 goal	W2–0

League Cup

v Notts County (h)	2nd round 1st leg	3 goals	W4–1
v Notts County (a)	2nd round 2nd leg	3 goals	W7–1

FA Cup

v Coventry City (h)	3rd round	1 goal	W2–0
v Luton Town (h)	4th round		D1–1
v Luton Town (a)	4th round replay		L0–2

Premiership 1994/5

v Leicester City (a)	League	1 goal	W3–1
v Coventry (h)	League	1 goal	W4–0
v Southampton (h)	League	2 goals	W5–1
v West Ham United (a)	League		W3–1
v Chelsea (h)	League	2 goals	W4–1
v Arsenal (a)	League		W3–1
v Liverpool (h)	League		D1–1
v Aston Villa (a)	League	1 goal	W2–0
v Blackburn Rovers (h)	League		D1–1
v Crystal Palace (a)	League		W1–0
v Sheffield Wed. (h)	League	1 goal	W2–1
v Ipswich Town (h)	League	1 goal	D1–1
v Tottenham Hotspur (a)	League		L2–4
v Leicester City (h)	League		W3–1
v Coventry (a)	League		D0–0
v Leeds (a)	League		D0–0
v Norwich City (a)	League		L1–2
v Manchester City (h)	League		D0–0

League Cup

v Barnsley (h)	2nd round 1st leg	1 goal	W2–1
v Barnsley (a)	2nd round 2nd leg	1 goal	W1–0
v Manchester United (h)	3rd round		W2–0
v Manchester City (a)	4th round		D1–1
v Manchester City (h)	4th round replay		L0–2

FA Cup

v Blackburn Rovers (h)	3rd round		D1–1

UEFA Cup

v Antwerp (a)	1st round 1st leg		W5–0
v Antwerp (h)	1st round 2nd leg	3 goals	W5–2
v Athletico Bilbao (h)	2nd round 1st leg	1 goal	W3–2

MANCHESTER UNITED

Jan 1995–

1994/5:	18 League Games, 12 Goals
1995/6:	34 League Games, 11 Goals; 7 FAC (2); 1 LC; 1 UEFAC
1996/7:	20 League Games, 7 Goals; 3 FAC; 5 EC (1)
1997/8:	33 League Games, 16 Goals; 3 FAC (5); 1 LC; 1 CS; 7 EC (5)
1998/9:	32 League Games, 17 Goals; 7 FAC (2); 1 CS; 10 EC (5)

Premiership 1994/5

v Blackburn Rovers (h)	League		W1–0
v Crystal Palace (a)	League		D1–1
v Aston Villa (h)	League	1 goal	W1–0
v̄ Manchester City (a)	League	1 goal	W3–0
v Norwich City (a)	League		W2–0
v Everton (a)	League		L0–1
v Ipswich Town (h)	League	5 goals	W9–0
v Wimbledon (a)	League		W1–0
v Tottenham Hotspur (h)	League		D0–0
v Liverpool (a)	League		L0–2
v Arsenal (h)	League		W3–0
v Leeds United (h)	League		D0–0
v Leicester City (a)	League	2 goals	W4–0
v Chelsea (h)	League		D0–0
v Coventry City (a)	League	2 goals	W3–2
v Sheffield Wed. (h)	League		W1–0
v Southampton (h)	League	1 goal	W2–1
v West Ham United (a)	League		D1–1

FA Premiership 1995/6

v West Ham United (h)	League		W2–1
v Wimbledon (h)	League	1 goal	W3–1
v Blackburn Rovers (a)	League		W2–1
v Everton (a)	League		W3–2
v Liverpool (h)	League		D2–2
v Manchester City (h)	League		W1–0
v Chelsea (a)	League		W4–1
v Middlesbrough (h)	League	1 goal	W2–0
v Arsenal (h)	League		L0–1
v Southampton (h)	League	1 goal	W4–1
v Coventry City (a)	League		W4–0
v Nottingham Forest (a)	League		D1–1
v Chelsea (h)	League		D1–1
v Sheffield Wed. (h)	League		D2–2
v Liverpool (a)	League		L0–2
v Leeds United (a)	League	1 goal	L1–3
v Newcastle United (h)	League	1 goal	W2–0
v QPR (h)	League	1 goal	W2–1
v Tottenham Hotspur (a)	League	1 goal	L1–4
v Aston Villa (h)	League		D0–0
v West Ham United (a)	League		W1–0
v Wimbledon (a)	League	1 goal	W4–2
v Blackburn Rovers (h)	League		W1–0
v Everton (h)	League		W2–0
v Bolton Wanderers (a)	League	1 goal	W6–0

v Newcastle United (a)	League		W1–0
v QPR (a)	League		D1–1
v Arsenal (h)	League		W1–0
v Tottenham Hotspur (h)	League		W1–0
v Manchester City (a)	League	1 goal	W3–2
v Coventry City (h)	League		W1–0
v Southampton (a)	League		L1–3
v Leeds United (h)	League		W1–0
v Middlesbrough (a)	League	1 goal	W3–0

League Cup

v York City (a)	2nd round 2nd leg		W3–1

FA Cup

v Sunderland (h)	3rd round		D2–2
v Sunderland (a)	3rd round replay	1 goal	W2–1
v Reading (a)	4th round		W3–0
v Manchester City (h)	5th round		W2–1
v Southampton (h)	¼ final		W2–0
v Chelsea (Villa Park)	semi-final	1 goal	W2–1
v Liverpool (Wembley)	Final		W1–0

UEFA Cup

Rotor Volgograd (h)	1st round 2nd leg		D2–2

Premiership 1996/7

v Leeds	United (a)	League	W4–0
v Nottingham Forest (h)	League		W4–1
v Aston Villa (a)	League		D0–0
v Nottingham Forest (a)	League	1 goal	W4–0
v Leeds United (h)	League		W1–0
v Aston Villa (h)	League		D0–0
v Tottenham Hotspur (a)	League		W2–1
v Wimbledon (h)	League	1 goal	W2–1
v Southampton (h)	League		W2–1
v Arsenal (a)	League	1 goal	W2–1
v Chelsea (a)	League		D1–1
v Coventry City (h)	League	1 goal	W3–1
v Sunderland (a)	League		L1–2
v Sheffield Wed. (h)	League	1 goal	W2–0
v Derby County (h)	League		L2–3
v Blackburn Rovers (a)	League	1 goal	W3–2
v Liverpool (a)	League	1 goal	W3–1
v Leicester City (a)	League		D2–2
v Middlesbrough (h)	League		D3–3
v Newcastle United (h)	League		D0–0

FA Cup

v Tottenham Hotspur (h)	3rd round		W2–0
v Wimbledon (h)	League		D1–1
v Wimbledon (a)	League		L0–1

Champions League

v Juventus (a)	Group		L0–1
v Rapid Vienna (h)	Group		W2–0
v Porto (h)	¼ final	1 goal	W4–0

v Borussia Dortmund (a)	semi-final		L0–1
v Borussia Dortmund (h)	semi-final		L0–1

FA Premiership 1997/8

v Everton (a)	League		W2–0
v Coventry City (h)	League	1 goal	W3–0
v West Ham United (h)	League		W2–1
v Bolton Wanderers (a)	League		D0–0
v Chelsea (h)	League		D2–2
v Derby County (a)	League	1 goal	D2–2
v Barnsley (h)	League	3 goals	W7–0
v Sheffield Wed. (h)	League	2 goals	W6–1
v Arsenal (a)	League		L2–3
v Wimbledon (a)	League	1 goal	W5–2
v Blackburn Rovers (h)	League		W4–0
v Liverpool (a)	League	2 goals	W3–1
v Aston Villa (h)	League		W1–0
v Newcastle United (a)	League	1 goal	W1–0
v Everton (h)	League	1 goal	W2–0
v Coventry City (a)	League		L2–3
v Tottenham Hotspur (h)	League		W2–0
v Southampton (a)	League		L0–1
v Leicester City (h)	League		L0–1
v Bolton Wanderers (h)	League	1 goal	D1–1
v Aston Villa (a)	League		W2–0
v Derby County (h)	League		W2–0
v Chelsea (a)	League		W1–0
v Sheffield Wed. (a)	League		L0–2
v West Ham United (a)	League		D1–1
v Arsenal (h)	League		L0–1
v Wimbledon (h)	League		W2–0
v Blackburn Rovers (a)	League	1 goal	W3–1
v Liverpool (h)	League		D1–1
v Newcastle United (h)	League		D1–1
v Crystal Palace (a)	League	1 goal	W3–0
v Leeds United (h)	League		W3–0
v Barnsley (a)	League	1 goal	W2–0

Charity Shield

v Chelsea			D1–1

League Cup

v Ipswich Town (a)	3rd round		L0–2

FA Cup

v Chelsea (a)	3rd round	2 goals	W5–3
v Walsall (h)	4th round	2 goals	W5–1
v Barnsley (a)	5th round replay	1 goal	L2–3

Champions League

v Kosice (a)	Group	1 goal	W3–0
v Feyenoord (h)	Group		W2–1
v Feyenoord (a)	Group	3 goals	W3–1
v Kosice (h)	Group	1 goal	W3–0
v Juventus (a)	Group		L0–1
v Monaco (a)	¼ final 1st leg		D0–0
v Monaco (h)	¼ final 2nd leg		D1–1

Andy Cole

Premiership 1998/9

v Leicester City (h)	League		D2–2
v West Ham United (a)	League		D0–0
v Charlton Athletic (h)	League		W4–1
v Liverpool (h)	League		W2–0
v Southampton (a)	League	1 goal	W3–0
v Wimbledon (h)	League	2 goals	W5–1
v Derby County (a)	League		D1–1
v Everton (a)	League	1 goal	W4–1
v Newcastle United (h)	League		D0–0
v Blackburn Rovers (h)	League		W3–2
v Sheffield Wed (a)	League	1 goal	L1–3
v Leeds United (h)	League		W3–2
v Aston Villa (a)	League		D1–1
v Tottenham Hotspur (a)	League		D2–2
v Chelsea (h)	League	1 goal	D1–1
v Middlesbrough (h)	League		L2–3
v Chelsea (a)	League		D0–0
v West Ham United (h)	League	2 goals	W4–1
v Leicester City (a)	League	2 goals	W6–2
v Charlton Athletic (a)	League		W1–0
v Nottingham Forest (a)	League	2 goals	W8–1
v Arsenal (h)	League	1 goal	D1–1
v Coventry City (a)	League		W1–0
v Southampton (h)	League		W2–1
v Newcastle United (a)	League	2 goals	W2–1
v Everton (h)	League		W3–1
v Wimbledon (a)	League		D1–1
v Leeds United (a)	League	1 goal	D1–1
v Liverpool (a)	League		D2–2
v Middlesbrough (a)	League		W1–0
v Blackburn Rovers (a)	League		D0–0
v Tottenham Hotspur (h)	League	1 goal	W2–1

Charity Shield

v Arsenal			L0–3

FA Cup

v Middlesbrough (h)	3rd round	1 goal	W3–1
v Liverpool (h)	4th round		W2–1
v Fulham (h)	5th round	1 goal	W1–0
v Chelsea (h)	¼ final		D0–0
v Chelsea (a)	¼ final replay		W2–0
v Arsenal	semi-final		D0–0aet
v Newcastle United	Final		W2–0

Champions League

v LKS Kodz (h)	Prelim	1 goal	W2–0
v Brondby (a)	Group	1 goal	W6–2
v Brondby (h)	Group	1 goal	W5–0
v Barcelona (a)	Group	1 goal	D3–3
v Bayern Munich (h)	Group		D1–1
v Inter Milan (h)	¼ final 1st leg		W2–0
v Inter Milan (a)	¼ final 2nd leg		D1–1
v Juventus (h)	semi-final 1st leg		D1–1
v Juventus (a)	semi-final 2nd leg	1 goal	W3–2
v Bayern Munich	Final		W2–1